THE HOLY BOOK

in
Comparative
Perspective

Studies in Comparative Religion

Frederick M. Denny, *Editor*

THE HOLY BOOK

in
Comparative
Perspective

EDITED BY
Frederick M. Denny
&Rodney L. Taylor

UNIVERSITY OF SOUTH CAROLINA PRESS

FIRST EDITION

Published in Columbia, South Carolina,
by the *University of South Carolina Press*

Manufactured in the United States of America

Library of Congress Cataloging-in-Publication Data
Main entry under title:

The Holy Book in comparative perspective.

   Includes bibliographies and index.
   1. Sacred books—History and criticism.   I. Denny,
Frederick Mathewson.   II. Taylor, Rodney Leon,
1944–
BL71.H63   1985   291.8'2   85-8473
ISBN 0-87249-453-5

CONTENTS

PREFACE

This volume originated as a related series of plenary papers that were delivered at the annual meeting of the Rocky Mountains–Great Plains Region of the American Academy of Religion–Society for Biblical Literature, which met at the University of Denver in April of 1982. Because of the warm and thoughtful reception the papers received, it was decided to publish them together in a convenient format intended for a wide, non-specialist readership. The original series of papers has been augmented by contributions from Harry Y. Gamble, Reginald A. Ray, and Laurence G. Thompson.

The editors have received encouragement and guidance from a number of persons, whom they gratefully acknowledge. Frederick Greenspahn of the Center for Judaic Studies of the University of Denver was a strong supporter of the original program featuring papers on scripture when he was president of the regional AAR-SBL in 1982. Charles L. Long of the University of North Carolina-Chapel Hill and Duke University provided helpful advice about producing a book from papers. William A. Graham of Harvard University, James C. Livingston of the College of William and Mary, and Frank E. Reynolds of the University of Chicago carefully read the manuscript and offered valuable suggestions and comments, all of which we soberly considered even when, at points, we went our own way. Kenneth J. Scott, Acquisitions Manager of the University of South Carolina Press, was of the greatest help from the first time he learned about the project from the editors. His generous and energetic counsel, informed by a sound vision of what can be accomplished in religious scholarly publishing, has been instrumental in making this publication possible.

The editors are most grateful to all the contributors, who expended great amounts of time and energy transforming their papers into articles. As is often the case in such circumstances, the pieces needed to be substantially rewritten in order to conform to the aims of this volume. Three contributors generously consented to write articles from scratch, in support of the project and to round out its coverage. Their names have been gratefully recalled above.

The Editors
Boulder
Summer, 1984

THE HOLY BOOK

in

Comparative Perspective

INTRODUCTION

Since its invention over five thousand years ago, writing has possessed both a prestige and a power that have often been sacral. The revolutionary breakthrough of writing and literacy made possible large, complex civilizations, the recording of events as history, the codification of law, and the preservation and transmission of sacred traditions. In light of such achievements, it is little wonder that writing may be thought to have had a divine origin.

But sacred traditions—the myths, stories, legends, mysteries, and highest values of peoples—do not themselves require the technology of writing in order to be conserved, handed down, and dynamically embodied in life. It is obviously not necessary to be literate in order to be religious, or even to transmit, authentically and over long periods, the patterns and processes of belief and behavior.

Whether people are able to read or not, all religious experience leads to concrete, intelligible forms of expression. These forms may be conceptual or theoretical or ideational in nature, such as symbols, myths, creeds, doctrines, histories, laws, and theologies. Or the forms may be more concrete and dynamic, as in ritual and devotional practices. Finally, religious experience expresses itself in specifically religious forms of community life, ranging from small, select groupings all the way to global communities of faith. Every religion possesses all three distinct means of expression: the conceptual, the practical, and the social.[1] All three dimensions are in dynamic interaction with each other. One may dominate in a given tradition, or at a given time period; but religion requires some sort of integration and harmonious balance of all three in order to survive.

Although it is doubtful that there has ever been religion without language, the ways in which language symbolizes, communicates, informs, regulates, unites, inspires, and motivates religious belief and action differ between literate and nonliterate traditions, or rather, between traditions which possess a sacred scripture of some kind and those which do not. Yet, it is also true that language of belief may be appropriated and enjoyed in similar ways by literate and nonliterate people. This is especially true of songs, stories, liturgies, and recitations. The sacred word is always and everywhere prominent in religion, because it is the link between humans and the sacred realm.[2] Its forms are as diverse as the ways in which humans use language in pursuit of spiritual goals, whether by means of mantra, oracle, prayer, hymn, chant, spell, creed, confession, doctrinal exposition, calligraphy, or canon.

Scripture or holy book—we use the two interchangeably—is in many ways but one complex category of holy words. Some sort of sacred literature occupies a position of central importance in each of the world religions. The goal of this collection of articles is to provide reliable, nontechnical introductions to the scriptures of most of them.[3] Each chapter has been written by a specialist in the particular tradition who also shares a common concern with the other authors for the study of religion as an academic discipline in which there are many facts and values that can be viewed comparatively.

The chapters often differ significantly from each other, not only stylistically, but also in their conception of the nature of scripture, its functions, and the appropriate ways in which it may be approached as a theoretical issue. This variety of treatments reflects the different religious traditions themselves and allows each to be approached with due regard for its own internal logic and processes. At the same time, each chapter in its own way addresses three main aspects of scripture, whether viewed as a universal category or as a specific phenomenon: its origin, forms, and functions.

ORIGINS

Whence does scripture arise? This is an important question for all religions that possess a holy book, because the answer reveals central convictions of the believers and gives insight into the essence of each tradition. Divine revelation of sacred writ is a widespread claim, especially among the Abrahamic religions of Judaism, Christianity, and Islam. But the precise meaning of revelation in those traditions varies, sometimes even within a single tradition. Muslims consider their Qur'an to contain the verbatim record of God's special revelation to the Prophet Muhammad through the angel Gabriel. All true scripture originates with God, in a "preserved tablet," according to Islam. But Jews and Christians, while they certainly embrace doctrines about divine inspiration and even direct verbal divine authorship, also recognize a vast assortment of writings by humans, in history, as possessing a special sacred authority. In the case of Judaism and at least the Latter Day Saints variety of Christianity, scripture can and does continue to emerge within the historical process. Zoroastrians also have a strong tradition of prophetic revelation, but there is difference of opinion over whether scripture is basically liturgical performance of written text to be studied and transmitted as such.

The question of origins in such traditions as Hinduism and Buddhism requires a grasp of basic metaphysical assumptions which govern the ways in which the believers view language, writing, the transmission of tradition, and the goal of human life. *Veda*, the Sanskrit word for scripture, which literally means "knowledge," originates in the eternal realm of truth, beyond the more concrete notion of a theistic deity who reveals texts to prophets or visionaries. Veda originates as sound rather than as written word, although in evolved Hindu scripture it is both. In a related manner, Buddhist scripture emerges from what is believed to be the Buddha's "word." This word is variously considered to be an actual body of doctrine and discourse or, in a manner parallel to Hinduism, the transcending nature of things. Both Hinduism and Buddhism recognize the different levels of scripture as originating in eternal truth, on the one hand, and its having been produced as actual text in history, on the other.

Chinese religious thought, as contained in the Taoist and Confucian traditions, differs from both the Abrahamic and the Indic traditions, while it resembles both in specific features. That is, Taoists of different types recognize either a divine revelation of scripture by intentional deities through select individuals—a parallel to some Abrahamic notions of prophetic inspiration—or a product of the experiencing of the transcendental Tao or Way of the universe, which is beyond personality and language. It matters greatly when considering Taoist scripture whether one is referring to religious or philosophical Taoism; the former can superficially resemble other theistic religions on the question of the origins of scripture, whereas the latter parallels to some extent the Vedic doctrine, at least in recognizing a transpersonal, trans-historic source.

The Confucian tradition also focuses on the Tao or "Way of Heaven." But there is much more of a historical and communal context for the generation of the ancient "classics" of Chinese literature which comprise what we would classify as scripture in the tradition. Sagehood plays an important role in maintaining a continuing sense of the truth of Heaven's Way, whenever and wherever it is discerned. Confucianism thus relates the present to the past, while benefiting from the long tradition of scholarly and moral discipline that makes possible a direct apprehension of Truth through meditation and study. In simpler words, it is not only because the Confucian Classics are from an age of the sages of antiquity that they are venerated and cultivated; it is because they are true, as evidenced by the continuing tradition of the experience of the sage in each generation.

In our attempt to discern and understand scriptural origins, we have to take into account what a tradition says and believes about itself, first of all. But we also are required by the rules of scholarly investigation to engage in historical criticism, or at least to recognize that there may be crucial differences between what the followers of a religious way say about the origins of their most sacred texts and what a detached observer might conclude, after pondering historical, environmental, linguistic, cultural, aesthetic, and other factors pertaining to religious systems. The contributions to this book all in some way or other acknowledge the distinction and, sometimes, the tension between a religious insider's appreciation of sacred scripture and the necessarily more neutral position of the outside scholar-observer.

Beyond the level of speculating about whether a scripture actually originated in the fertile mind of a prophet rather than in direct divine inspiration from above, or whether a great leader actually received God's commandments on engraved stones, or whether the transcendental Tao can be captured in any sense within a text, the question of scriptural origins needs to be viewed within the context of religious experience, in fact, as one of its most pervasive and enduring expressions. As will be seen in a number of the discussions, the religious experience that inspires scripture production does not stop with the prophet or founder or ancient sage. It continues to recur and seek expression, maintaining the original message and insight while extending them in new directions and by means of new forms.

FORMS

All scriptures have in common a special language through which basic concepts and insights have been generated. This language must be understood by a sufficiently broad range of people, whether such knowledge includes technical literacy or not, before any scripture can emerge that has canonical status. That is, there is a strong dimension of consensus in the formation of scripture in any religion. The form of a scripture, for example on the linguistic level, has much to do with its function. The Qur'an is considered to be originally an oral verbal message, and it is in the continued live recitation of it that Muslims rediscover the primal power of the revelation. In this respect, the Vedas are similar. So, although both Veda and Qur'an came to have written forms, with associated high arts of calligraphy and illumination, the use of the scriptures in chanting remains primary. The Qur'an, which means "recitation," is not "The Recitation" unless it is recited. So, Muslims recognize two main forms for their revelation: the written and the recited. The two mutually reinforce each other, providing both a visual and an aural pathway to God.

The "special language" does not mean an arcane or secret language. Rather it refers to a language by which religious concepts and expressions establish their native genius. It is not necessary for the language in which a scripture first finds expression to continue as the only means of conveying the tradition, but it is often the case that a scriptural language is also a sacred and thus an indispensable language. Christianity, including the Mormons, does not insist on any single language as the necessary vehicle for its scriptures. The myriad translations of the Bible bear witness to this absence of a sacred, orthodox language. The Bahais have a similar disregard for special scriptural languages, as do also most Buddhists who have preserved their texts in a number of languages, such as Pali, Tibetan, and Chinese. The Buddhist canon, in fact, varies importantly in the several major regions where it was preserved, both as to content and extent of writings.

The scriptures of Hinduism, Islam, Zoroastrianism, and Judaism all have sacred languages which comprise fundamentally important dimensions of their meanings and uses. Aramaic and Hebrew studies are indispensable for Jewish reading, reciting, and study of scripture, as is Sanskrit for the transmission of Veda, Avestan in Zoroastrian scripture-based liturgy, Arabic for the recitation of the Qur'an, and Chinese for both Confucianism and Taoism.

Beyond the linguistic form of a scripture are the genres of literature that make up a canon. These vary greatly around the world. The Chinese classics contain oracle, philosophic discourse, poetry, chronicle, ritual matter, and divination. Taoist scripture contains a similar wealth and variety. The Qur'an is highly oracular, but it also contains stories, prayers, parables, maxims, proverbs, and oaths. Its external form and divisions are not necessarily a product of revelation, but they are nonetheless held in the deepest respect and are never significantly altered. But external form of scriptures is not always a matter for strict observance. The collection of sources that form the Bible of the Christians and the Jews contains history, legend, prophecy, chronicle, biography, myth, proverb, theology, hymns, poetry, preaching, epistles, apocalyptic, law, and ritual procedures. The Torah scroll of the synagogue is an enduring sacred form, setting the Pentateuch apart from all other Jewish religious texts.

Every scriptural religion recognizes some kind of canon of authoritative, inspired, or otherwise official writings. Sometimes the canon is closed, as in Islam, although even that revelation-based tradition recognized Muhammad's sayings as a kind of scripture, though not prophecy.

Sometimes there is a recognized collection of definitive classics, as in Confucianism, which nevertheless can be added to by certain schools and movements, as in Neo-Confucianism in which the sage figures prominently. Judaism recognizes several levels of canon, beginning with the Torah as fundamental and proceeding through the rest of the Bible, through Talmudic legal, ritual, and exegetical commentary, all the way to responsa and other writings down to contemporary times. The Christian canon was a long time in the making and depended heavily on the emerging testimony and self-interpretation of the various bodies of believers in the ancient Mediterranean world.

The written form of a scripture's language is an important matter in some traditons, for example Confucianism, Taoism, Islam, Buddhism, and Judaism. Calligraphy can often be both a visual reinforcement of a scripture's distinctive authority and beauty as well as a form of spiritual discipline, if not religious power itself. Calligraphy sometimes provides objects for meditation, too. For example, the Islamic arabesque, which is always taken from the Qur'an, offers a visual pathway into the mysteries of God's revelation. The only decoration permissible in a mosque is nonfigural, based on the Arabic calligraphy of the Qur'anic text, sometimes enlisting floral and vegetal motifs. Buddhists, Confucians, and Taoists place great amphasis on mastery of ink and brush and often focus upon a single phrase or even a single word which will become the quintessential expression of religious discipline and spiritual insight as well as the summation of a scripture's teaching.

The forms which scripture takes range throughout the genres which any literature may feature, with the exception that certain kinds of literary expression are uniquely and definitvely religious in nature. These often originate in oral tradition and require ritual performance. Prophecy, oracle, hymn, creed, spell, homily, prayer, liturgical rubric, koan, mantra, apocalyptic, myth, history, sacred litany and confession of sin all have distinct forms and often contribute to scriptural canons, whence they enter into the religious life at all levels and are preserved unchanged.

The most significant thing about scripture as a form, beyond the question of the forms which scripture takes, is its general accessibility and standardizing influence. Not all religions allow nonspecialists or persons of lower degree access to scripture (e.g., medieval Catholic Christianity, Brahmanical Hinduism, respectively). But the fact of an enduring, replicable, written form makes possible a level and extent of authority and influence of sacred writings that is impossible in nonliterate traditions, regardless of the sublimity, originality, and attractiveness of their central myths and teachings. Scripture is the most potent medium for the propagation, maintenance, and regulation of religion yet devised. Without some sort of scripture, world religions would be impossible.

But scripture, when it comes to predominate as the source of knowledge and inspiration about a religion, sometimes exacts a heavy price when viewed from the perspective of nonliterate traditions. Scripture may so heavily influence people in the direction of textual preservation and study as to rob the devotional-ritual and communal dimensions of a religion of their dynamism and spontaneity. Put another way, hard and fast written texts reduce things to their own terms, not because they intend to, but because people let them. The Biblical maxim, "The letter killeth, but the Spirit giveth life," is never truer than when scriptural texts are allowed to dominate over what originally they were generated to safeguard and proclaim: the core experiences and insights of a religious way.

There is a great range within which scripture may exercise influence on its tradition. Sometimes it is appropriate for scripture to dominate faith and practice; at other times such dominance is an aberration. What we have been opening up in the last two paragrphs are functions of scripture rather than forms. But it should be obvious that scriptures, by their enduring literary forms, develop functions that persist over time, especially in uniting communities around common convictions and memories. We turn now to consider some of the chief functions of sacred scriptures.

FUNCTIONS

Beyond the questions of origins and forms of scripture, the essays in this book also address the subject of how scripture functions in its living context. Something of the unconscious and autonomous function of scripture was suggested in the preceding section. Here we intend to introduce the issue of how a religious community uses its scripture. It may be convenient to borrow from contemporary ritual studies the distinction, as phrased by Sam D. Gill in his essay in this collection, between "informative" and "performative" functions of language. Scriptures have both of these functions, in greater or lesser degree and proportion to each other, just as the myths, symbols and oral traditions of nonliterate peoples do.

The close relationship between informative and performative functions in nonliterate traditions is closely paralleled in such scriptural religions as Hinduism, Judaism, Taoism, Zoroastrianism, and Islam. Veda is not Veda if it is restricted to a written text. It must be recited out loud, from memory, by a qualified specialist who is ritually pure and of proper status. Nor is it possible to listen to Veda being recited unless certain ritual requirements are met. Similar restrictions and conditions surround Jewish recitation of Torah, Muslim recitation of the Qur'an, the liturgies of religious Taoism, and especially Zoroastrian liturgies in which the scripture comes to life, as it is meant to do. In traditions which place heavy emphasis on ritual performance of recitation, the informative dimensions are balanced by the need to engage in a dynamic ritual activity, which involves much more than the conceptual, mental, literal levels associated with mere reading and study for information, knowledge, and guidance.

To acknowledge the heavily performative functions of scripture in certain religions is not to deny their important informative functions. It is significant that word and act continue to work intimately with each other in a total configuration of scripture-centered piety. Other traditions, most notably Christianity, Confucianism, and Buddhism, tend to stress the informative over the performative functions of their scriptures although the performative is not necessarily absent. That is, those traditions concentrate more on the conceptual and doctrinal content of their sacred texts, so as to relate them to life. The notion of performative simply plays less of a role when a scriptural message is used primarily for purposes of religious, legal, and ethical guidance. To acknowledge this textual function is not to denigrate it; it is to distinguish it from more liturgical engagements with scripture. But even in heavily textualist—sometimes to the point of literalist—traditions, as certain forms of Protestantism, the scripture also has a performative function as symbol and presence, if not as means of devotion through recitation or liturgical functions or mantra-style meditation. The open copy of the Bible on the pulpit symbolizes that scripture's absolute authority for its congregation. The lifting up on high of the Bible by the impassioned preacher symbolizes its omnicompetent capacity as final arbitrater of all matters in heaven and on earth. Similarly, the use of the Bible as witness to courtroom oaths in America is a function that is more performative than informative.

The essays in this volume describe many ways in which scripture functions in the various traditions treated. Beyond the useful distinction between informative and performative functions, which fairly reflect the conceptual and practical dimensions of religious expression, with which this chapter opened, is the social, or community-enhancing function, that third necessary dimension of religion. Scriptures are produced by and for their communities. Whether a given tradition emphasizes the informative, or the performative functions, or some balanced combination of the two, there is always the community-enhancing function that ensures continued survival of the tradition.

The relationship between a scripture and its community is mutual and vital. For example, the New Testament was produced within the context of the early Christian community. When the collection of texts had reached a canonical status, it continued to guide and preserve the community which had in the first place generated it as a continuing testimony to its profound religious experience of the risen Christ. This process of scripture formation and scripture conservation in canon is often paralleled, if not duplicated, in other traditions, as the chapters in this book demonstrate.

Regardless of the specifics of scripture origins and canon-formation, there is always a powerful bond between the text and its human context in every scriptural tradition. If that bond is ever broken, the religious system that was produced by it will decay and eventually vanish. Perhaps fear of such an outcome is the greatest motivating factor in the strenuous efforts at scripture preservation, and often propagation, that can be seen across the religious world, such as the engraving in stone of the entire Pali Canon of Theravada Buddhism in nineteenth-century Mandalay, the preserving of the Chinese Classics in stone as Confucianism became state orthodoxy, and the Qur'an and Bible societies that prosper in many places in our time.

NOTES

1. We are indebted, for this three-part model, to Joachim Wach, *The Comparative Study of Religion* (New York: Columbia University Press, 1958). There Wach writes of religious expression in terms of "thought," "action," and "fellowship." In another place, he prefers the labels "theoretical," "practical," and "sociological." "Universals in Religion," in the author's collection of essays, *Types of Religious Experience: Christian and Non-Christian* (Chicago: University of Chicago Press, 1951), p. 34.

2. A detailed study is Gustav Mensching, *Das Heilige Wort: Eine religionsphänomenologische Untersuchung* (Bonn: Ludwig Röhrscheid Verlag, 1937). The relationship between oral and written word is discussed on pp. 71–88.

3. Some useful studies of the phenomenon of scripture and specific scriptural traditions are: L. Koep, *Das himmlische Buch in Antike und Christentum* (Bonn: 1952); Alfred Bertholet, *Die Macht der Schrift in Glauben und Aberglauben* (Berlin: 1949); G. Lanczkowski, *Heilige Schriften* (Stuttgart: 1956; E. T., 1966); J. Leipoldt and Siegfried Morenz, *Heilige Schriften* (Leipzig: 1953); Charles S. Braden, *The Scriptures of Mankind* (New York: 1952); F. F. Bruce and G. Rupp, eds., *Holy Book and Holy Tradition* (Manchester: 1968); and Neal E. Lambert, ed., *Literature of Belief: Sacred Scripture and Religious Experience* (Provo, Utah: Religious Studies Center, Brigham Young University, 1981).

✡ JUDAISM:
Torah and Tradition

Jonathan Rosenbaum

The holy literature of Judaism is broad and deep. Including the oral traditions which are often thought to underlie it, this literature may stretch over an historical expanse of almost four millenia. It is not limited to Biblical writ but rather constitutes a constantly developing organism that bears new young in each generation. Jewish holy literature defies stereotype and rejects easy categorization. It is neither exclusively legalistic nor narrative, is neither history nor poetry. Certain holy books are recognized by all Jews; others are sectarian, their holiness limited to a specific Jewish group, their sanctity possibly temporary.

Jewish holy literature includes sagas, satires, homiletical material, history, intellectual dialects, philosophy, legends, liturgy, and, of course, law. Jewish legal literature is almost never static or literal and has invariably been open to interpretation. Indeed, no major Jewish holy text can be studied without a commentary. Jews do not "read" the Bible or Talmud; they "learn" it. Learning requires not only a precise study of the text, but also and traditionally a careful survey of the commentators who have preceded the student. For two thousand years scholars have provided explanations and interpretations of Jewish holy literature. The works of these contributors have in turn taken on the quality of holiness. Thus, the Jewish holy book is not one tome, but many; not static, but dynamic; not just old, but modern, even futuristic; not literal, but a constant source of interpretation.

The present work seeks to introduce the reader to Jewish holy literature and its development. The subject is vast and cannot be more than outlined here. Nevertheless, an acquaintance with definitions and methods as well as an awareness of the breadth of the study is attainable. Important secondary literature will be available in the notes that were composed more for the informed layman than the scholar. History's most enduring stereotypes, libels, and misconceptions about Jewish holy literature will be held up to the light of evidence. Gradually, an accurate picture—albeit in broad strokes—should emerge.

MISCONCEPTIONS ABOUT JEWISH HOLY LITERATURE

The concept of the holy book in Judaism had stimulated strong positions within the other Abrahamic traditions. As these positions have colored both popular and scholarly views of Judaism within Christianity and Islam, a review of such statements should provide a fitting backdrop against which Judaism's own position may be compared.

The Pauline epistles provide early indications of Christian discomfort with Jewish holy literature. While maintaining that the Hebrew Bible ("Old Testament") reaches fulfillment in the life and crucifixion of Jesus, the subsequent relevance of Jewish Written and Oral Law is directly challenged by Paul. "For no human being will be justified in (God's) sight by the works of the law since through the law comes knowledge of sin" (Rom. 3:20; compare 7:7–13), he writes. The Mosaic covenant is "a dispensation of death, carved in letters on a stone . . . a dispensation of condemnation . . . (which) fades away." By contrast the new covenant is the "dispensation of the spirit" (2 Cor. 3:7–11). Paul further states that " . . . the law brings wrath, but where there is no law there is no transgression" (Rom. 4:15). To those who accept Jesus, he states, "Likewise, my brethren you have died to the law through the body of Christ, so that you may belong to another . . ." (Rom. 7:4). Within the same spirit, Paul is the moving force behind the early Church's permission to accept Gentile converts without the requirement of Mosaic law (Acts 15).[1]

Though Paul's antilegalism was not totally accepted by the later Church which saw the need for religious law, his attitude toward Jewish holy books—Written and Oral—within their legal context would have a continuing impact upon the Church. Political, social, and economic restrictions imposed upon Jews by the Church would begin in the fourth century with the advent of Christianity as the official Roman state religion.[2] However, direct campaigns to proscribe Jewish literature would not arise until the thirteenth century. From that time until the middle eighteenth century, periodic burnings of Jewish holy books, particularly the Talmud, would plague the Jews of Europe.[3]

The Protestant Reformation did not provide improvement. Martin Luther's pamphlet, *Dass Jesus Christus ein geborene Jude sei* ("That Jesus

Christ was Born a Jew," 1523) held that Jews and Jesus were of the same stock and that the former had been correct in refusing to accept what Luther called "the papal paganism." However, some twenty years later Luther's realization that Jews had also refused to adopt Lutheran Christianity brought its founder to suggest the total restriction or expulsion of Jews from Protestant lands and the confiscation "of their prayer-books and Talmuds (sic) in which such idolatry, lies, cursing, and blasphemy are taught." In tandem with this suggestion to nobles under his influence, Luther also prescribed forbidding rabbis to teach under threat of death.[4]

Such violence toward Jewish literature did not generally accompany Islam. Nevertheless, Islam's position that it is the final dispensation following the abrogation of Judaism and Christianity led to a critique of the Hebrew Bible. Jews were accused of distorting the text in reading or interpretation and some of the Scriptural stories were considered to be unworthy or senseless within a divine book.[5]

CATEGORIES AND DEFINITIONS

The target of such interreligious antagonism is the holy literature best known as Torah. The word Torah is a nominal form of the Hebrew root, yod-reš-he, and clearly has the meaning of "instruction, teaching." Within the Pentateuch the word generally applies to a body of laws referring to a specific topic.[6] In a few passages (e.g., "this is the Torah that Moses said before the Children of Israel" [Deut. 4:44]; "Moses commanded us a Torah, an inheritance of the congregation of Jacob" [Deut. 33:4]; "the Torah of Moses" [Ezra 3:2; 7:6; Neh. 8:1]; "the Torah of God" [Neh. 8:8]), the term may well refer to the Pentateuch itself.[7] This denotation is also an accepted restricted meaning of the word in later Jewish literature.

A fuller extension of the term comes in Jewish sources which distinguish the Written Torah (Tôrāh še-biktāb; hereafter: Torah she-biktav with the k pronounced like the ch in Scottish loch) and Oral Torah (Tôrāh š-běʿal peh; hereafter: Torah she-ba'al peh). From the early Rabbinic period onward, there is a fundamental assumption that much of the Oral Torah was given to Moses on Sinai simultaneously with the Written. The well-known Mishnaic Tractate of ʾAbôt (hereafter: Avot) begins, "Moses received the Torah at Sinai and transmitted it to Joshua, Joshua to the elders, and the elders to the prophets, and the prophets to the men of the Great Assembly." Questions concerning the dates of the inception and demise of the Great Assembly, its system of organization, functions, and authority remain unanswered by classical or modern sources. According to the *Avot de-Rabbi Natan* (Text II: ch. 1, p. 2), the men of the Great Assembly received the Torah from Haggai, Zechariah, Malachi. The size of the Great Assembly is given as 120 (*Meg.* 17b) and alternatively as 85 (*y. Meg.* I, 5; 70d). It has been suggested that the fact that late first-century historian, Josephus, fails to mention the Great Assembly of the Persian period indicates that it may have been a body without political powers.[8] In any case, the Great Assembly was responsible for a number of rabbinic directives (*taqqānôt*; hereafter *taqqanot*) some of which share basic similarities to those that are ascribed to Ezra and Nehemiah. (See Figure 1 for this and following discussions.)

"Simon The Just was one of the last Great Assembly," continues *Avot* (1:2). This person is either Simon Ben Onias I, high priest between 310 and 291, or, his grandson Simon II, high priest between 219 and 199 B.C.E. "Antigonous of Socho received (tradition) from Simon the Just" (*Avot* 1:3). The Greek name and other factors have suggested that Antigonus lived in the first century of Greek rule. According to Rabbinic testimony, the schism between the Sadducees and Pharisees originated with some of Antigonus' disciples. His activities thus probably do not extend much beyond the year 200 B.C.E.[9]

The first of the *Zûgôt* (hereafter: *Zugot*; i.e., "Pairs") received the Torah either from Antigonus or unnamed sages between him and them. During the Hasmonean (142 B.C.E. to 63 B.C.E) and the Herodian periods (63 B.C.E. to 66 C.E.), the *Zugot* were the heads of the supreme court of Jewish law, the Sanhedrin. The list of the members of the *Zugot* supplied in *Avot* concludes with the most famous of their number, Hillel and Shammai. The latter establish the fundamental schools of thought which influence much of the Mishnah. For his part, Hillel, the dominant scholar of his day (*ca.* the turn of the Era), founds the Patriarchate which lasts for over four hundred years and remains the administrative focal point of Jewish practice for half of that period.

Thus, from the standpoint of Jewish tradition, holy literature is bipartite. The Written Law must be interpreted and applied in tandem with the Oral, a circumstance which consistently militated against literalistic applications of that law. Any concept of the holy book in Judaism must take both Oral and Written Law into account.

THE WRITTEN LAW

For Jews the primary holy book (*kĕtāb qōdeš*; hereafter; *ketav qodesh*) is the Torah in its restricted sense of the Five Books of Moses. The final

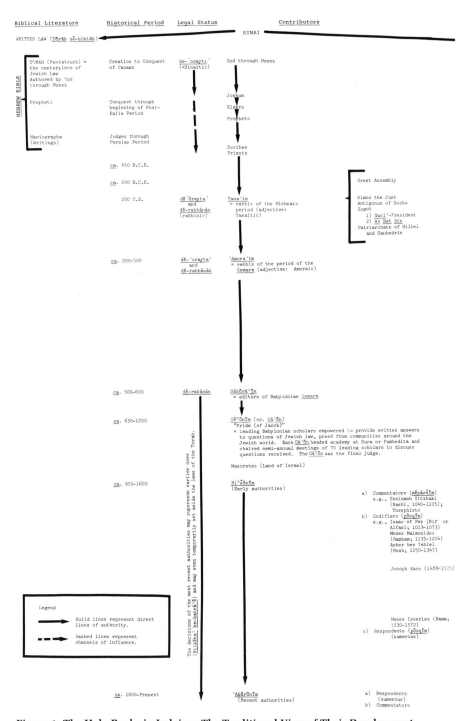

Biblical Literature	Historical Period	Legal Status	Contributors

SINAI

WRITTEN LAW (Tōrāh še-biktāb)

TORAH (Pentateuch) = the centerpiece of Jewish Law Authored by God through Moses — Creation to Conquest of Canaan — de-'orаytа' (=Sinaitic) — God through Moses

Prophets — Conquest through beginning of Post-Exile Period — Joshua / Elders / Prophets

Hagiographa (Writings) — Judges through Persian Period — Scribes Priests

ca. 450 B.C.E.

ca. 200 B.C.E. — Great Assembly

200 C.E. — də-'orаytа' and də-rabbānān (rabbinic) — Tana'im = rabbis of the Mishnaic period (adjective: Tanaitic) — Simon the Just / Antigonus of Socho / Zugot / 1) Nasi'-President / 2) Av Bet Din / Patriarchate of Hillel and Sanhedrin

ca. 200-500 — də-'orаytа' and də-rabbānān — 'Amora'im = rabbis of the period of the Gemara (adjective: Amoraic)

ca. 500-600 — də-rabānān — Sābōrā'īm = editors of Babylonian Gemara

ca. 650-1050 — Gə'ōnīm (sg. Gā'ōn) "Pride (of Jacob)" = leading Babylonian scholars empowered to provide written answers to questions of Jewish law, posed from communities around the Jewish world. Each Gā'ōn headed academy at Sura or Pumbedita and chaired semi-annual meetings of 70 leading scholars to discuss questions received. The Gā'ōn was the final judge.

Masoretes (Land of Israel)

ca. 950-1600 — Rī'šōnīm (Early authorities)

a) Commentators (məpāršīm) e.g., Shelomoh Yitzhaki (Rashi, 1040-1105); Tosephists
b) Codifiers (pōsqīm) e.g., Isaac of Fez (Rif or Alfasi; 1013-1073) Moses Maimonides (Rambam; 1135-1204) Asher ben Yehiel (Rosh; 1250-1347)

Joseph Karo (1488-1575)

Moses Isserles (Rama; 1530-1572)
c) Respondents (pōsqīm) (numerous)

ca. 1600-Present — 'Ahārōnīm (Recent authorities)

a) Respondents (numerous)
b) Commentators

The decisions of the most recent authorities may supersede earlier ones and may even temporarily set aside the laws of the Torah. (Hilkātā' ke-batrā'ē)

Legend

→ Solid lines represent direct lines of authority.

⇢ Dashed lines represent channels of influence.

Figure 1: The Holy Books in Judaism: The Traditional View of Their Development

Non-Biblical Literature

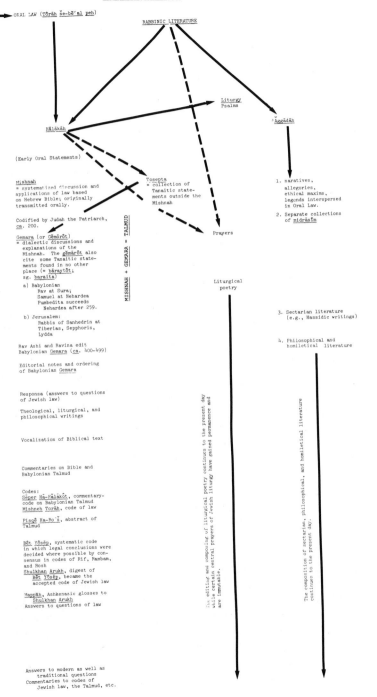

ORAL LAW (Tōrāh še-bĕʿal peh)

RABBINIC LITERATURE

Liturgy
Psalms

ʾAggādāh

Hālākāh

(Early Oral Statements)

Mishnah
= systematized discussion and
applications of law based
on Hebrew Bible; originally
transmitted orally.

Codified by Judah the Patriarch,
ca. 200.

Gemara (or Gĕmōrōt)
= dialectic discussions and
explanations of the
Mishnah. The gĕmārōt also
cite some Tanaitic state-
ments found in no other
place (= bāraytōt;
sg. baraita)

a) Babylonian
Rav at Sura;
Samuel at Nehardea
Pumbedita succeeds
Nehardea after 259.

b) Jerusalem:
Rabbis of Sanhedrin at
Tiberias, Sepphoris,
Lydda

Rav Ashi and Ravina edit
Babylonian Gemara (ca. 400-499)

Editorial notes and ordering
of Babylonian Gemara

Responsa (answers to questions
of Jewish law)

Theological, liturgical, and
philosophical writings

Vocalization of Biblical text

Commentaries on Bible and
Babylonian Talmud

Codes:
Sēper Ha-Hălākôt, commentary-
code on Babylonian Talmud
Mishneh Tōrāh, code of law

Pisqē Ha-Roʾš, abstract of
Talmud

Bēt Yōsēp, systematic code
in which legal conclusions were
decided where possible by consensus in codes of Rif, Rambam,
and Rosh
Shulkhan Arukh, digest of
Bēt Yōsēp, became the
accepted code of Jewish law

Mappāh, Ashkenazic glosses to
Shulkhan Arukh
Answers to questions of law

Answers to modern as well as
traditional questions
Commentaries to codes of
Jewish law, the Talmud, etc.

Tosepta
= collection of
Tanaitic state-
ments outside the
Mishnah

Prayers

1. naratives,
allegories,
ethical maxims,
legends interspersed
in Oral Law.

2. Separate collections
of midrāšīm

3. Sectarian literature
(e.g., Hassidic writings)

4. Philosophical and
homiletical literature

MISHNAH + GEMARA = TALMUD

Liturgical
poetry

The editing and composing of liturgical poetry continues to the present day
while certain central prayers of Jewish liturgy have gained permanence and
are immutable.

The composition of sectarian, philosophical, and homiletical literature
continues to the present day.

collecting, fixing, and preservation of the Pentateuch took place in the Babylonian Exile (Ezra 7:14, 25) though many of its elements clearly precede this period and, as we have noted, the completed text was probably in Ezra's hands.[10]

The remaining parts of the Hebrew Bible, Nĕbî'îm (prophets; hereafter: Nevi'im) and Kĕtûbîm (Hagiographa; hereafter: Ketuvim) are of somewhat lesser holiness in Jewish thought. (The first letters of all three sections, Torah, Nevi'im and Ktuvim, are used to form the acronym Tanak, which is the common term used by Jews to denote the Hebrew Bible.) On the one hand, commandments and prohibitions which are found in the Prophets or the Hagiographa are usually considered Sinaitic on the assumption that the prophets received or interpreted from them ongoing laws (hălākāh; hereafter: halakah), given to Moses at Sinai (e.g., Git. 36a). On the other hand, the later Talmudic authorities (ca. 300 to 500 C.E.) often cite a verse from the Prophets or Hagiographa as a "supporting text" ('asmaktā' hereafter: asmakta) which is not considered Sinaitic law. Jewish tradition regards the last of the prophets, Malachi (ca. 450 B.C.E.), as the final speaker in the prophetic tradition. "Henceforth, no prophet may make innovations" (Siprā', bĕḥuggōtay, 13:7) is the basic rule. Later prophecies were discredited and the responsibility for the legislation of ritual and moral standards based on Written Law passed (as we have seen in Avot) to the scholars who would ultimately develop Pharisaic and later Jewish tradition.

Much debate has recently centered over the date and process of canonization of the entire Hebrew Bible. The fact that the early Church included the Apocrypha in its canon while Judaism excluded these materials has recently stimulated new discussion. There is no direct evidence for exact canonical decision-making at the Synod of Jabneh (usually dated 90–100 C.E.) which is traditionally credited with this process. Many indirect indications show that the Roman suppression of the first Jewish Revolt (66–73 C.E.), with the accompanying destruction of the Second Temple and the consequent displacement of fundamental Jewish institutions, traumatized Jewry's surviving leadership into formalizing the canon of Written Law. Nevertheless, it seems clear that the Synod of Jabneh did not have the final word. Rabbinic debates imply that by the time of Jabneh most books of the Hagiographa were included in the Canon with the exception of Ecclesiastes and Song of Songs (Yad. 3:5) around which controversies remained.[11] However, later debates concerning Esther (Meg. 7a), Proverbs (Šabb. 30b), Ecclesiastes (m. 'Ed 5:3) and Ezekiel (e.g., Šabb. 13b; Hag. 13a) continued into subsequent generations.[12] Further, as late as the middle of the second century, it was necessary to emphasize the uncanonical status of the *Wisdom of Ben Sirah* (*t. Yad.*, 2:13) and to forbid its public reading (*y. Sanh.* 10:1, 28a). This fact demonstrates fluidity in the corpus of the Hagiographa, especially when juxtaposed with the statement of a late third-century Babylonian *amora* who actually cites Ben Sirah as part of the Hagiographa (*B. Qam.* 92b). Thus, the Hebrew Bible, which *is* basically the Written Law and, therefore, the fundamental holy book of Judaism, was not fully defined and limited until more than two and a half centuries after its latest component part (Daniel)[13] was completed.[14]

RABBINIC LITERATURE
ʾAggādāh (*hereafter:* aggadah)
Before we examine the *halakah* in some detail, we should note that just as the Written Law is paralleled by the Oral Law, *halakah* is balanced by *aggadah*. *Aggadah* is commonly found within the literature of the Oral Law. It includes interpretation and exegesis of various portions of the Bible and may take the form of narratives, allegories, history (legendary or otherwise), ethical maxims, explanations of the prophets, sagas, and legends about the rabbis and their contemporaries. The factor which unites all *aggadot* (plural) is that they are not binding in a legal sense. *Aggadah* helps to illustrate the law, but its interpretations do not in themselves have the force of law. Nevertheless, *aggadot* were *not* composed as intellectual exercises but as moral teachings. In addition to the Talmudic literature, they are also found in independent collections of *midrāšîm* (hereafter: midrashim) beginning with the Mishnaic period.[15] *Aggadot* should be included with the holy books of Judaism, but with the limitations just noted.

Halakah
The Pentateuch (Torah in its restricted meaning) and, to a lesser degree, of the Prophets/Hagiographa[16] represent two of the primary sources of the Jewish legal system. As has been noted, much of the Oral Law is also considered to be Sinaitic. In Rabbinic sources, laws are commonly designated as either *dĕ-ʾôraytāʾ* ("of the Torah," hereafter: de-orayta) or *dĕ-rabbānān* ("of the Rabbis," hereafter: de-rabbanan; sometimes also known as *middibrê sôprîm*, "from the words of scribes"). The first category means of Sinaitic authority, while the second denotes rabbinic authority. However, the concepts are not so much chronological as qualitative. The medieval scholars Maimonides and Nahmanides differed on the definitions of these categories. Maimonides held that any law inferred by interpretation is *de-rabbanan* unless it is supported by an established tradition; Nahmanides argued that anything derived by interpretation is *de-orayta* whether or not

supported by Talmudic tradition *unless* the Talmud states explicitly that it is *de-rabbanan.*[17]

Though the modern critical scholar quite logically assumes that halakic innovations of many types are not Sinaitic even when the Talmudic texts claim such to be the case, the problem of these claims was not lost upon the contributors to the Talmud. Two Tanaitic [18] *aggadot* illustrate. In the first we read:

> When Moses went up to heaven (i.e., after his death), he found the Holy One Blessed Be He (i.e., God) sitting and connecting crowns to the letters.[19] He said to him, "Lord of the Universe, considering all that you have written, is it necessary to add crowns to the letters?"[20]
>
> God answered, "There will be one man in the future at the end of several generations and Akiva the son of Joseph[21] is his name. It is he who in the future will interpret every jot and tittle of Jewish laws (*halakot*)."
>
> Moses responded before him, "Lord of the Universe, show him to me."
>
> God said to him, "Return from whence you came." (Moses) went and sat at the end of the eighth row (in the academy of Akiva) and he did not understand anything which (the scholars) were saying. His strength was growing weaker when (Rabbi Akiva) reached a particular point at which his students said to him, "Rabbi, from where do you derive this?"
>
> (Rabbi Akiva responded to them,) "It is the *halakah* of Moses from Sinai."
>
> (At that point Moses) was satisfied. (Menaḥ. 29b)

This famous *aggadah* clearly illustrates the Rabbinic recognition of (1) the right of scholars (i.e., Pharisees, and, later, rabbis) to develop Jewish law by logical deduction, and (2) the ambiguity of considering some laws *de-orayta* and some *de-rabbanan.*

Another aggadic passage further shows that logical deduction had totally superseded any post-Biblical prophecy which might be considered to be the direct word of God. At the beginning of the second century C.E., Rabbi Eliezer ben Hyrcanus, the brother-in-law of the Patriarch Gamaliel II, was involved in an argument of law with his colleagues.

> On that day, though Rabbi Eliezer brought forward every imaginable argument, they did not accept any of them. So he said to them, "If the *halakah* agrees with me, let this carob-tree prove it."
>
> The carob-tree was uprooted one hundred cubits out of its place . . . (but) they said, "No proof can be brought from the carob-tree."
>
> He continued and said to them, "If the *halakah* agrees with me, the (stream of) water will prove (it)." (Immediately,) the stream of water turned around and flowed backwards.

They responded, "One cannot bring proof from a stream of water."

Again, he said to them, "If the *halakah* agrees with me, the walls of the academy will prove (it)."

The walls of the academy tilted (and were about) to fall (when) Rabbi Joshua[22] scolded them saying to them, "When scholars best one another in halakic debate (literally, 'in *halakah*'), how is it your right (to interfere)?" (The walls thus) did not fall out of respect for Rabbi Joshua, but they also did not stand upright out of respect for Rabbi Eliezer. Indeed, they are still standing on an incline.

Again, he (i.e., Rabbi Eliezer) said to them, "If the *halakah* agrees with me, from heaven will come the proof."

(Immediately,) the still, small, heavenly voice[23] went out and said, "How can you have (a problem) with Rabbi Eliezer when the *halakah* in fact agrees with him in every case?!"

Rabbi Joshua then rose to his feet and cried, "'It is not in heaven'" (Deut. 30:12). What did he mean by this Biblical quotation? Rabbi Joshua responded, "Since the Torah was already given at Mount Sinai, we may no longer rely on a heavenly voice, for you (i.e., God) have already written in the Torah at Mount Sinai." (Thus the rule is:) "According to the majority must one incline."

Sometime later, Rabbi Nathan met Elijah (the Prophet).[24] He said to him, "What did the Holy One, Blessed be He, do at that hour" (i.e., the hour of the dispute described above)?

(Elijah) responded to him, "He smiled and said, 'My children have bested me, my children have bested me!'" (B. Meṣ 59b)[25]

While this *aggadah* is often quoted, the material, which follows it is not. Rabbi Eliezer was excommunicated for attempting to use prophetic means to prove his argument and thereby deny the authority of the majority.[26]

In a modern epilogue the Hazon Ish (Abraham Y. Karelitz, 1878–1953), a leading halakic authority of the present century, ruled that even if the actual Torah which Moses received were discovered and found to be different from the Masoretic Text, it would be halakically irrelevant and the developed law would require no emendation.[27] Thus, we have definite support—ancient and modern—for the holiness of post-Biblical Jewish law.

The Development of Jewish Law

As these remarks are primarily aimed at those who are not specialists in *halakah*, it is appropriate to outline the main events in the development of Oral Law. As we have previously seen, the origin of Oral Law can be traced at least to the *Zugot*, possibly to the Great Assembly and Ezra, and by tradition, to Moses himself. From the time of Hillel and Shammai onward, large collections of *halakah* were assembled and transmitted orally from teacher to student to avoid any challenge to the Written Law. However, between 66 and 135 C.E., three Jewish revolts erupted against the Romans, two of them in the land of Israel itself. They resulted in the brutal suppression of Jewish religious rights and scholarly leadership. For this reason, Rabbi Judah the Patriarch reduced to writing the fundamental Oral Law, ca. 200 C.E. His compendium, the Mishnah, was divided into six orders and 63 tractates.[28] Between ca. 220 and 470 rabbinical academies in Babylonia and the Land of Israel produced dialectics on Mishnaic law. These dialectics were ultimately edited and codified in the Jerusalem and Babylonian gĕmārôt (hereafter: gemarot; singular, gemara) which were completed ca. 400 and 500,[29] respectively. The Babylonian gemara together with the Mishnah forms the Babylonian Talmud which is more developed and comprehensive than its counterpart, the Jerusalem Talmud (the Mishnah + the Jerusalem gemara). Further, the textual condition of the Babylonian Talmud was preserved more satisfactorily. Thus, it gradually gained hegemony in the teaching of Jewish law.

1. COMMENTARIES AND CODES

After the final editing and redaction of the Babylonian Talmud in the sixth century,[30] the responsibility for halakic interpretation passed to the heads of the Babylonian academies who bore the title Gaon (Excellency). From the mid-eighth century, the Geonic codes and responsa appear until the suppression of the entire institution in the middle of the eleventh century. By that time, the center of Jewish learning had shifted to North Africa and western Europe.

In these regions, two main types of legal scholars arose: commentators (mĕparšîm, pronounced "mefareshim") and codifiers or decisionmakers (pôsqîm) though the two titles are not mutually exclusive.[31] The best known of the commentators is certainly Rabbi Shelomo Yitzhaki (1040–1105) who wrote in the French province of Champagne. In addition to composing a major Biblical commentary, Rashi, as he is commonly known, wrote a massive commentary on almost all of the Babylonian Talmud. His extraordinary work was succeeded by other commentaries provided by his grandchildren, particularly Rabbi Jacob Ben Meir Tam (1100–1171; also known as Rabbenu Tam). At the same time, the first of the major codifiers of Jewish law was writing in Morocco. Rabbi Isaac of Fez (Alfasi; 1013–1073) produced a codex (Sēper Hā-Hǎlākôt; hereafter: Sefer Ha-Halakot) which closely followed the Talmud, but excluded aggadic passages and included only those halakic opinions accepted as Jewish law.

In the twelfth century, the famous Moses Maimonides (1135–1204) of Spain and, later, of Egypt wrote a brilliant code of Jewish law which he named without excessive modesty, Mišneh Tôrāh (hereafter: Mishneh

Torah), "Second Torah"). This code was meant to supplant the need to refer to the Talmud and other legal sources. The fact that its form omitted citations of legal authorities and tended to ignore the views of Franco-German scholars altogether caused it to gain critics until a series of commentaries loosely called *nôs³ê kēlāw*, "its armor bearers," made it more acceptable to the majority of Jewish scholars.

The thirteenth century witnessed the rise of several major codes and commentaries which attempted to provide a union of Spanish and Franco-German interpretations. Among these are the *Sēper Miṣwôt Gādôl* ("The Great Book of Commandments," known by its acronym as *SeMaG*) of Moses of Coucy. The work is based on the *Mishneh Torah* but includes the works of prominent Franco-German scholars. It thus represents the first attempt to reconcile differing decisions of these two schools. It was divided into positive and negative commandments and thus differed in format from the *Sēper Miṣwôt Qātān* (called *SeMaQ*; "The Small Book of Commandments") which was keyed to the days of the week and appeared some time afterward. Other thirteenth century works include the *Mŏrdĕkay* of Rabbi Mordecai ben Hillel of Nürnburg (1240?–1298), a massive compendium of opinions and responsa; *Bêt Ha-Bĕḥîrāh*, a lucid halakic commentary to most of the tractates of the Babylonian Talmud compiled by Menahem ben Solomon Meiri (1249–1316); the *novellae* and commentaries on various tractates by Nahmanides (R. Moses ben Nahman, or Ramban, 1195–1270); and similar works by the latter's pupil, R. Solomon ben Adret (or Rashba, 1215–1310). Despite such prolific writers, the most influential contributor to Jewish law in the thirteenth century was R. Asher ben Yehiel of Toledo (Rabbenu Asher or Rosh, 1250–1327). His *Pisqê Ha-Ro³š* was an abstract of the Talmud which took precedence in some eyes over the *Mishneh Torah* and Alfasi's *Sefer Ha-Halakot*.

Rabbenu Asher's son, Jacob (*ca.* 1270–1340) wrote a comprehensive code which noted the conclusions of both Franco-German and Spanish schools and is entitled ³*Arbaʿāh Tûrîm* ("Four Rows": commonly known as the *Tur*). Structurally, the *Tur* was innovative in that it divided Jewish law into four general subject areas, a form which made it an especially accessible reference. However, its method of deducing the actual law from many opinions and its reconciliation of Franco-German halakic commentaries and Spanish codes are its most important contributions.

In the two centuries after the completion of the *Tur* no complete code emerged, but a large number of scholars appeared who wrote commentaries on the codes, *novellas* on the Talmud, and responsa. In the sixteenth century, however, the *halakah* reached a new plateau with the works of

Joseph Karo (1488–1575). Karo took the codes of Alfasi, Maimonides, and Asher ben Yehiel and combined them methodically in his own great code *Bêt Yôsēp* (hereafter: *Bet Yosef*), which was framed as a commentary on the *Tur* and explores each law from its place in the Talmud through the latest sources. After completing this monumental work, Karo wrote a short synopsis of it which he called *Šulḥān ʿArûk* (hereafter: *Shulkhan Arukh*), the "Set Table." This two-part presentation freed him from the criticism, previously leveled at Maimonides, of not citing sources while it simultaneously allowed him to offer an uncluttered digest of Jewish law. Together with *Mappāh* ("Table Cloth"), a series of glosses describing European (i.e., Ashkenazic) divergences and written by the Polish authority, R. Moses Isserles (1530–1572),[32] the *Shulkhan Arukh* became the basic code of Jewish law and remains so for traditional Jewry to the present day.[33] Its acceptance gave rise to a stream of later commentaries and abridgments which has continued to flow into the twentieth century.[34]

2. RESPONSA

From the Geonic period to the present, another vital vehicle for the application of Jewish law has been the responsa literature. Consisting of answers by *posqim* to questions asked by scholar and laymen alike, responsa have grown to comprise thousands of decisions which are only now being made fully accessible by computer projects sponsored through Yeshiva University and Bar-Ilan University in cooperation with the Institute for Computers in Jewish Life in Chicago.[35]

It might be assumed that by now only the smallest minutiae of Jewish practice would be subject of modern responsa. To the contrary, the fundamental halakic principle of *hikĕtāʾ kĕ-batrāʾê* ("The law is according to the latest *halakic* authorities.") means that modern answers to new and, in some cases, older questions are attainable. Thus, modern authorities can deal with the very heart of Jewish observance. Jewish law provides a variety of measures through which modern halakic scholars may even set aside, if temporarily, basic provisions of even the Written Law when the religious well-being of the community is at stake. The issuance of *taqqanot* (directives enacted by a body of halakic scholars which enjoy the force of law) is one major method of such legislation. Even the community at-large has the capacity to affect the law and thus the holy literature. Communal contributions tend to arise in the form of custom the legitimacy of which was recognized in the halakic rule, *Minhāg mĕbattēl hǎlākāh* ("A custom may abrogate a law.").

As an example of the currency of the modern responsa which constitute the largest segment of more recent Jewish holy books, we may note that there is a voluminous literature on such modern biomedical questions as artificial insemination, therapeutic abortion, and prolongation of life through extraordinary means.[36] Many of these responsa have influenced not only the personal observances of Jews, but also their attitudes in issues of public policy. The modern movement of Jews to places which they had never previously inhabited has also inspired new responsa. The success of explorations of space has led authorities to discuss how an inhabitant of the moon, for example, will observe the Sabbath which normally begins on Earth at sunset on Friday. The most plausible answer was actually established during World War II when, for the first time, Jews in some numbers lived above the Arctic Circle: one utilizes the Sabbath times of one's home town or another city of one's choosing.[37] Clearly, Jewish law and the holy books which comprise it stretch from the Biblical period to the present moment.

This flexibility of Jewish law is also illustrated by its capacity to permit disagreements even among contemporary scholars in which each takes a position diametrically opposed to the other. Two recent examples are appropriate here. Rabbi Ovadia Yosef, the former Sephardic chief rabbi of Israel, wrote a responsum in which he permitted a certain type of palm branch (*lulav*) to be used in observance of the Sukkot festival. In a responsum written within a year of the publication of Rabbi Yosef's work, one of the leading Ashkenazic rabbis in the world, Rabbi Moshe Feinstein, prohibited the same palm from use.[38] It is worthy of note that the rabbis seem to define the plant in question differently and wrote their responsa independently without reference to the other's work. In another case, Rabbi Yosef prohibited participation by Sephardic Jews in a national lottery in Israel which provides funds for educational purposes. Within a week, his ruling was contradicted by both current chief rabbis.[39]

THE BREADTH OF JEWISH HOLY LITERATURE
Operational Considerations

There is a good deal of halakic literature on the definition and treatment of holy books themselves. As early as the Mishnaic tractate *Yadayim* (ch. 3), the holy books (*kitve ha-qodesh*) were defined as those that "soiled the hands."[40] In addition, holy books are commonly described as those materials which are written in "Assyrian script," a technical term referring to texts written in the normal Hebrew alphabet.[41] These general technical descriptions serve not to exclude, but rather to identify likely candidates for holy literature. Though the "Assyrian" script is used to write Hebrew, it is also utilized for Aramaic, a language in which much rabbinic literature appears from the days of the *gemarot* to the technical terminology and idiomatic phrases favored by contemporary rabbis. Further, while Hebrew, known in Jewish tradition as "the Holy Tongue," is the preferred language of holy literature, every work written in Hebrew is not by definition Jewish holy literature.[42] The format and content of a work as well as the attitude of its writer clearly plays a role in defining the work as holy.[43] Secular literature written in Hebrew or religious literature which utilizes sacred texts but seeks to draw the reader away from Judaism—even if written in Hebrew—would not be considered holy. On the other hand, sincere explications of the Biblical or rabbinic texts, even if composed by students takes an aspect of holiness. Thus, in many traditional rabbinic academies (*yeshivot*), it is customary for students' notes on their studies to be discarded in a special drawer or cabinet for subsequent burial with tattered holy books. This custom acknowledges an ongoing chain of Jewish tradition which is exemplified in the actions of the learned in each generation.

The *Shulkhan Arukh* provides an outline of the various laws regarding holy literature and lists by example works which clearly qualify as holy. It states that it is a *mitzvah* (religious obligation) for every Jew to write a Torah scroll or to participate in such a project. Joseph Karo adds that "in our time it is also an obligation to write the Pentateuch, Mishnah, Gemara, and their commentaries." This statement clearly extends the definition of holy literature to later works. Other works clearly qualify as holy. Among these is the whole corpus of Jewish liturgical literature. Such works include prayer books for the Sabbath, Festivals, and the High Holy Days.[44]

Additional qualifying characteristics of holy books can be found in descriptions of their treatment. Holy books must be treated with a respect almost equal with that accorded the Pentateuch. They should be acquired and not sold except to provide one with an opportunity for additional study of Torah or to garner funds for one's marriage (*Yŏreh Dē⁽āh*, 270). If they are on a bench, one is forbidden to sit on that bench unless they are raised. It is also forbidden to place such books on the floor. They may not be discarded or burned[45] but must rather be secreted in a special closet (*genizah*) and/or eventually buried in a Jewish cemetery. They may not be thrown even if they are only *aggadah*(*Yoreh De ah* 285:5). They cannot be used for one's own physical comfort such as to screen the sun from one's eyes. Finally, if a fire which does *not* threaten life breaks out on the Sabbath, the Rabbis enjoined the Jew from putting it out. Only clothing which can be worn and food which can be carried to a place where it is permissible to carry may be taken out of the burning area. However, sacred books whether written or printed may be saved from the fire and they may be carried even to a place where it is normally forbidden to carry them. These holy books include those printed in ink or in other colors whether they are written in Hebrew or in other languages (ʾŌrah Ḥayyîm 334:12 and Mišnāh Běrûrāh).

The Status of Philosophical Works

Many Jewish philosophical tomes have also taken on the aspect of holiness. These include such works as the classics of Jewish mysticism, the most famous example of which is the *Zohar*. This work which claims to consist of words of *tana'im* and *amora'im* was mainly written and compiled in thirteenth-century Spain. Together with later works including the writings of Rabbi Isaac Luria (1534–1572), the *Zohar* has become the foundation of Kabbalistic studies. Despite the fact that these studies are rarely more than a peripheral part of even a deep Jewish education, their holiness has enjoyed wide acceptance from the sixteenth century to the present.

Other Jewish philosophical works experienced a more difficult road to acknowledgment as holy literature. A classic case is the *Guide of the Perplexed*. Moses Maimonides wrote this work and considered it to be his *magnum opus*. The *Guide of the Perplexed* dealt with the reconciliation of the science of the day (primarily, Neoplatonic Aristotelian ideas) with Jewish tradition. It was written originally in Arabic, the intellectual language of Sephardic Jewry as well as the Muslim world. In addition to appealing to more widely educated Jews, its language made it less accessible to possible opponents who eschewed secular studies. Maimonides understood the *Guide's* potential for contention. He published it privately and couched its more controversial passages in cryptic language. In the generations which followed him, however, his precautions were to no avail. Shortly after his death in 1204, bitter controversies arose concerning the acceptability of the *Guide* and rabbis in France as well as certain other parts of Europe banned it. Nevertheless, the *Guide of the Perplexed* gradually gained acceptance as holy literature. An affirmation of its holiness is demonstrated by the fact that modern Jewish scholars will occasionally quote the *Guide* as a support for decisions of Jewish law appearing in responsa.[46] Jewish philosophical literature generally gains sanctity more slowly than legal or homiletical works, but the gradual acceptance of Maimonides' *Guide of the Perplexed* suggests that works of this genre can and do reach the status of holy literature.

The Torah Scroll: A Summit of Holiness

The rough road to holiness over which philosophical works must pass dramatizes the hierarchy that exists in Jewish holy literature. Just as Written Law takes precedence over Oral Law and pronouncements *de-orayta* are superior to those *de-rabbanan*, so Jewish holy books are endowed with levels of sanctity. For example, it is customary to place a Pentateuch on top of a text of the Talmud while, in turn, later scholarly writings would be placed below the Talmudic text. Further, a substantial literature exists concerning the *halakah* which governs the scribal arts. The holiest text is of course the Torah scroll. The writing of such a scroll is only undertaken by an accomplished and pious scribe after years of training and study. The act of such writing is viewed as holy work and is executed according to spiritual as well as technical and artistic requirements.[47] The writing of the Torah scroll can take an accomplished scribe a full year of work. Once completed, the parchment and ink must be maintained precisely. As the ink has a tendency to chip with time, the Torah scroll must be periodically examined by a certified scribe who touches up the text and refurbishes the parchment. Figure 2 illustrates some of the many flaws which can disqualify a Torah scroll from ritual use.[48]

The Torah scroll itself is treated with great respect and love. As part of traditional Jewish liturgical ritual, its mantle is kissed by congregants. Great care is taken to keep it from unclean places and to guard it from falling to the ground. If it should be dropped, the incident is traditionally regarded as a communal disaster and the giving of charity and sometimes fasting is prescribed.

Other Biblical manuscripts written under prescribed *halakot* require a respect which is almost equal to that shown the Torah scroll itself. Thus, phylacteries, mezuzot, and scrolls from the Prophets and Writings are subject to displays of reverence similar to those accorded a Torah scroll. As we have seen, printed holy books also deserve honored treatment, but their means of production makes such requirements less stringent.

Sectarian Literature

Jewish history is replete with groups and sects which have sanctified certain writings not recognized by the whole of Jewry. Thus, the community of Qumran which produced the Dead Sea Scrolls also composed its own sectarian literature including a manual of discipline and laws which it regarded as holy, but which the rest of the Jewish community ignored. Ultimately, the holiness of Qumran's sectarian literature proved fleeting: no Jewish group has recognized its sanctity since the demise of the Qumran sect. On another level, we noted earlier that certain aprocryphal books were regarded as canonical by some even after the canonization of the Hebrew Bible. In modern times, specific groups within Judaism have produced writings which they regard as holy but which are perceived as sec-

Acceptable

ואת ממלכת עוג מלך הבשן הארץ לעריה בגבלת
ערי הארץ סביב ויבנו בני גד את דיבן ואת עטרת
ואת ערער ואת עטרת שופן ואת יעזר ויגבהה
ואת בית נמרה ואת בית הרן ערי מבצר וגדרת
צאן ובני ראובן בנו את חשבון ואת אלעלא ואת
קריתים ואת נבו ואת בעל מעון מוסבת שם ואת
שבמה ויקראו בשמת את שמות הערים אשר
בנו וילכו בני מכיר בן מנשה גלעדה וילכדה
ויורש את האמרי אשר בה ויתן משה את
הגלעד למכיר בן מנשה וישב בה ויאיר בן

Defective

ואת נוטלכת עוג מלך הבשן הארץ לעריה בגבלת
ערי הארץ סביב ויבנו בני גד את דיבן ואת עטרת
ואת ערער ואת עטרת שופן ואת יעזר ויגבהה
ואת בית נמרה ואת בית הרן ערי מבצר וגדרת
צאן ובני ראובן בנו את חשבון ואת אלעלא ואת
קריתים ואת נבו ואת בעל מעון מוסבת שם ואת
שבמה ויקראו בשמת את שמות הערים אשר
בנו וילכו בני מכיר בן מנשה גלעדה וילכדה
ויורש את האמרי אשר בה ויתן משה את
הגלעד למכיר בן מנשה וישב בה ויאיר בן

1. Letter broken.
2. Superfluous quill-stroke.
3. Letter incomplete.
4. Ink disintegrated.
5. Letter illegible.
6. Word altered by defective letter.
7. Word altered by superfluous quill-stroke.

Figure 2: Disqualifying Defects in the Torah Scroll

ondary or even secular by the bulk of other Jews. For example, many Hassidic groups have produced their own philosophy and prescriptions for observance. While some of these writings are studied by Jews outside the Hassidic sect which reveres them, most of these works seem unlikely to gain acceptance by all Jews. In an ironic twist, one should also remember that while normative Judaism has historically recognized the holiness of the Talmud, a few sects (e.g., the Karaites) have denied the sanctity of all but Biblical literature.

From a different perspective, liturgical, philosophical, homiletical, and halakic works produced within the Conservative, Reform, and Reconstructionist movements have clearly been sanctified by rabbis and lay people within these movements. For example, the legal decisions of the Conservative rabbinate's Committee on Law and Standards have defined the range of acceptable ritual and moral practices for that movement and, in unanimous cases, are considered legally binding on all Conservative Jews.[49] At the same time, the Reform movement has published *responsa* many of which have been composed by the leading Reform scholar in this area, Rabbi Solomon Freehof.[50] The Reconstructionist movement grew out of the philosophy espoused by the late Rabbi Mordecai Kaplan (1881–1983) and for the committed Reconstructionist, Kaplan's works possess a genuine sanctity. All three non-Orthodox movements have edited and published their own prayer books with liturgies which sometimes vary substantially in both length and content from the liturgies of Orthodoxy. To varying degrees these works among others have been recognized as holy by their respective movements. At the same time, however, most Orthodox Jews have vehemently rejected the religious writings of the Conservative, Reform, and Reconstructionist movements even when they are produced by scholars of international acclaim utilizing traditional sources and methods.[51] Orthodoxy's reasons for this rejection are often related to the very positions which many non-Orthodox Jews have taken toward holy literature. By and large, most Reform and Reconstructionist theologians and many within the Conservative movement would deny that Moses received the Written (as well as the Oral) Law at Sinai. In Orthodox terms this rejection of what for Orthodoxy is a theological axiom disqualifies a person as an author of holy literature regardless of his/her credentials.

THE GENERAL USE OF JEWISH HOLY BOOKS

The vast number and substantial complexity of Jewish holy books have not made them unavailable or unused. Jews have been proud to be identified as the "People of the Book" and do not restrict the study of holy works to a scholarly elite. Jewish holy literature has classically played a central role in the life of every community. Scholarship was never simply the domain of religious leaders, but was the responsibility of the common member of the community. Thus, traditional Jewish education began at the age of four or five and produced generations where illiteracy was virtually unknown. From the Middle Ages onward, the Jewish boy would begin his studies with Leviticus and, would almost simultaneously be introduced to commentaries. As he progressed, he would be exposed to the Talmud. Girls too were invariably taught to read and write and many were provided with substantial backgrounds in holy texts.

This tradition of access to primary holy literature by the community-at-large remains an often accomplished ideal in modern Jewish societies. In North America even the smallest communities provide a Hebrew education which includes an average of six hours a week of religious education for youngsters from the primary to the high school years. In the United States, virtually every Jewish community of more than five thousand Jews sponsors at least one day school. These schools combine both general and Jewish studies and provide youngsters with an exposure to the varieties of Jewish holy literature. Thus, it is not uncommon to see adult Jewish lay people participating in relatively advanced Jewish studies. Despite substantial assimilation in the United States and other Western countries, trends indicate that Jewish parochial schools have increased in number yearly since the end of World War II. Further, even the most assimilated Jewish homes normally possess a Bible in Hebrew and English as well as a selection of prayer books for the various calendrical observances.

Jewish liturgy itself actually includes study sessions as part of the service. In the daily morning service, the introductory prayers incorporate not only selections from the Pentateuch, but also materials from the Mishnah and *gemarot*. Many of the prayers themselves are taken directly from the Bible. In both the traditional and liberal wings of Judaism, prayer is a thrice daily event which constantly reinforces the adherent's understanding of Jewish holy literature.

The Torah scroll which, as we have seen, is painstakingly written and maintained is not simply an object of reverence. Rather, its public reading is an integral part of the liturgy. On Sabbath mornings a portion of the scroll is read serially so that the reading of the entire Pentateuch is completed annually. The first section of each portion is also read at the preceding Saturday afternoon, Monday morning, and Thursday morning services. On the festival Simhat Torah (the second day of Shmini Atzeret, observed as one day in Israel), the final chapter of Deuteronomy is ceremoniously completed and immediately followed by the first of Genesis.

Special readings are assigned for the Festivals, the High Holy Days, and other calendrical occasions. Both the Sabbath and special readings are generally followed by parallel selections from the Prophets. In addition, the Writings are acknowledged by public readings of the five Megillot (Song of Songs, Ruth, Lamentations, Ecclesiastes, and Esther) each of which is permanently assigned to the three Pilgrim Festivals (Sukkot, Pesah, and Shavu'ot), Purim, and the Ninth of Ab. The Pentateuch, Prophets and Megillot are chanted according to traditional melodies assigned to each type of literature.

Parchment scrolls containing holy literature are not limited to public readings; they also have private uses. Phylacteries containing Biblical texts are worn on head and weaker arm as part of the morning service. Further, *halakah* mandates that every entrance to every room in a Jewish home (with the exception of bathrooms) must have a mezuzah affixed to the right side of the door as one enters. The mezuzah, a small scroll containing Deut. 6:4–9, is placed in a decorative container and nailed to the doorpost within thirty days of one's domicile in the building.

Jewish learning is a constant daily activity throughout life. Beyond prayer, public readings, and ritual objects, Jewish holy books are the foci of study sessions which are common in the adult Jewish community. Within the last fifty years, the study of the Talmud on a daily basis after completion of one's education has been formalized within the program known as *Daf Yomi* ("A Daily Page"). The *Daf Yomi* program seeks to complete one folio page (two sides) of the Talmud each day. This is a substantial undertaking and if the student is successful, he can study the entire work on at least an elementary basis in "just" seven years! Nevertheless, thousands of learned Jewish students around the world participate in the *Daf Yomi* program. Less arduous, but still intensive study of holy texts is also available to the adult community in the form of adult education programs offered in almost every synagogue and community.

CONCLUSION

The holy books of Judaism are not limited to the Biblical and the Talmudic literature; they comprise a much larger corpus. This corpus includes both *halakah* and *aggadah* and, especially in the case of the former, extends to the present day and is still developing. Far from being obsessed with the minutiae of obscure legalisms, Jewish law constantly continues to confront major social and moral issues as well as innovative questions spawned by ongoing advances in science. *Halakah* possesses mechanisms which allow modern authorities to propose sometimes radical applications and modifications founded on earlier sources. This flexibility is not new. As we have seen, the right of decision by the scholarly majority was accepted in the Talmudic period. In sum, far from being the overly stringent legalistic material known in the popular mind as well as in Christian and Muslim literature, *kitve ha-qodesh* (Jewish holy writings) comprise an expanding corpus of flexible law and lore which strives to be as useful and sanctified in the present as it has been in the past.

NOTES

1. For a fuller discussion of Paul's feelings about the Jewish law, see E. P. Sanders, *Paul and Palestinian Judaism* (Philadelphia: Fortress, 1977), especially 475–97; Samuel Sandmel *The Genius of Paul* (New York: Farrar, Straus, & Cudahy, 1958), 48, 55–60, 106–7; *idem, Anti-Semitism in the New Testament* (Philadelphia: Fortress, 1978), 16–18. It should be noted that the references cited in these notes have been chosen for the person who is a nonspecialist in Jewish law. Unless absolutely necessary technical literature in languages other than English has been limited. Further, the general accessibility of materials to those who lack academic libraries of Jewish studies has also influenced the choice of sources. Talmudic citations are from the Babylonian Talmud unless otherwise noted.
2. See Jacob R. Marcus, *The Jew in the Medieval World* (New York: Harper/ Torchbook, 1965), 3–7.
3. Y. Glikson, "Talmud, Burning of," *Encyclopedia Judaica* (hereafter: *EJ*; Jerusalem: Keter, 1972) 15: cols. 768–771.
4. Marcus, *The Jew in the Medieval World*, 167.
5. For a fuller discussion, see Salo W. Baron, *A Social and Religious History of the Jews* (Philadelphia: Jewish Publication Society, 1952–   ) 3 (1957): 76–85, 87, 156–57; 5 (1957): 82–105, 117–121, 136, 326–37.
6. See, for example, *A Hebrew and English Lexicon of the Old Testament* (eds. F. Brown, S. R. Driver, C. A. Briggs; Oxford: Oxford University, 1966), 435–36.
7. It seems quite possible that Ezra read the completed Pentateuch to the people (Ezra ch. 8). See John Bright, *A History of Israel* (3rd ed.; Philadelphia: Westminster, 1981), 433–34.
8. Alexander Guttmann, *Rabbinic Judaism in the Making* (Detroit: Wayne State University, 1970), 5–7.
9. Ibid., 11–12.
10. See citation in note 7 as well as N. M. Sarna, "Bible," *EJ*, 4: col. 823.
11. Mishnaic citations require comment. Those lacking comfort with the original text often seem to prefer the translation by H. Danby, *The Mishnah* (London:

Oxford University, 1933). More detailed in commentary (though some acquaintance with Hebrew is helpful) are P. Blackman, *Mishnayot* (New York: Judaica Press, 1965) and the voluminous works by J. Neusner and his students. H. Albeck, *Šišāh Sidrê Mišnāh* [The Six Orders of The Mishnah] (Jerusalem: Mosad Bialik/Tel Aviv: Devir, 1958) represents a fine commentary in modern Hebrew.

12. For a full discussion of the classical sources, see G. F. Moore, *Judaism in the First Centuries of the Christian Era.* (New York: Schocken, 1971). 1:238– 2447.

13. Bright, *A History of Israel*, 423– 24.

14. For further descriptions of the scholarly questions concerning canonization, see J. A. Sanders, "Adaptation for Life: The Nature and Function of Canon," *Magnalia Dei: The Mighty Acts of God* (eds. Frank M. Cross, Werner E. Lemke, Patrick D. Miller; Garden City, NY: Doubleday, 1976), 531–60; David N. Freedman, "Canonization of the OT," *IDB Sup*, 135; Sarna, "Bible," cols. 816–35. esp. cols. 824–25 and the bibliography, col. 835.

15. For further information, see a still superb but often forgotten description of independent *aggadot*: J. Theodor, "Midrash Haggadah," *Jewish Encyclopedia* (ed. I. Singer; New York: Funk and Wagnalls, 1907), 8:550–69.

16. The Prophets and Hagiographa are generally placed in the halakic category of Kabbalah (received tradition) to differentiate them from Torah.

17. A lucid explanation of these complicated categories can be found in Benjamin De-Vries, "Halakhah," *EJ* 7: cols. 1156–1161; Menachem Elon, "Mishpat Ivri," *EJ* 12: cols. 113–115.

18. The term "Tanaitic" refers to the period of the Mishnah (i.e., the *tana'im, ca.* 200 B.C.E. to 200 C.E. See the discussion of the development of Jewish law provided below.

19. In the Jewish scribal tradition the letters are written with decorative hooks or "crowns."

20. The translation here is based on the commentary of Rashi (Rabbi Shelomo Yitzhaki, 1040–1105), who is the premier authority in this field. Literally, the clause might be rendered: "What delays your hand?"

21. Akiva ben Joseph (*ca.* 50–135 C.E.) was the leading rabbinic intellect of the first third of the second century C.E. When Simon bar Kochba rebelled against Rome in 132, Akiva proclaimed him the messiah and was ultimately martyred by the Romans.

22. Rabbi Joshua ben Hananiah (*ca.* 50–130 C.E.) was, like Rabbi Eliezer ben Hyrcanus, one of the leading disciples of Rabbi Yohanan ben Zakkai, the key preserver of Oral Law immediately after the Roman destruction of the Temple in 70.

23. The *bat qôl*, "the still, small voice," is a special term for direct communication from God. It was, for example, the *bat qol* which spoke to Elijah on Mt. Horeb (1 Kings 19:12).

24. Since the Bible described Elijah as having been taken bodily and alive to heaven (2 Kings 2:11), Rabbinic tradition stated that he was still alive and appeared to the Rabbis of the Talmudic period.

25. The implication is that Rabbi Joshua and the majority have understood God's point: the responsibility for deciding law is in their hands.

26. For an excellent discussion of the decision-making process in Jewish law, see Aaron M. Schreiber, *Jewish Law and Decision Making: A Study Through Time* (Philadelphia: Temple University, 1979), especially 191–225.

27. Zvi A. Yehuda, "Hazon Ish on Textual Criticism and Halakhah," *Tradition* 18 (1980), 172–80, esp. 178–80.

28. It should be noted that in addition to the Mishnah, outside Tanaitic statements (called *bāraytôt*; singular, *baraita*) have been preserved in (1) the *gemarot* themselves; (2) in the Tosepta, an independent collection of laws many of which were not included in the Mishnah; and (3) in the Tanaitic *midrashim* on Exodus, Leviticus, Numbers, and Deuteronomy (*Měkîltā' Siprā', and Siprê*).

29. The dates for the conclusion of the two *gemarot* are approximate. The finalization of both works seems to have been occasioned by external pressures. In the Land of Israel, the Roman commander Ursicinus' attack on the three Jewish academies at Tiberias, Sepphoris, and Lydda in 351 hastened the end which came officially with the abolition of the Patriarchate in 421. In Babylonia, the great academies were closed down for a substantial time in the last quarter of the fifth century. The final period of the Babylonian *gemara* is associated with Ravina (died 499), the head of the academy at Sura, who concluded the work of his predecessor, R. Ashi (*ca.* 335–428) and is generally considered the concluding internal editor and last *amora*. It should be noted that the complete English translation of the Babylonian Talmud (ed. I. Epstein; London: Soncino, 1935–52) is available and that the Jerusalem Talmud is now appearing under the editorship of Jacob Neusner as *The Talmud of the Land of Israel* (Chicago Studies in the History of Judaism; Chicago: University of Chicago, 1982–).

30. This work was accomplished by scholars known as *sābôrā'im* to differentiate them from the contributors to the *gemorot*, the *amora'im*, and those of the Mishnah, the *tana'im*. Except for a work by R. Shevira Gaon, some other Geonic fragments including *Sēder Tanā'îm wě-Āmôrā'im*, and the works of Abraham Ibn Daud, there is little material that describes the *savora'im*.

31. Among the earliest important figures of the North African school is R. Hananel ben Hushi'el (died 1055/56) who wrote an early halakic commentary on the Babylonian Talmud much of which is printed in modern standard editions of same. The commentary relied heavily on materials of the *Geonim* particularly the writings of Hai Gaon (939–1038) as well as the Jerusalem Talmud, the Tosepta, and the traditions of western rabbis. It was a strong influence on Isaac of Fez.

32. Karo wrote from the Sephardic (i.e., of Spain, North Africa, the Levant, Turkey, and the rest of the Near East and Orient) tradition, a fact which limited the usefulness of his work to the European community, where different decisions had in some cases gained force. Isserles' contribution preserves Karo's text, while appending the European consensus.

33. The importance of the *Shulkhan Arukh* as a watershed in the history of Jewish law is demonstrated by the fact that scholars from the end of the Geonic period through Karo are known as *rîʾšônîm* ("Early Authorities") while those who follow him (i.e., post-1600) are *ʾaḥărônîm* ("Later or Recent Authorities").

34. Such works are far too numerous to list, but we might mention the halakic commentary of Karo's contemporary, Solomon Luria of Posen (1510–1573), which was written as a response to Karo's method. Other, more modern tomes include the *ʾArûk Ha-Šûlḥān*, a compendium of later authorities up to the beginning of the twentieth century. Written by R. Yehiel Epstein (1829–1908), it covers all sections of the *Shulkhan Arukh*. For the section which deals primarily with holiday observance and other ritual law (*ʾŌraḥ Ḥayyîm*), another popular modern commentary is the *Mišnāh Bĕrûrāh* (hereafter: *Mishnah Berurah*) which was composed by the Hafetz Hayyim (R. Israel Meir Ha-Kohen Kagen, 1838–1933). All of these writings and others testify to the continuing impact of Karo's original contribution.

35. Searches of the database which includes responsa from the eighth century to the present are available through Responsa Project Coordinator, Institute for Computers in Jewish Life, 845 North Michigan Avenue, Suite 843, Chicago, Illinois 60611. The fullest written work on responsa is *Otzar HaPoskim*, a major undertaking by scholars in Jerusalem. See also Solomon B. Freehof, *The Responsa Literature and a Treasury of Responsa* (New York: KTAV, 1973) and S. Tal, "Responsa," *EJ*, 14: cols 83–95 for a general histories and surveys of the literature in English.

36. See, for example, David Feldman, *Birth Control in Jewish Law* (New York: New York University, 1968) and J. David Bleich, *Contemporary Halachic Problems* (New York: KTAV, 1977), 325–93.

37. Bleich, *Contemporary Halachic Problems*, 211–12.

38. Ovadai Yosef, *Yĕḥawweh Daʿat* (Jerusalem: 1977), v. 1, 197–99 and Moshe Feinstein, *ʾIqrôt Mōšeh*, (Brooklyn, N.Y.: Moriah, 1982), v. 6, no. 123, pp. 214–15.

39. *Jerusalem Post International Edition*, 1213 (February 5–11, 1984), p. 16; 1215 (February 12–18), p. 16.

40. It might seem curious that holy works were designated capable of causing disqualification. However, the rabbinic intent seems to have been to make sure that the texts would not be used for mundane purposes. See *m. Yad.* 4:6.

41. At the height of the neo-Assyrian period (ninth to seventh centuries, B.C.E.), Aramaic became the language of diplomacy in the Near East (see 2 Kings 18:26). At the same time, the Hebrew and Aramaic scripts diverged. When Aramaic became the official language of the Persian empire (539–331), its script gradually replaced the Hebrew hand. However, the original Hebrew script was preserved in certain official and holy documents and appears sporadically as late as the manuscripts from Qumran (popularly known as the Dead Sea Scrolls, which date from the second century B.C.E. to the first century C.E.). Nevertheless, for most Jewish documents, Aramaic script became

the basic medium for writing the Hebrew language. The term "Assyrian script" thus seems to harken back to the period in which Aramaic first became prominent.

42. It should be noted that some scholars have held that by and large only documents written in Hebrew are holy books. (See for example the responsa of the Radvaz, vol. 3, no. 513)

43. See responsum no. 109 in *Hawwôt Yāʾir*, no. 109.

44. See, for example, *Těrûmat Ha-Dešen*, vol. 1, no. 17.

45. See Jeremiah 36 for what might be a Biblical acknowledgment of this rule.

46. See, for example, Yosef, *Yehawweh Da'at*, v. 1, p. 142.

47. In the *Mishneh Torah*, Maimonides (*Sēper ʾAhăbāh, Hilkôt Sēper Tôrāh*, chapter 10) elucidates twenty defects which disqualify a Torah Scroll. Many of these factors are not related to the form of the letters but rather to the religious attitudes and qualifications of the scribe.

48. The illustration was supplied through the kindness of T.B.M. (S.T.M. Scribes Ltd.) 200 West 86th Street, New York, NY 10024.

49. For a digest of some of the earlier writings and legal decisions of the Conservative movement, see Mordecai Waxman, *Tradition and Change* (New York: Burning Bush, 1965). Later legal materials can be found periodically in issues of *Conservative Judaism* and the newsletter of the Rabbinical Assembly which publishes the minutes of the Committee on Law and Standards.

50. Rabbi Freehof's many volumes of responsa have been published by the Hebrew Union College and Jewish Publication Society. In addition, his *Responsa Literature and a Treasury of Responsa* includes an excellent history of the whole of this literature.

51. For a careful survey of the impact of liberal movements on Jewish law, see A. Guttmann, *The Struggle Over Reform in Rabbinic Literature* (New York: World Union for Progressive Judaism, 1977).

✝ CHRISTIANITY:
Scripture and Canon

Harry Y. Gamble, Jr.

It has been customary for historians and phenomenologists of religion to regard Christianity as a scriptural religion and even to represent it as a paradigm among the major religious traditions of what it means to be a scriptural religion. It would be foolish to quibble with such a description, since it is obvious that Christianity has a scripture, and indeed a closely defined sense of what writings constitute it; and since in its historic forms Christianity has paid deference to the authority of its scripture. Nevertheless, such generalizations must be qualified by the more specific facts that Christianity has not always had its own scripture, has not always been agreed about what constitutes scripture, and has not always ascribed to its scripture the same type or degree of religious authority.

It may even be said that the inner diversity of Christianity is thrown into its sharpest relief precisely in connection with the concept of scripture. Certainly it is apparent in the modern era that the concept of scripture has been highly divisive, splitting the Western Christian tradition into Catholic and Protestant segments and generating innumerable sectarian forms of Protestantism. Yet the very fact that such major consequences have followed from disagreements about scripture indicates very well the fundamental importance of scripture within Christianity. When the necessary qualifications are taken into account, it is not at all easy to answer the question of the significance of scripture for Christianity, and hence of the character of Christianity as a scriptural religion. This essay aims to illuminate the problem from a historical perspective. Such an approach will not address directly the modern Christian uses of and debates about scripture, but it will help to clarify some basic and perennial issues.

THE INFLUENCE OF JEWISH SCRIPTURE

Since Christianity came into being not as a new and independent religion but as a particular type of ancient Judaism, it has been said that Christianity was "born with a Bible in its cradle." This is true, but it is also misleading. For although Christianity from the beginning had recourse to the scriptures of Judaism, Christianity was not originally a scriptural religion in the same sense as Judaism, and the fact that it employed the Jewish scriptures does not mean that Christianity was in its essence, or was necessarily destined to become, a scriptural religion in its own right. Rather, the faith of the earliest Christians was evoked by and focused on a person, Jesus of Nazareth, and he was apprehended by the primitive Christian communities not first of all in texts, but in missionary preaching, oral tradition, and charismatic experience. Only secondarily were the sacred writings of Judaism called into service, and their function was to confirm and defend the Christian message. They did not constitute its basis, or even give it adequate expression. The controlling authorities were, instead, the "words of the Lord" (i.e., the teachings of Jesus, preserved mainly in oral tradition) and the "testimony of the apostles" (i.e., the teachings of qualified messengers).[1] The appeal to Jewish scriptures was consequent upon these, and the nature of that appeal was determined by these. Thus the Jewish scriptures did not have an independent standing.

This is shown by the fact that the early Christian use of the scriptures of Judaism was selective in both content and method of interpretation.[2] As to content, there was a decided preference for the prophetic books (including the Psalms, which were taken to be prophetic). The books of Moses were, to be sure, also used, yet not in terms of their prescriptive and practical import, which constituted their preeminent value to Judaism generally, but in terms of their narrative structure and substance, which offered a historical scheme and prefigurative possibilities which were specifically amenable to Christian claims. Broadly speaking, then, the relative values of the main portions of the Jewish scriptures, namely Torah and Prophecy, were reversed in early Christianity, and a prophetic-predictive sense was ascribed to the whole.

But within this general tendency there was also a Christian predilection for specific books and for particular passages in those books (e.g., Genesis, Exodus, Isaiah, Jeremiah), and at the same time a studied neglect of others. Along with such discrimination among the contents of the Jewish scriptures early Christianity gave full play to allegorical and typological interpretations which were capable of eliciting specifically Christian meanings from the ancient texts. These methods of interpretation were by no means Christian innovations, but they acquired in Christianity an importance unparalleled in Judaism, and were taken to be the only means by which the scriptures of Judaism could be properly understood. Conversely expressed, these interpretive methods offered the only means by which Christianity could appropriate the Jewish scriptures to its own purposes. Thus although the early church took up the scriptures of Judaism, it invested them with a very different meaning. The perspective which furnished this meaning was not the scriptures themselves, but the confession of Jesus as Messiah: the scriptures were seen to prefigure him, and he was seen to fulfill them. Consequently, the function of the Jewish scriptures within Christianity was decidedly different from their function in Judaism, and there is little to be compared in these two orientations, even though the texts as such are the same.

Whereas Christianity inherited from Judaism very many scriptural documents, it did not receive from Judaism a fixed and definite collection of such documents, that is, a canon, for the simple reason that in the period of Christian beginnings Judaism itself had not fashioned a fixed collection.[3] Therefore the number of Jewish writings valued as scripture by the early church was not only large but also fluid, and included not a few writings which Judaism was ultimately to reject when it fashioned a canon, and some of these have continued to form part of some Christian Bibles down to the present.[4] What Christians regard as the "Old Testament" was not, then, simply taken over from Judaism, even though it consists of Jewish scriptures. As a collection, the Christian "Old Testament" is as much a product of Christian usage and reflection as the "New Testament."[5]

Even though by the time of Christian origins Judaism had become largely a religion of the Book, and even though Christianity made use of Jewish scriptures for its own purposes, this does not entitle the claim that Christianity was or was obliged to become a scriptural religion. Equally, it does not imply that Christianity would as a matter of course fashion its own scriptures as a correlative or supplement to the scriptures it took over from Judaism. In fact, the idea of a distinctively Christian scripture was entirely remote from the early Christian mind, for in its early stages Christianity was not even a literary movement, much less a scriptural one.[6]

The earliest extant Christian literature, namely the letters of Paul, dates from the middle of the first century, and it was only in the last three decades of the first century that other Christian writings began to be composed in any appreciable quantity, so that writings which can be confidently dated within a half century of Christianity's beginnings are relatively few. Beyond their paucity, their character is also noteworthy, for all such writings were occasional, that is, were evoked by and were calculated to address specific circumstances within various early Christian communities. None was composed as Christian scripture. While it is true that some religious authority was either claimed by their authors (when they did not remain anonymous) or was implicit in their content (when it was traditional), this alone did not constitute them as scripture. Throughout the first century and well into the second the Christian conception of scripture continued to be restricted to Jewish writings, in spite of the increasing availability of specifically Christian literature.[7]

Theoretically this situation might have obtained indefinitely, but it did not. Gradually Christian writings acquired broad currency and esteem in Christian circles, were increasingly read in worship and employed in teaching along with the Jewish scriptures, and eventually came to be regarded as scriptures in their own right with a religious authority approximating to that of the Jewish scriptures. How, when, and why this development took place cannot now be determined with much precision because the evidence is sparse, leaving ample room for uncertainty and conjecture. Still, the broad lines of the development, and the nature of the forces behind it, are clear enough.

THE EMERGENCE OF CHRISTIAN SCRIPTURE

The emergence of a distinctively Christian scripture was a gradual process stretching from the composition of Christian literature in the first and early second centuries, through the dissemination and use of these writings in the second and third centuries, to the fixation of a definitive collection (canon) of Christian scripture in the fourth and fifth centuries. This process was not only gradual, but was also uneven, moving at a different pace and even in somewhat different directions in the various regional constituencies of the ancient church. And furthermore, this process was not consistently deliberative and self-conscious, but at many points was indebted to merely circumstantial contingencies as well. With these qualifications in mind, we may sketch out the emergence of Christian scripture.

The Letters of Paul

The letters of the apostle Paul, the earliest surviving Christian writings, were in many respects very unlikely candidates for scriptural regard, chiefly because they are real letters and, as such, documents of the moment tailored to the specific concerns of the individual Christian congregations to whom Paul wrote. Their particularity and the geographical disparities of the congregations to which they were sent augured against even their preservation. In spite of this, many of Paul's letters were not only preserved but by the end of the first century had been gathered up into a collection, and so were regarded and employed as a group. It is not clear how much this development owed to a random and informal exchange of Paul's letters among such churches as possessed any, and how much it was due to the systematic efforts of associates and admirers of Paul who, after the apostle's death, sought to promote Pauline teaching by preserving, collecting, and disseminating his letters.[8]

In either case, by the early second century Paul's letters were known to Christians over a wide area stretching from Syria through Asia Minor to Rome, and were available in one or more editions which presented them under the rubric of "letters to seven churches."[9] The idea that Paul wrote to precisely seven churches was conceived as a way of overcoming the particularity of Paul's correspondence: the number seven was a symbol of wholeness, and it was supposed that by writing to seven churches Paul actually meant to speak to the whole church. Thus a perception and assertion of the general relevance of Paul's letters was prerequisite to an acknowledgment of their religious authority, which did not accrue to them merely because they were written by an apostle.[10]

In spite of the general availability of the collected letters of Paul by the early second century, they had not by then attained the status of Christian scripture. It is remarkable that the works of Christian writers through most of the second century show little or no knowledge of Paul's letters and seem innocent of their influence.[11] A notable exception to this rule is provided by Marcion (fl. 140–150), a radical Paulinist who considered Paul the only true apostle, repudiated the scriptures of Judaism, and insisted that Paul's letters were the only authoritative resource for authentic Christian teaching. Marcion is the first person known to us to set up a distinctively Christian scripture, and his scripture consisted strictly of Paul's letters and the Gospel of Luke (or a form of it).[12] Besides Marcion, Paul's letters also served as a court of appeal for various gnostic-Christian teachers of the second century, even though their basic concepts seem not to have been drawn from Paul but were only buttressed from Paul's letters.

The use of Paul's letters by marcionites and gnostics, groups which were progressively labeled heterodox, has sometimes been thought to have discredited Paul in the eyes of others, and so to explain the apparent neglect of Paul's letters by other writers.[13] But this seems unlikely because by the end of the second century Paul's letters were being confidently invoked by Irenaeus of Lyons, Tertullian of Carthage, and Clement of Alexandria. The esteem in which the letters are held by such geographically widespread figures implies that the letters must have experienced a broad-based and continuous use through the second century, even if this is not evident in the literature preserved from that period. In any event, by the end of the second century Paul's letters were believed to have ecumenical relevance and authority despite their exaggerated particularity, and had attained the status of Christian scripture.

The Gospels

From the beginning Christianity had acquiesced in the authority of the sayings of Jesus, not so much because of their intrinsic merits as because of the Christian identification of Jesus as the Messiah. The authority of the sayings was rooted in the authority of the teacher. But narratives about Jesus also had their value, serving to underline his messianic identity, to represent him as the fulfillment of Israelite prophecy, and to provide paradigms for missionary preaching and moral instruction. Originally and for several decades the traditions of the words and deeds of Jesus were preserved only by memory and transmitted by word of mouth. Only gradually, and then by no clear necessity, did these traditions begin to be committed to writing.

The earliest extant Gospels are partial deposits of this primitive oral tradition, Mark dating from 65–70, Matthew and Luke from 80–90, and John from 90–100, though behind these larger accounts there lay some earlier and smaller written collections of traditions about Jesus. But the oral tradition was sufficiently rich in content and well-established by custom that it persisted well beyond these early written Gospels. Through the first half of the second century oral tradition continued to enjoy a prestige greater than any of its redactions and to furnish materials for the composition of many additional Gospel-type documents.[14]

The composition of written Gospels represents an effort, on the one hand, to collect and codify traditions about Jesus, but on the other hand, also to interpret those traditions in the service of particular constructions of the meaning of Christianity. The interpretations offered by the early Gospels are quite distinctive among themselves, and each arose in response to a different situation.[15] Hence the Gospels, no less than the letters of Paul, are occasional documents, composed in and directed toward specific and local constituencies. Accordingly, it was at first customary for any particular Christian group to know and to use only one such document. The authority of these documents was implicit: their authors remained anonymous and relied on the authoritative force of the traditions themselves. The authority of written Gospels was also limited for a time by the coexistence of oral tradition. But as the Gospels became more widely known, and as oral tradition began to dissipate and grow wild, Gospel documents were increasingly appreciated and employed.

It was somewhat contrary to their actual character as interpretations of the Jesus-traditions that the Gospels came to be valued first as historical records, and not as scripture.[16] This perspective became problematical, however, when Christian communities became acquainted with a multiplicity of such documents, for although a plurality of historical testimonies had its own uses, the ancient church was well aware that among the Gospels there were obvious discrepancies that were not easily to be reconciled.[17] This fact, together with the fixed custom of employing only one Gospel and the idea that the Christian message (which was itself traditionally known as "gospel") must be unitary and coherent, militated against any easy acknowledgment of numerous Gospels. Thus the history of Gospel literature in the second century was marked by two opposing tendencies: on the one hand the desire for a comprehensive and theologically adequate Gospel led to a proliferation of such documents, and on the other hand the desire for a single and self-consistent Gospel tended to reduce the number, either by championing one Gospel against the rest or by conflating several such documents into one.[18] The signal example of this latter tendency is provided by the *Diatessaron* of Tatian, who, about 170, ingeniously wove the contents of Matthew, Mark, Luke, and John, as well as some other written and/or oral traditions, into a single narrative. This effort (and the very broad popularity of its result) not only symptomizes the problem posed by a multiplicity of Gospels, but shows very clearly that the Gospels, while they were valued for their contents, had not acquired sacrosanct status as individual texts.

Ultimately neither an indefinite plurality of Gospels nor the exclusive use of a single Gospel proved acceptable. Instead, the ancient church settled on a compromise, namely, a collection of four Gospels. None of these four, however, was considered as *the* Gospel proper; rather, each was seen as a (partial) witness to the gospel message, and therefore each member of the collection was known as the gospel *according to* its putative author.[19] Hence the tension between plurality and unity was not resolved but only perpetuated in manageable form. The formation of this "fourfold Gospel" occurred relatively late in the second century in Western Christianity, but its general acceptance occurred only in the third century. It is notable that the Gospels acquired their scriptural standing as a group and not individually, and that religious authority was vested precisely in their collectivity.

Other Writings

Beyond the collected letters of Paul and the fourfold Gospel, a very considerable number of other writings acquired the status and function of scripture in ancient Christianity, though not all of them retained this distinction. Several apocalypses were held in high regard by reason of their claim to impart inspired revelation. The *Apocalypse of Peter* and *The Shepherd of Hermas* were scarcely less popular in the second century than the *Revelation to John*. Various compositions of the Acts-type, retailing stories about the apostles, were current as well. But an even larger number of letters, apart from Paul's, were in use. The prominence of the letter-genre in early Christian literature was due in part to the practical necessities of communication among geographically distant Christian groups. But many of the "letters" which were accorded scriptural value were not actual pieces of correspondence, but theological, ethical and apologetical tracts dressed out with epistolary conventions.[20] The stimulus for this must have been provided in part by the letters of Paul which, because they were widely current, became something of a standard, at least in outward form, for later would-be Christian teachers. And not a few of these letters were pseudonymous, being given out in the name of some apostolic figure (Paul, Peter, James, Jude, Barnabas, or even of all the apostles together!) and being received as statements of "apostolic" teaching.[21]

In sum, during the second century many individual pieces of Christian literature came into circulation, attained wide currency, and acquired the function, if not always the designation, of scripture. These were used along with the scriptures of Judaism as resources of Christian preaching, teaching, worship, ethical instruction, and apologetics.[22] Some of these (the letters of Paul and the Gospels) had been gathered into discrete collections and were known and used in collective form, but other writings continued to have largely individual histories of use. But if by the end of the second century Christianity had generated many scriptural documents of its own, their number was still indefinite and their nature was diverse in both form and content. And even though these documents had the functional role of scripture, that is, were understood to be religiously authoritative, they were not yet thought to have the sort of oracular and inspired character which had traditonally been ascribed to the scriptures of Judaism.[23] Consequently, the idea of distinctively Christian scriptures remained without clear textual or conceptual definition, and this circumstance persisted into the fourth century.

The next stage in the formation of Christian scripture was the creation of a formal canon, that is, a definitive list of those writings which were received by the church for use in worship and teaching. While a measure of discrimination among Christian writings was already at work in the late second century and during the third, it was fitful and led to no clear results.[24] The effort to consolidate Christian scriptures into a fixed canon, and thus to make a determination as to which writings were genuinely authoritative and which were not, belongs for the most part to the fourth and fifth centuries. During this period actual lists began to be drawn up.

One of the earliest and most interesting of these is provided by Eusebius of Caesarea in the course of his *Ecclesiastical History*, composed about 325. He sorted a large number of Christian writings into three categories, "acknowledged," "disputed," and "heretical." The acknowledged books, so designated because they had been in long and wide use and were unanimously esteemed in Eusebius' day, numbered only 21 (18 of these were comprised by the four Gospels and 14 letters of Paul). The disputed books, so called because although they were known to most their genuineness was often doubted, numbered 11 (including, interestingly, 6 which ultimately found their way into the canon nevertheless). The heretical books extended to a large number, but are only partially named by Eusebius.[25]

The earliest list of acknowledged and authoritative books which agrees exactly with the canon of historic Christianity was laid down by Athanasius, bishop of Alexandria in Egypt, in 367, who named 27 documents as alone comprising Christian scripture. Other lists of the same or closely similar scope were set forth by various local or regional ecclesiastical councils of the late fourth century, so that by the early fifth century there had emerged a widespread unanimity about the extent of Christian scripture.[26] The "books of the new covenant" were taken to be 27 in number, and precisely these documents have stood as the exclusively normative Christian scriptures, taking their place alongside the scriptures of Judaism, from the fifth century to the present.

It is important to note that this canon was never authorized and mandated by any *ecumenical* (general) council of the ancient church, even though it was adopted by various regional bishops and councils, and therefore it had no strictly official status in the church at large. Its authority, rather, was de facto, resting upon a consensus which had emerged through centuries of experience with a much larger body of scriptures than that limited number which attained canonical standing. The first official and binding pronouncement of the church upon the content of Christian scripture was not made until the sixteenth century by the Council of Trent. This was a pronouncement of the Roman church, made in reaction to the Protestant Reformation, and consequently it had no force for Protestant churches, nor for that matter, for the orthodox communions of the East. Nevertheless, the early and largely informal consensus of the ancient church has remained effective in practice for all branches of Christianity up to the present.[27]

THE EVOLUTION OF A CHRISTIAN SCRIPTURAL CANON

It is clear that over a period of four centuries Christianity evolved from a non-scriptural religion into a fully scriptural religion possessing a canon of specifically Christian texts. But a tracing of that evolution is neither complete nor instructive without an explanation of its causes and an assessment of its consequences, and it is to these matters that we may now turn.

It is not possible to specify a single cause which alone or above all others led to the formation of Christian scripture. The emergence of Christian scripture, which taken as a whole must include the composition of early Christian literature, its selective use as scripture and its eventual consolidation into a formal canon, and which extended over a long period, can only be understood as an aspect of the historical development of the Christian religion itself, and therefore as contingent upon a complex interplay of forces. Even so, some factors were more significant than others and may be singled out for discussion.

The appeal to the scriptures of Judaism, although very important in the early period of Christianity, could not finally suffice for Christian needs. The specifically Christian interpretation of those writings was challenged and repudiated by Judaism itself on a variety of grounds.[28] More problematical still was the fact that this interpretation could not be taken for granted even within Christianity itself, as some Christians, sensitive to the diversity of the Jewish scriptures and to the points of basic difference between Judaism and Christianity, rejected the authority of certain parts of those scriptures, or even of the entire body of Jewish texts.[29] These difficulties went hand in hand with the success of the Christian mission beyond the confines of Judaism, which resulted in a predominantly non-Jewish constituency neither well-acquainted with the scriptures of Judaism nor conditioned to presume their authority. In this situation the force of appeals to Jewish texts was inevitably weakened and the utility of specifically Christian resources was increasingly felt.

But the role of the Jewish scriptures was, even at the beginning, only ancillary to the direct testimony about Jesus which consisted in the tradition of his words and deeds and in the witness of the apostles in preaching and teaching. These were the primitive and preeminent authorities upon which faith and practice depended. For half a century and more the words and deeds of Jesus were adequately accessible in oral tradition, and for decades too the apostles were living authorities among Christian congregations, but in the nature of the case this situation could not persist indefinitely.

With the passage of time, the demise of apostolic teachers, the geographical expansion of Christianity and its concurrent cultural and linguistic diversification, reliance upon oral tradition became increasingly tenuous. The foundational testimony on which the church had depended had to be cast into forms and modes which would enable it to be sustained over a longer time and under changing circumstances. In these conditions, then, the impulse toward the textualization of tradition originated. The products of this impulse were, variously, the composition of Christian writings, the valuation of Christian writings as scripture, and ultimately the formation of a formal canon of Christian scriptures. The composition of Christian literature occurred, to be sure, at different times and in different specific situations, and not many early Christian documents may be understood simply as efforts to preserve tradition: most of them aimed also, and even more, to interpret and apply tradition and thus to mediate its meaning. Nevertheless they had the effect of preserving and fixing tradition, and were subsequently valued just for that reason.[30]

The interest in tradition is also reflected in the composition of writings under the names of apostles, who were understood as the ultimate sources and guarantors of tradition, and in the attempts to associate even anonymous writings with apostolic figures.[31] Since Christianity was dependent from the first upon dominical and apostolic tradition, it is possible to regard the emergence of a scriptural canon consisting of Gospels and apostolic writings as a necessity inherent in the nature of Christianity.[32] But it must be emphasized that this was not so much a logical necessity as a historical necessity, for the textualization of tradition was dictated by a continuation of history which had not been anticipated in earliest Christianity and which increasingly distanced the church from its generative testimony. Scripture was simply the form in which tradition came to be preserved under the duress of the church's on-going historical experience, and the means by which the church sought to sustain continuity with its origins.

The emergence of Christian scriptures, however, needs to be distinguished from the creation of a canon of scripture, that is, the determination of a fixed group of scriptures which are held to be exclusively authoritative. The church possessed scriptures long before it possessed a canon. The existence of scriptures is, of course, prerequisite to the creation of a canon, but not sufficient for it, and therefore additional causes must be discovered for the determination of a canon.

The development of a canon of Christian scripture was part of a larger movement in the ancient church toward religious self-definition. This movement towards the consolidation and standardization of Christian belief and practice arose in the second century amid progressively diverse conceptions of the substance of Christian teaching and the authorities for it. Persisting into the fifth century, this movement resulted in the articulation of Christian orthodoxy and the disenfranchisement of deviant interpretations.[33] The doctrinal controversies of this period acutely posed the problem of the legitimate resources and authorities of Christian belief. As early as the late second century the need was felt to discriminate more carefully among the large number of Christian writings which were in use and to inquire after their pedigrees. At the same time, doctrinal debates tended to shift the accent from the popular and liturgical uses of Christian writings to the question of their theological content and authority. A selective delimitation of Christian scripture leading to a formal canon was one means by which the fundamental resources of Christian faith could be defined and variations of Christian teaching could be controlled.[34]

These interests are evident in the principles which were invoked by the ancient church to affirm or deny the authority of individual writings. These so-called criteria of canonicity were numerous, but the most prominent among them were apostolicity, catholicity, orthodoxy, and established usage.[35]

The notion of the apostolicity of a writing was often articulated in terms of authorship by an apostle, but it was in fact a much broader and more flexible concept than this, and could signify, besides actual authorship, derivation from the apostolic period, or even simply the agreement of a document's content with what the church took to be apostolic teaching.[36]

The question of a document's catholicity concerned its relevance to the church as a whole. This principle reveals the church's preference for writings which were broadly accessible and widely pertinent as over against esoteric and idiosyncratic documents.

Still more crucial was the standard of orthodoxy: no document was to be received as authoritative unless it conformed to, or at least did not manifestly contradict, right teaching. That such a criterion could be invoked means that the true faith was capable of being apprehended independently of scripture, specifically in what was known as the *regula fidei*, the "rule of faith," a traditional summary formulation of fundamental articles of faith. Here it is obvious that even in the period when the canon of scripture was taking shape there was no idea that scripture was the sole repository of authoritative teaching. To the contrary, the authority of scripture was gauged against authoritative yet unwritten tradition.[37]

No less important was the question of established usage, that is, whether a writing had been customarily employed from an early time in worship and widely acknowledged. This principle, which appealed to standing practice rather than to the intrinsic character of a document, became explicit only in the third and fourth centuries, by which time the church was in a position to assess its own past. Nevertheless, traditional usage had in fact been the major force in promoting documents toward canonical status before it was articulated as a principle of canonicity.

Even though the criteria of canonicity professed by the ancient church show well enough that canon-formation involved a measure of reflective deliberation, it is difficult to regard these criteria as the effective *reasons* for the canonization of any particular document. What these criteria reveal, rather, are the desiderata of the church for its scripture, and therefore they tell us more about the canon-shaping church than the writings which came to be canonized or the actual causes of canonization. Apostolicity, catholicity, orthodoxy, and traditional usage are conceptual warrants that served to confirm and legitimize the standing of documents which had become authoritative for other and more practical reasons, namely their traditional utility for Christian teaching. The writings included in the canon do not fully satisfy these criteria, whereas many pieces of early Christian scripture which were finally omitted from the canon satisfy them equally well. Consequently, from a historical point of view it has to be said that the boundaries of the canon are arbitrary, and that the canon is deeply indebted to historical contingency.[38]

But precisely for this reason it was necessary to insist the more strongly upon the correctness of these boundaries and to stress the noncontingent character of the collection as such. This was achieved by two claims which were not altogether compatible. The propriety of the canon's limits was defended on the basis that only these documents derive from the apostles, so that their authority rests on *historical* proximity to the events of revelation. But this claim was accompanied by the growing belief that the authority of the canon rested upon the inspiration of its contents by God himself, an idea which supersedes and to some extent contravenes the argument from apostolicity. By these means the ancient church sought both to affirm the historical authority of the canon and yet to preserve that authority from historical contingency.[39]

The emergence of Christian scriptures and the formation of a canon of Christian scripture are therefore to be understood as stages of a gradual transition within Christianity from living authorities to written authorities, and from functionally authoritative writings to formally authoritative writings. The variety of forces contributing to this development from within and from without must not be underestimated, though they will probably never be fully detailed.[40] For present purposes, however, it is more important to canvass the consequences of the formation of a scriptural canon.

THE EFFECTS OF CANON FORMATION ON THE CHURCH

Short of a full survey of the history of the use and interpretation of the Bible in subsequent Christianity, it would be difficult to grasp the rich results of the creation of a canon of scripture. But several of its most decisive and far-reaching effects may be briefly sketched.[41]

The creation of a canon of scripture stabilized in written form the traditions which derived from the period of Christian beginnings, were instrumental to its early development, and had been more or less continuously useful in the life of the ancient church. This stabilization had two aspects:

1. It insured the preservation of those traditions, and through their preservation the ancient church sought both to affirm its continuity with its foundational past and to maintain access to the primal revelation from which the church had taken its rise.
2. It reduced the scope of earlier tradition by acknowledging as authoritative only what was believed to be authentic and original tradition.

In this way the broad diversification of Christian belief and practice, which increasingly threatened the theological and social coherence of Christianity, was checked. Thus the canon of scripture is not simply a collection of early written traditions, but a selection of certain traditions from a larger pool of possibilities.

But while this selection was made from the point of view of emerging Christian orthodoxy and in the service of greater uniformity, the canon itself is not narrowly ideological. Its relatively broad compass was dictated by the long usage of these various writings in the earlier period as well as by their general currency in the fourth and fifth centuries. Although canonization did effectively preserve a significant body of early Christian tradition, its limiting function was no less successful. Virtually no primitive Christian tradition persisted outside the canon, and ancient Christian writings omitted from the canon have survived only accidentally, if at all.[42]

The establishment of a canon of scripture also served to formalize the authority of its contents as media of revelation for subsequent Christianity. The authority of these writings was, to begin with, of a functional sort, resting upon their contents and utility. The process of canonization, however, led to an ever greater correlation between these documents and apostolic figures, and the authority of the writings was increasingly legitimized by the assumption that they derived from apostles, directly or indirectly. The apostles, for their part, were regarded as the immediate witnesses of the revelation and thus uniquely qualified to attest it. In this way the authority of the documents was made formally dependent upon their authors. But once these writings came to be viewed as embodying direct apostolic testimony in virtue of which they were indispensable *means* to the apprehension of the revelation in Jesus of Nazareth, it was but a short and easy step to understand these writings as *part of* the revelation, and as being revelatory in and of themselves.

This altered the basic conception of the nature and authority of scripture: instead of being the church's tradition of testimony to the revelation, the scripture is now seen as God's revelation to the church; instead of being the words of the apostles, it is now seen as the word of God mediated through the apostles; and correspondingly, the ultimate authority of scripture is rooted not merely in the historical proximity of the apostles to Jesus, but equally in its divine "inspiration."[43] So, just as the composition and use of early Christian writings had the effect of textualizing tradition, the later canonization of those writings had the effect of literalizing revelation insofar as it assigned to the texts an intrinsic and formal authority.

Another major consequence of the canonization of scripture is that later Christian tradition acquired a fundamentally exegetical character. The task of exegesis was posed by the existence of a holy book, but for two different reasons. The first was the nature of the canon itself as a collection of writings which derived from diverse circumstances and embodied divergent viewpoints. Since, however, the collection was defended on the basis of the apostolic character of its contents and regarded as the fruit of divine inspiration, the internal inconsistencies of the canon had to be overcome in the interest of the coherence and authority of the whole. The canonical documents were therefore subjected to a harmonizing interpretation which aimed to show that perceived incongruities were only apparent and that, rightly interpreted, all the constituent parts of the New Testament were in agreement and that the truth of the scriptures was unitary.[44]

The second and more far-reaching compulsion to exegesis lay in the nature of the canon as a closed and fixed body of texts. Precisely because the canon was a delimitation of authentic and authoritative tradition, the only means for the continuing appropriation of that tradition was interpretative commentary upon the canonical texts. If it was the function of canonization to reduce and stabilize the resources of Christian teaching, then it has been the role of exegesis to enlarge and variegate the meanings of those texts in order to make them fruitful for the on-going life of the Christian church.[45] Only in this way has it been possible for a canon of ancient texts to retain their relevance, and so also to retain an effective authority, amid the ever-changing needs of the community, and, conversely, only in this way has the church again and again been able to submit itself to the authority of its scripture.

It needs to be emphasized that the exegetical endeavors of the church have always had a thoroughly practical objective, namely, the edification and doctrinal instruction of the faithful.[46] This purpose, together with the presumption that the ultimate author of scripture is God himself, has meant that the church could never be content with the merely literal and historical sense of these texts. Although that meaning has never been denied, it has rarely had a controlling or preeminent importance, but has provided the starting point for the discovery, by allegorical methods, of the more profound spiritual and moral truths which the scripture is believed to embody. In this way any single passage of scripture is subject to a plurality of interpretations, and the legitimacy of such interpretations, so long as they fall within the broad perimeters of orthodox doctrine, is determined only by their relevance and usefulness in their own settings. The history of the interpretation of the scriptures within Christianity is therefore characterized by a rich diversity, and even though much of it must appear to the modern mind as fanciful and arbitrary, its success can be measured only by the extent to which it has enabled the Bible to remain a powerful force in the long life of the church.[47]

THE FUNCTIONS OF SCRIPTURE IN CHRISTIAN COMMUNITY AND INDIVIDUAL LIFE

It remains to make some brief remarks about the ways in which scripture has functioned and continues to function both with the life of the Christian community and in the lives of individual believers. In this connection it is difficult to formulate valid generalizations since the role of the Christian Bible has varied in different historical periods and in different branches of Christendom, not to mention among groups and individuals within them. The broad observations which follow are therefore liable to many particular qualifications.

The primary context of the use of scripture in Christianity has always been the service of worship, in which scripture is regularly read and expounded. This practice goes back to the earliest days of Christianity, and was taken over, along with Christianity's earliest scriptures, directly from Judaism. In the ancient synagogue it was customary for portions of the Law and the Prophets to be read to the congregation, and then to be interpreted, on each Sabbath. In Christian worship, at first only the scriptures of Judaism were read, as no distinctively Christian scriptures were yet available. But as specifically Christian writings gained currency and value, they began to be read alongside the Jewish scriptures in the worship setting. This practice, which is evidenced already in the mid-second century but was undoubtedly earlier even than that, enhanced the authority of Christian writings and was an important factor leading to their later canonization.[48]

The formation of a canon of Christian scriptures then permitted the development of a lectionary system providing a fixed schedule for the liturgical reading of scripture passages throughout the year, thus promoting, over time, a broad acquaintance with scripture in the worshipping community. This practical effect was blunted, however, as the readings, which were at first lengthy, were gradually reduced in extent so that other liturgical elements could be incorporated in the service, and as relatively brief passages were used without attention to their larger literary contexts. As a result the scripture was read and heard in church in largely piecemeal fashion. If this was, to some extent, a circumstantial necessity, it was not at odds with the oracular conception of scripture which prevails widely in historic and contemporary Christianity.[49]

The reading of scripture has customarily been accompanied by the sermon or homily which, in its classical form, constitutes an interpretation, exposition and application of the text(s) previously read, and aims at the instruction and edification of the worshippers. The sermon, then, has historically been the primary and recurrent occasion for the interpretation of scripture in the church. It may be informed by great learning, but its chief aim is to give scripture a direct, *ad hoc* relevance to the congregation.[50]

In addition to the reading and exposition of scripture in corporate worship, the private devotional reading of scripture has also had its place. The currency of this practice has depended historically on two factors, the availability of scriptural texts for private use, and the availability of those texts in the vernacular. These conditions have been amply satisified in the modern period, and they were apparently adequately met in the early centuries of the church.[51] But this was not always so.

During the middle ages there was a long hiatus, at least in the Western church, in the private use of scripture, and this was due to a sharp decline in the production of Bibles and to widespread illiteracy. The latter had its consequences even for the reading of scripture in worship, for the Latin of the Vulgate, which was the standard text for Western Christianity, was simply unintelligible to the majority of worshippers. Thus the scriptures for a long time had little direct impact on the ordinary believer either through worship or private reading. Even in this situation, however, the influence of scripture was not eclipsed. Christian art during the middle ages has appropriately been called "the people's Bible," since through painting, sculpture, carved wood and colored glass there was vivid depiction of scriptural personages, events, images, and themes, instructing the illiterate by the language of symbols.[52] Scripture also found representation in the liturgy, both through the drama of the sacraments and through formulae, prayers and hymns imbued with scriptural language and ideas.

A direct acquaintance with and use of scripture by the ordinary Christian had an unprecedented revival in the fifteenth and sixteenth centuries. The invention of the printing press suddenly made Bibles available in great number and at modest cost.[53] Not long afterward, the Protestant Reformation gave a new emphasis to the authority of scripture, energetically promoted its translation into the vernacular, and prescribed an intimate, first-hand knowledge of scripture as a primary religious duty of the individual believer. Consequently, Protestant Christianity has been the context in the modern period where the private reading of scripture is most assiduously pursued. For many Protestants, the Bible is a *vade mecum* daily studied for instruction and consulted for guidance in everyday life, and so serves as the chief instrument of personal piety. As a result, Protestants are, on the whole, much more closely familiar with scripture than Roman Catholic or Orthodox Christians.[54] But the reasons for this feature of Protestantism lie within its special conception of the authority of scripture.

The role of scripture within Christianity tends to be most diverse, both in theory and in practice, in connection with its function as a theological and doctrinal norm among the various branches of Christianity. The theological authority of the Bible is, of course, fully conceded on all sides, and yet the ways in which this authority is conceived and implemented vary widely.

Within the Roman and Orthodox settings there is the closest correlation between scripture and the tradition of the church's faith: scripture is a dimension of tradition, distinguished not so much by its antiquity as by its literary character. Here the church is understood as the source of scripture and as the proper context of scripture. The church collected the scripture, vouches for its authority, and is the arbiter of scripture's meaning. Therefore the correct interpretation of scripture is available only through the historic community of faith. Hence Roman Catholic and Orthodox appeals to scripture are made in accordance with the tradition of the church's teaching and in reliance upon the interpretations developed by the ancient ecclesiastical authorities, the "fathers" of the church. Conceived in this way, scripture does not constitute a viable theological norm in and of itself, but only when it is rightly understood, and this understanding occurs in the light of and in conformity with the faith believed, confessed, and taught by the church.[55]

Over against this unitary, organic relationship between scripture and tradition, Protestant Christianity has insisted upon the preeminent and exclusive authority of scripture in matters of faith and practice, such that even the tradition of the church's faith is accountable at the bar of scripture. Here the appeal to scripture is made directly to the plain sense of the text by the individual believer, without recourse to interpretive authorities. The essential clarity of the text and its capacity to serve as its own interpreter are emphasized. Consequently, in Protestant opinion scripture may serve in and of itself as a thoroughly sufficient norm for faith.

The evolution of these different viewpoints and their particularized formulations in modern Christian thought are too complex for brief description.[56] For present purposes what needs to be noticed is that the doctrinal function of scripture is much more pronounced in Protestantism than in other forms of Christianity, and that the demotion or repudiation of other doctrinal authorities has prompted not only a much heavier reliance on scripture, but also a much stronger emphasis on its *intrinsic* authority. But in spite of its common deference to scripture as the controlling theological norm, Protestantism has achieved no unanimity about the precise nature of biblical authority nor about the appropriate methods of biblical interpretation. As a result, scripture operates somewhat differently as a doctrinal standard among various Protestant groups.[57]

The functions of scripture within Christianity are only partially, and perhaps even superficially, characterized by reference to its liturgical, devotional, and doctrinal uses, for while these are important in themselves, they are also the media by which scripture shapes the imaginations and sensibilities of individual Christians in subtle yet far-reaching ways. But both the formal and the personalistic functions of scripture take effect in different proportions and to different results over the broad spectrum of Christian faith and life. To speak of Christianity as a scriptural religion is to point to its consistent reliance upon the Bible for the nurture and instruction of the believing community, and to the remarkable capacity of the Bible to be continually reappropriated as a source of religious insight under the most diverse conditions. These are valid observations, but they must not be taken to suggest that scripture has the same importance or plays a uniform role in Christendom as a whole.

NOTES

1. It does not appear, however, that these two authorities were always correlative in function or equal in force. So, for example, in the synoptic sayings source ("Q") which lies behind the Gospels of Matthew and Luke, full authority seems to have been vested simply in the sayings of Jesus. In the case of the letters of Paul, on the other hand, relatively slight appeal is made to the sayings of Jesus, and the chief authority is the apostolic witness.

2. For discussions of the early Christian use of the scriptures of Judaism, see the classic study of C. H. Dodd, *According to the Scriptures: The Sub-structure of New Testament Theology* (London, 1952), B. Lindars, *New Testament Apologetic: The Doctrinal Significance of the Old Testament Quotations* (London, 1961), and the useful survey of D. M. Smith, "The Use of the Old Testament in the New," in J. M. Efird, ed., *The Use of the Old Testament in the New and Others Essays: Studies in Honor of W. F. Stinespring* (Durham, N.C., 1972), 3–65, with references to most of the pertinent literature.

3. This has been shown by A. C. Sundberg, *The Old Testament of the Early Church* (Harvard Theological Studies, 20; Cambridge, 1964). His findings are summarized in "The Old Testament of the Early Church," *Harvard Theological Review* 51 (1958) 205–26.

4. While all branches of Christianity use the same New Testament, they are not agreed on the scope of the Old Testament: Protestants subscribe to the Hebrew canon of 39 books, but the Roman and Orthodox churches acknowledge additional books which belonged to the Greek version of the Jewish scriptures, the Septuagint. The Septuagint, not the Hebrew, was the version of the Jewish scriptures employed in ancient Christianity, so that the Protestant adherence to the Hebrew canon is innovative. Most of the additional books contained in the Septuagint are fully employed as scriptural by early Christian authorities. For discussion of these differences and of the "deuterocanonical" literature itself see B. M. Metzger, *An Introduction to the Apocrypha* (New York, 1957).

5. A. C. Sundberg, "The Protestant Old Testament Canon: Should It Be Re-

examined?" *Catholic Biblical Quarterly* 28 (1966) 194–203, and "The 'Old Testament': A Christian Canon," *Catholic Biblical Quarterly* 30 (1968) 143–55.

6. Two of the factors at work in this were the disposition of the Jewish environment in favor of oral tradition and the highly eschatological orientation of earliest Christianity. Both militated against the composition of Christian literature.

7. The references to "scripture" in Christian writings through most of the second century are almost unexceptionally to Jewish writings. For the very occasional application of the term *graphe* to Christian documents and the question of its meaning ("scripture," "writing," "document") see the remarks of R. P. C. Hanson, *Tradition in the Early Church* (Philadelphia, 1962), 205–8.

8. The former has been the traditional explanation, but the evidence actually favors the latter: some Pauline letters have been subjected to secondary editorial revision, and the collection contains numerous pseudonymously Pauline letters. See H.-M. Schenke, "Das Weiterwirken des Paulus und die Pflege seines Erbs durch die Paulusschule," *New Testament Studies* 21 (1975) 505–18.

9. For early editions of the letters of Paul, consult J. Finegan, "The Original Form of the Pauline Collection," *Harvard Theological Review* 49 (1956) 85–103; H. J. Frede, "Die Ordnung der Paulusbriefe und der Platz des Kilosserbriefs im Corpus Paulinum," *Vetus Latina. Die Reste der altlateinischen Bibel*, 24/2 (Freiburg, 1969), 290–303; and N. A. Dahl, "The Origin of the Earliest Prologues to the Pauline Letters," *Semeia* 12 (1978) 233–77.

10. K. Stendahl, "The Apocalypse of John and the Epistles of Paul in the Muratorian Fragment," in W. Klassen and G. Snyder, eds., *Current Issues in New Testament Interpretation* (New York, 1962), 239– 45.

11. On the use of Paul's letters in the second century see especially the studies of A. Lindemann, *Paulus im ältesten Christentum* (Beiträge zur historischen Theologie, 58; Tübingen, 1979), and D. Rensberger, *As the Apostle Teaches: The Development of the Use of Paul's Letters in Second Century Christianity* (Yale diss., 1981).

12. On Marcion generally see A. von Harnack, *Marcion: Das Evangelium von fremden Gott*, 2nd ed. (Leipzig, 1924), and with regard to Marcion's significance for Christian scripture see J. Knox, *Marcion and the New Testament* (Chicago, 1942), and H. von Campenhausen, *The Formation of the Christian Bible* (Philadelphia, 1972). All of these, however, overplay the importance of Marcion for the creation of a canon of Christian scripture.

13. So, for example, W. Bauer, *Orthodoxy and Heresy in Earliest Christianity* (ET Philadelphia, 1971) 226–28; Campenhausen, *The Formation of the Christian Bible*, 144–45; W. Schneemelcher, "Paulus in der griechischen Kirche des 2. Jahrhunderts," *Zeitschrift für Kirchengeschichte* 75 (1964) 1–20. This view has been fully discussed and successfully refuted by Rensberger, *As the Apostle Teaches.*

14. This is shown not only on the explicit remarks of Papias, bishop of Hierapolis in the early second century, as preserved by Eusebius (*Church History* 3. 39. 4), but also by the use made of traditions about Jesus among the Apostolic Fathers, on which see H. Köster, *Synoptische Überlieferung bei den apostolischen Vätern* (Texte und Untersuchungen, 65; Berlin, 1957). The many Gospel-type documents composed in early Christianity and still extant may be consulted in E. Hennecke and W. Schneemelcher, eds., *New Testament Apocrypha*, 1 (ET Philadelphia, 1963).

15. This has been made abundantly clear by that method of New Testament study called "redaction criticism." For a survey of the method and a summary of its results, see J. Rohde, *Rediscovering the Teaching of the Evangelists* (ET London, 1968).

16. Thus the Gospels were first called *apomnemoneumata*, "memoirs" or "reminiscences" of the apostles. For the sense of the term see R. Grant, *The Earliest Lives of Jesus*, 14–20.

17. This problem is surveyed by H. Merkel, *Die Widersprüche zwischen den Evangelien. Ihre polemische und apologetische Behandlung in der alten Kirche bis zu Augustin* (Wissenschaftliche Untersuchungen zum Neuen Testament, 13; Tübingen, 1971).

18. O. Cullmann, "The Plurality of the Gospels as a Theological Problem in Antiquity," in *The Early Church* (Philadelphia, 1956), 39–54. A collection of texts reflecting this problem is provided by H. Merkel, *Die Pluralität der Evangelien als theologisches und exegetisches Problem in der alten Kirche* (Berne, 1978).

19. This was possible only because of a changed estimate of the Gospels, as Cullmann (ibid.) points out: they were viewed less as historical records than as testimonies of faith.

20. This must be said of Hebrews, James, and 1 John at least (and 1 John does not even have the form of a letter, though it has been traditionally regarded as one).

21. Here too the letters of Paul were probably influential in promoting the idea that "apostolic" teaching was to be found in "apostolic" letters. The pseudonymous issuing of letters in the names of apostles is counterpart to the tendency of the second century to associate anonymous documents with apostles also, and both illustrate the church's desire to certify its received teaching with the authority of the apostles. For the idea of apostolicity in relation to the authoritative status of Christian writings see further below.

22. Undoubtedly there was much more scriptural literature in the ancient church than we can now know since some of it has long since perished and finds no mention in ancient sources. For writings which did not finally gain a foothold in the canon but are still extant by happy accident, though sometimes only in fragments, see below, note 42.

23. Inspiration was not attributed to Christian writings in the early period, except in the case of several apocalpytic texts which by their nature constituted (inspired) revelations: the Apocalypse of John, The Shepherd of Hermas, The

Apocalypse of Peter. Apart from these, the scriptural valuation of Christian texts was not dependent on a concept of their inspiration. The idea that Christian scriptures were, like the Jewish scriptures, inspired, did not take hold until the third century and later. See further below, note 39.

24. A famous annotated listing of writings received by the church as scripture is the so-called Muratorian Canon, a Western document from the late second or early third century, but it represents only a preliminary stage in the process of shaping a canon of Christian writings. The great Alexandrian scripture scholar of the early third century, Origen, made many judgments about the authenticity and authority of the various writings known to him, but formulated no list of authoritative books.

25. *Church History* 3. 35. 1–7.

26. Syrian Christianity lagged considerably behind this broad development. Traditionally, the Syrian church admitted as scripture only the four Gospels, Acts and the letters of Paul; and the *Diatessaron* of Tatian, rather than the four separate Gospels, continued to have great popularity there during the fourth century. The acceptance of other writings was slow, and in the first half of the fifth century the Syrian canon typically comprised only 22 books.

27. Technically, therefore, the canon of scripture has never been closed for Christianity as a whole, and the scope of the traditional canon is not an item of Christian doctrine.

28. These grounds were textual, historical, and hermeneutical. Their character is well-represented in the mid-second-century tract of Justin Martyr, *Dialogue with Trypho the Jew*, which, though it is a set-piece of Christian apologetics, accurately reflects Christian-Jewish debates of the period.

29. On the intra-Christian debate about the Jewish scriptures see the discussion by Campenhausen, *The Formation of the Christian Bible*, 21–102.

30. This is preeminently true of the Gospels, but also of the Pauline letters (at least in the churches which traced their origins to Paul).

31. For the techniques and functions of pseudonymity in the early church see N. Brox, *Falsche Verfasserangaben. Zur Erklärung der frühchristliche Pseudepigraphie* (Stuttgarter Bibelstudien, 79; Stuttgart, 1975).

32. W. G. Kümmel, "Notwendigkeit und Grenze des neutestamentlichen Kanons," *Zeitschrift für Theologie und Kirche* 47 (1950) 277–313.

33. In contrast to the long-standing ecclesiastical idea that heterodox movements are late deviations from an aboriginal body of orthodox belief, it is now widely recognized that early Christianity was characterized by a broad and tension-laden confessional pluriformity, of which traditional Christian "orthodoxy" is a subsequent consolidation and refinement. On this see especially the influential study of W. Bauer, *Orthodoxy and Heresy in Earliest Christianity*, and also the more recent work of J. D. G. Dunn, *Unity and Diversity in the New Testament* (Philadelphia, 1977). Various aspects of the movement toward consolidation are discussed in E. P. Sanders, ed., *Jewish and Christian Self-Definition*, 1, "The Shaping of Christianity in the Second and Third Centuries" (Philadelphia, 1980).

34. It must be emphasized that the formation of a canon of scripture was, in itself, inadequate to this purpose, simply because it did not decide the problem of the *interpretation* of scripture. Hence additional controls were necessary, and these were provided in the teaching authority of ecclesiastical offices and in the formulation of creed-like summaries of the faith.

35. A thorough examination of the criteria of canonicity is provided by K. -H. Ohlig, *Die theologische Begründung des neutestamentlichen Kanons in der alten Kirche* (Dusseldorf, 1972).

36. Ohlig (ibid.) sums up the sense of "apostolicity" in the term *Urkirchlichkeit*, "what is characteristic of the early church."

37. Nevertheless, the tradition of the church's faith had developed to no small extent under the influence of many of the writings which eventually became canonical. For this reason the criterion of orthodoxy involved a circular argument: documents were received as authoritative if they conformed to the rule of faith, but at the same time the rule of faith was validated by appealing, among other things, to those very documents. Hence Christian writers of the late second and early third centuries were unwilling to allow any thoroughgoing distinction between the scriptures and the rule of faith. On this problem, see E. Flesseman-van Leer, *Tradition and Scripture in the Early Church* (Assen, 1954), and R. P. C. Hanson, *Tradition in the Early Church*.

38. This is not to deny that a canon must, by definition, have boundaries, but only that the actual boundaries of the Christian canon have no compelling basis or explanation.

39. As noted above (note 23) inspiration was not generally attributed to Christian scripture before the third century. Here it needs to be noted also that inspiration did not constitute a criterion of canonicity, and no early Christian writing gained or failed to gain canonical standing on this basis. On this see E. Kalin, *Argument from Inspiration in the Canonization of the New Testament* (Harvard diss., 1967), and A. C. Sundberg, "The Bible Canon and the Christian Doctrine of Inspiration," *Interpretation* 29 (1975) 352−71. It is instructive in this connection that those early Christian writings which most explicitly claimed to be inspired were also the ones which had the most difficulty in gaining general authority, and in the end only one of them, the Apocalypse of John, was canonized. Thus the popular Christian claim that the books of the New Testament are unique and authoritative precisely because they are inspired has no foothold in the actual history of the canon. On the modern Christian concepts of and debates about inspiration see the useful discussion of P. Achtemeier, *The Inspiration of Scripture: Problems and Proposals* (Philadelphia, 1980).

40. Even so non-religious a factor as the technology of book manufacture in Graeco-Roman antiquity cannot be left out of account. The evolution of the canon was related in part to the development of the codex or leaf-book, which was used by Christianity virtually from the beginning, instead of the scroll or roll-book, which was the format of the scriptures in Judaism. On this see C. H. Roberts and T. C. Skeat, *The Birth of the Codex* (London, 1983). Only in the

third and fourth centuries did codices become available which could accommodate a large number of writings within a single book. The limits of the canon were therefore not only theological, but to some extent technological as well. In any case, it was only with the transcription of all these writings within a single codex that the idea of a Christian canon of scripture gained clear and tangible expression.

41. Very few historians of the canon have undertaken an assessment of its consequences, but a notable exception is A. von Harnack, *The Origin of the New Testament and the Most Important Consequences of the New Creation* (ET London, 1925), esp. 115–63.

42. Two major bodies of early Christian writings, many of which were once esteemed as scriptural, are now known under the collective titles of "The Apostolic Fathers" and "New Testament Apocrypha." The former is conveniently available in K. Lake, ed., *The Apostolic Fathers*, 2 vols. (Loeb Classical Library; Cambridge, Mass., 1912–13), the latter in E. Hennecke and W. Schneemelcher, eds., *New Testament Aprocrypha*, 2 vols. (ET Philadelphia, 1963–64).

43. On the problem of whether or not this development may be regarded as appropriate or constructive, see the remarks of C. F. Evans, *Is "Holy Scripture" Christian? and Other Questions* (London, 1971), 21–36.

44. Harmonistic exegesis was employed not only to overcome disparities within the New Testament, but also to maintain the unity between the distinctively Christian scriptures and the scriptures which had been taken over from Judaism. Thus the unity of scripture, which is a correlative of the authority of a scriptural canon, does not reside in the texts as such. They are the locus of the problem. Their unity and coherence can be claimed only by means of interpretation. The interest in securing the unity of the texts, or at any rate of resolving patent disparities, was strong enough that it sometimes went beyond interpretation and resulted in the alteration of the texts themselves. The manuscript tradition preserves many instances of this in the Gospels, where differences were least tolerable on account of the common subject matter.

45. For a highly suggestive exposition of this point from a phenomenological perspective see J. Z. Smith, "Sacred Persistence: Toward a Redescription of Canon," in *idem, Imagining Religion: From Babylon to Jonestown* (Chicago Studies in the History of Judaism; Chicago, 1982), 36–52.

46. Concise discussions of the history and character of the exegesis of scripture in Christianity may be found in R. M. Grant, *A Short History of the Interpretation of the Bible* (rev. ed., New York, 1963), and in various essays included in P. R. Ackroyd, C. F. Evans, et al., eds., *The Cambridge History of the Bible*, 3 vols. (Cambridge, 1963–70).

47. It should probably be observed in this connection that the modern historical-critical method of biblical interpretation, which aims to recover the "original" meaning of the biblical texts and represents this meaning as the "true" interpretation, is, for all its values, far-removed from the methods and aims of traditional Christian exegesis. But this is also true, ironically, of the funda-

mentalist type of biblical interpretation which has so energetically opposed historical criticism. Different as their presuppositions are, both mute the multivocacy which has enabled scripture to retain its vital authority within the church.

48. The term "canon" was originally applied to Christian writings in the sense of "list" (rather than "norm"), and signified writings which were acceptable for reading in worship. Thus the question of liturgical propriety was uppermost, even if the issue of their doctrinally normative character followed close behind. For the uses of the term "canon" in the ancient church see esp. Th. Zahn, *Grundriss der Geschichte des neutestamentlichen Kanons* (Leipzig, 1904), 1–14, and H. W. Beyer, art. *kanon, Theological Dictionary of the New Testament* 3 (Grand Rapids, 1965), 596–602.

49. In any case, the reading of scripture in worship is a solemn and formal occasion surrounded by ritual words and actions highlighting the holiness of the book and its illuminating capacity. Within the elaborate Orthodox liturgy and the traditional Roman Mass the Gospel book is carried in procession, its reader is blessed, the book is kissed before reading, the congregation stands for the lection and responds with acclamations. Even in simple Protestant orders of service the reading of scripture is marked out by admonitions to attention and prayers of illumination. On the role of the Bible in Christian worship see, for the early period, the concise survey by J. A. Lamb, "The Place of the Bible in Liturgy," in P. Ackroyd and C. F. Evans, eds., *The Cambridge History of the Bible* 1 (Cambridge, 1970) 563–86, and more generally A. Baumstark, *Comparative Liturgy* (3rd ed., rev.; ET London, 1958), and J. A. Jungmann, *The Mass of the Roman Rite* (rev. and abridged ed.; ET New York, 1959).

50. The sermon has therefore been delivered in the vernacular, even when the scriptures were not read in the vernacular. P. Ricoeur has incisively noted that it belongs to the nature of preaching "to be always brought back from the written to the oral; and it is the function of preaching to reverse the relation from written to spoken. In that sense preaching is more fundamental to Hebrew and Christian tradition because of the nature of the text which has to be reconverted to word, in contrast with scripture; and therefore it is a kind of desacralization of the written as such by the return to the spoken word" ("The Sacred Text and the Community," in W. O'Flaherty, ed., *The Critical Study of Sacred Texts* [Berkeley Religious Studies Series; Berkeley, 1979], 275).

51. See A. von Harnack, *Bible Reading in the Early Church* (ET London, 1912).

52. For the middle ages see B. Smalley, *The Study of the Bible in the Middle Ages* (2nd ed.; Oxford, 1952).

53. W. C. Smith, "The Study of Religion and the Study of the Bible," *Journal of the American Academy of Religion* 39 (1971) 131–40, points up an interesting contrast (136): "The relation of printing to scripture is not straightforward. . . . In Christendom, the Bible was virtually the first thing to be printed, and was foremost in Western man's response to the medium; in the Islamic world, on the other hand, when printing was introduced it was agreed that

secular books might be printed but the Qurʾan deliberately was not." The relation of scripture to the mode of its reproduction deserves further exploration. The proscription against the printing of the Qurʾan was, of course, temporary, and it has been printed since the latter part of the nineteenth century. Like Christianity, Judaism showed no qualms about printing scripture: the earliest printed edition of the Hebrew Bible, together with the commentary of Rashi, dates from 1475. Nevertheless, the Torah scroll used in synagogue liturgy must be handwritten, and so too the texts for mezuzoth and phylacteries. Here there seems to be a closer correlation between specific modes of reproduction and specific religious uses of scripture.

54. For the frequencies of personal reading of the Bible among Catholics and Protestants, and among different Protestant groups, and for some comparative statistics on attitudes toward the Bible, see "Evangelical Christianity in the United States: National Parallel Surveys of General Public and Clergy," conducted for *Christianity Today* by The Gallup Organization, Inc. and the Princeton Religious Research Center (Princeton: n.d.).

55. It is an explicit promise of the convert to the Orthodox church that "I will accept and understand Holy Scripture in accordance with the interpretation which was and is held by the Holy Orthodox Catholic Church of the East, our Mother," as noted by T. Ware, *The Orthodox Church* (Baltimore, 1963), 208. The sentiment is no less appropriate to Roman Catholicism.

56. Useful discussions of this development are given by G. H. Tavard, *Holy Writ or Holy Church: The Crisis of the Protestant Reformation* (New York: 1959), and R. M. Brown, *The Spirit of Protestantism* (New York, 1961), esp. 67–80. For specific issues in contemporary Protestant-Catholic discussion see E. Flesseman-van Leer, "Present-day Frontiers in the Discussion about Tradition," in F. F. Bruce and E. G. Rupp, eds., *Holy Book and Holy Tradition* (Manchester, 1968), 154–70.

57. See the essay of R. J. Mouw, "The Bible in Twentieth-Century Protestantism: A Preliminary Taxonomy," in N. O. Hatch and M. A. Noll, eds., *The Bible in America: Essays in Cultural History* (New York, 1982), 139–62. The difficulties inherent in appeals to scripture alone as a formal authority for theology have become increasingly obvious even to Protestant scholars. See, e.g., E. Käsemann, "The Canon of the New Testament and the Unity of the Church," in idem, *Essays on New Testament Themes* (ET London, 1964), 95–107. Quite apart from the manifest theological diversities within the canon, to which Käsemann points, the possibility of theological/doctrinal appeals to scripture is limited by the fact that the major dogmatic teachings of Christianity are not derived exclusively from scripture, even though scripture has always been invoked for their support. On this see M. F. Wiles, *The Making of Christian Doctrine* (Cambridge, 1967), 41–61.

LATTER-DAY SAINTS:
A Dynamic Scriptural Process

Kent P. Jackson

REVELATION AND CANON

"We believe all that God has revealed, all that He does now reveal, and we believe that He will yet reveal many great and important things pertaining to the Kingdom of God."[1] These words, written by Joseph Smith, state concisely a major doctrine of the Church of Jesus Christ of Latter-day Saints (often called Mormons). Not only has God revealed his will in the past, adherents to that faith believe, but he does so now and will yet do so in the future. Latter-day Saints hold a view of canon that does not restrict itself to God's revelations of the past, whether they be those which they revere in common with their fellow Christians or those believed uniquely by the Saints. Their view is broader: the canon is not closed, nor will it ever be. To them, revelation from God has not ceased; it continues in the Church. Future revelation is not only viewed as theoretically possible, it is needed and expected, as changing circumstances in the world necessitate new communication from God. This view of canon and scriptural authority is the legacy of Joseph Smith, whom members of the Church of Jesus Christ of Latter-day Saints acknowledge as the founding prophet of their faith. Much of their theology and much of their lifestyle is influenced by a belief that the heavens are not closed but that revelation is a reality in their church.

Latter-day Saint theology demands adherence to sacred books of the past. Yet it requires equal belief in ongoing revelation to the Church in the present. Historically such a marriage of static and dynamic revelatory theology is uncommon; most faiths end the prophetic phases of their development in the process of the canonization of what has come before. Yet Mormonism has a system of belief in which both elements are viewed as vital. The prospect of future revelation poses no threat to the canonized words of earlier times. Latter-day Saint sacred literature reflects this mix-

ture of static and dynamic canon. With their fellow Christians they view
the Old and New Testaments of the Bible as the revelations of God. Yet they
have other books which they view as equally authoritative. Beginning with
Joseph Smith's first purported theophany, the Latter-day Saints have believed that ongoing revelation has been one of the hallmarks of their faith.
In the years that have passed since then, their canon has expanded as new
revelation has been received and published—a process that has operated
as recently as 1978.[2]

According to Latter-day Saint belief, Joseph Smith's revelatory experiences began when he was fourteen years old in the spring of 1820, when
God and Jesus Christ appeared to him in a wooded area near his home in
Palmyra, New York, in response to his inquiry concerning which of the
churches in his area he should join. Their message, as he reported it, was
that he should join no church, for none of the churches of his day enjoyed
divine approval.[3] Joseph Smith would be the prophet through whom Jesus
would restore to mankind his true church and the gospel that had been
taught in its purity in the days of Jesus and his apostles but was subsequently lost from the earth. Latter-day Saints believe that original Christianity, including the correct doctrines and the authority to act in Jesus'
name, was lost from the world after the deaths of the apostles. They believe
further that Jesus restored it through Joseph Smith, who received scores of
revelations from God over the next twenty-four years until his murder at
the hands of a mob in 1844. These revelations are combined in two volumes, the "Doctrine and Covenants" and the "Pearl of Great Price." Joseph
Smith also published the "Book of Mormon," which purports to be a translation of an ancient text delivered to him by a messenger from God. Together with the Bible, these books are called by Latter-day Saints the
"Standard Works." Within the Latter-day Saint tradition these four volumes are viewed as holy books. They are the focus of this essay.

THE BIBLE

James E. Talmage, an early twentieth-century apostle of the Latter-day
Saint Church and one of its foremost theologians, wrote:

> The Church of Jesus Christ of Latter-day Saints accepts the Holy Bible as the
> foremost of her standard works, first among the books which have been pro-
> claimed as her written guides in faith and doctrine. In the respect and sanc-
> tity with which the Latter-day Saints regard the Bible they are of like profes-
> sion with Christian denominations in general, but differ from them in the
> additional acknowledgment of certain other scriptures as authentic and holy,

which others are in harmony with the Bible, and serve to support and emphasize its facts and doctrines.[4]

Joseph Smith stated, "We believe the Bible to be the word of God as far as it is translated correctly."[5] Even with the implied uncertainty concerning the accuracy of modern translations, Latter-day Saints hold the Bible on equal footing with the Book of Mormon and the other LDS holy books. This has been the case since the days of their founding prophet, who proclaimed the Bible to be a "sacred volume."[6] Joseph Smith's original theophany came as the result of his reading from the Bible, from a passage admonishing praying for enlightenment (James 1:5–6).[7] In the years following the purported revelations that led to the founding of the new faith, the Mormon prophet's enthusiasm for the biblical record did not diminish, as is demonstrated by the fact that he preached from the Bible much more frequently than from the volumes of scripture that he himself had published.[8]

Brigham Young, Joseph Smith's successor in the leadership of the Church, taught, "We have a holy reverence for and a belief in the Bible."[9] He also taught:

> I believe the doctrines concerning salvation contained in that book are true, and that their observance will elevate any people, nation or family that dwells on the face of the earth. The doctrines contained in the Bible will lift to a superior condition all who observe them; they will impart to them knowledge, wisdom, charity, fill them with compassion and cause them to feel after the wants of those who are in distress, or in painful or degraded circumstances. They who observe the precepts contained in the Scriptures will be just and true and virtuous and peaceable at home and abroad. Follow out the doctrines of the Bible, and men will make splendid husbands, women excellent wives, and children will be obedient; they will make families happy and the nations wealthy and happy and lifted up above the things of this life.[10]

The view of the Latter-day Saints regarding the Bible has not changed since Brigham Young made that statement over a century ago.

Joseph Smith usually used the King James Bible, the common English Bible of his day. Yet he was not unaware of the problems of language and translation. He was interested enough in foreign languages that he gained some exposure to several, even receiving formal instruction in Hebrew.[11] Although he never became proficient in Hebrew, he often extolled the value of knowing it as a means of understanding the Bible,[12] and he used some of the insights that he had gained from his Hebrew studies in public addresses.[13] He often took exception with the King James text. In 1844 he called the German translation that he had studied "the most correct that I have found, and it corresponds the nearest to the revelations that I have given the last 16 years."[14] His feelings concerning biblical authority are expressed succinctly in these words: "I believe the Bible as it read when it came from the pen of the original writers."[15] As noted, he taught that the Bible is God's word "as far as it is translated correctly."[16] Joseph Smith's term "translated" means *transmitted*, and it includes the entire process of bringing ancient words from their original sources to modern-language publication. Following their prophet's teaching, Latter-day Saints regard the biblical record as God's message to mankind insofar as current texts and versions accurately represent the inspired intentions of the authors. They accept the Bible as authoritative, believing that God has spoken to men on earth and that his messages have been recorded in the Bible by his spokesmen, the prophets. Yet the uncertainty of its preservation and transmission leads them not only to allow for the theoretical possibility of inaccuracies in modern versions but to believe that such do in fact exist. Joseph Smith taught, "Many important points touching the salvation of men had been taken from the Bible, or lost before it was compiled";[17] and "Ignorant translators, careless transcribers, or designing and corrupt priests have committed many errors."[18]

The Latter-day Saint faith claims to be a restoration of truths that God had revealed by prophets in earlier times. This restoration was needed, in part, because many points of important theological understanding had been lost since the biblical authors wrote God's word. Through processes such as those suggested by Joseph Smith, many of the teachings of Jesus, his apostles, and earlier prophets had been lost, necessitating a complete restoration of doctrine in a pure and uncorrupted form. Joseph Smith is viewed as a modern-day prophet called by God to serve in the restoration of primitive Christianity to the world. Doctrinal truths were restored in numerous revelations and in the Book of Mormon, which contains, according to one of Joseph Smith's revelations, "the fulness of the gospel of Jesus Christ."[19] Many of these revelations have direct bearing on the biblical text, or on doctrines taught in the Bible. According to believers, these revelations constitute God's restoration to the world of all the doctrines and sacraments necessary for the salvation and eternal well-being of the human family—things that had been known by God's people in ancient Israel as well as in early Christianity but had not been preserved in the Bible. Thus the new volumes of sacred literature restore things "taken from the Bible, or lost before it was compiled."[20]

THE BOOK OF MORMON

In 1830, Joseph Smith published what he claimed was a new volume of Christian scripture. The product of his efforts, the Book of Mormon, is held by Latter-day Saints to be a sacred book similar to the Bible, with which it shares equal status.[21] It purports to be the record of a people that lived in the western hemisphere during parts of the first millennium B.C.E. and the first millenium C.E. Latter-day Saints believe that it records God's word as revealed to the ancient prophets of the Americas and that it presents the doctrines of Jesus in their purity, making it an important part of their faith.

Joseph Smith said that on the night of 21 September 1823, a messenger from God named Moroni appeared to him and told him of his calling to bring forth an ancient record that would be given into his care at some later time. He reported that he learned from Moroni that the record contained "an account of the former inhabitants of this continent [the Americas], and the source from which they sprang. He also said that the fulness of the everlasting Gospel was contained in it, as delivered by the Savior to the ancient inhabitants."[22] In the Book of Mormon account, Moroni was the last of a line of ancient American prophets and the one who completed the record and concealed it in the ground. Now he made its existence known to a modern counterpart, Joseph Smith. According to the latter, Moroni appeared to him often and instructed and trained him for his calling. At the appropriate time, the young prophet went to the burial spot, took possession of the record, translated it, and published his translation as the Book of Mormon.

The account in the book begins in Jerusalem just prior to its siege by the forces of Nebuchadnezzar early in the sixth century B.C.E. According to the record, a prophet named Lehi was instructed by God to take his family and several other followers from Jerusalem to find a new home. Their divinely directed travels eventually brought them to the Americas, where they built cities and created a civilization patterned somewhat after that from which they came. The Book of Mormon describes itself as the record of Lehi's people from the time they left Jerusalem until the fifth century C.E. It tells of the ministries of their prophets, whose roles in the book of Mormon resemble those of their counterparts in the Hebrew Bible. Lehi's people later divided themselves into two groups called Nephites and Lamanites after two of Lehi's sons. The record tells how they enjoyed prosperity and peace when they followed the direction of their prophets, and ruin and warfare when they disregarded it. According to the Book of Mormon, Christianity was revealed to and preached by the early American prophets. The book tells that even centuries before the birth of Jesus there were those among the Nephites and Lamanites who knew of his future coming and called themselves Christians. Jesus was known to them by name, and much of the Christian faith known from the New Testament was common knowledge among them. The Book of Mormon claims further that Jesus appeared personally to Lehi's decendants after his resurrection. He remained a number of days among the people, preached to them, and called twelve disciples. The Lamanite and Nephite nations were converted as a result of his appearance and the continued preaching of his disciples after he left. Jesus' visit ushered in an era of peace and unity which lasted for almost two hundred years, following which the early Americans began a long road of terminal decline. By C.E. 400 the Nephite nation had been destroyed—the result of armed hostilities and internal decay.

Among the last of the prophets was one named Mormon, who was commanded by God to write the account of his people from the time his ancestors left Palestine. The book tells that Mormon compiled his history by editing the records that had been kept by prophets and historians since Lehi's day, including in his record only those things that he felt inspired to pass on to later generations. Mormon's account was inscribed in a book made of thin gold plates, attached loosely at one end.

Because of Mormon's role as the primary author and editor of the book it bears his name. At his death his prophet son Moroni, the last prophet of the Nephite nation, continued the task and finished the book, which he buried so that it would be preserved until a later generation when the time would be right to make its message known to the world. Joseph Smith claimed that it was this same Moroni who, as a resurrected man sent from the presence of God, came to instruct him concerning the ancient record. He maintained that the gold book was placed in his care until the translation was completed, after which Moroni returned and took it from him.[23] Joseph Smith did not claim to have any linguistic skills that would enable him to translate from an unknown language but stated instead that he made the translation through the power of God. The book was published in Palmyra, New York, on 26 March 1830, shortly before the formal organization of the Church of Jesus Christ of Latter-day Saints, which took place on the 6 April 1830.[24] Joseph Smith was twenty-four years old. Since its original publication, more than 21 million copies of the Book of Mormon have been printed in the English language. All or parts of it have been translated into over 70 other languages, and almost 9 million non-English books have been printed.[25] The term "Mormon," which is used popularly to identify members of the Church of Jesus Christ of Latter-day Saints, derives from their belief in that book. The Book of Mormon became a key part of the

Latter-day Saint movement from its beginning and still remains today a feature that distinguishes it from all other Christian traditions.[26]

The Message of the Book of Mormon

In order to understand the role of the Book of Mormon as a holy book to Latter-day Saints, we must examine what the book says concerning itself. This can be done best by examining its Title Page, which, according to Joseph Smith, was written by Moroni after he had completed the record. The Title Page, which is published at the beginning of every copy of the book, reads as follows:

> The Book of Mormon: an account written by the hand of Mormon upon plates taken from the plates of Nephi. Wherefore, it is an abridgment of the record of the People of Nephi, and also of the Lamanites—Written to the Lamanites, who are a remnant of the house of Israel; and also to Jew and Gentile—Written by way of commandment, and also by the spirit of prophecy and of revelation—Sealed by the hand of Moroni, and hid up unto the Lord, to come forth in due time by way of the Gentile—The interpretation thereof by the gift of God. . . . Which is to show unto the remnant of the House of Israel what great things the Lord hath done for their fathers; and that they may know the covenants of the Lord, that they are not cast off forever—And also to the convincing of the Jew and Gentile that Jesus is the Christ, the eternal God, manifesting himself unto all nations.

Among the major statements made on the Title Page, the following are most significant: (1) the Book of Mormon is an ancient historical record, containing divine revelation and written for a specified modern audience; and (2) its purpose is to testify "that Jesus is the Christ." The Title Page reflects the content of the book, which centers on these two assertions. They are echoed throughout its pages.

The Book of Mormon purports to be an authentic ancient record that describes actual events. Latter-day Saint theology rules out any alternatives; it is held to be a true book, the record of ancient people, written in ancient times, and recovered anew in a modern day. Yet it is believed to be a book of a unique sort—a sacred chronicle made by inspired individuals under divine direction. Its value to believers goes far beyond that of an ancient history; to them it is scripture—the mind and will of God written and preserved for his people.

With a basic framework of historical narrative, the Book of Mormon teaches theology from the events of human experience. It chronicles dealings of God with people on both individual and national levels. It is similar, at least as far as the structure of the narrative is concerned, to the sections of the Hebrew Bible that purport to record historical events, both in the Pentateuch and in the historical books. Much of the Book of Mormon is analogous to books such as Genesis, Exodus, and Numbers in recording the sacred history of people who viewed themselves as chosen by God. And—as in those pentateuchal narratives—only the history of a selected group of people is important. Events that transpire elsewhere in the world are irrelevant, unless they directly involve in some way those with whom the narrative concerns itself. In the Book of Mormon, as in the Pentateuch and elsewhere in the Bible, history of God's interaction with mankind is what is important, not history of more mundane matters. Its history serves a theological purpose, as it is usually accompanied by a type of editorial moralizing that is common in the Hebrew Bible. Consider the following example from the account of a large battle:

> Notwithstanding the great destruction which hung over my people, they did not repent of their evil doings; therefore there was blood and carnage spread throughout all the face of the land, both on the part of the Nephites and also on the part of the Lamanites; and it was one complete revolution throughout all the face of the land. . . . And it came to pass that when I, Mormon, saw their lamentation and their mourning and their sorrow before the Lord, my heart did begin to rejoice within me, knowing the mercies and the long-suffering of the Lord, therefore supposing that he would be merciful unto them that they would again become a righteous people. But behold this my joy was vain, for their sorrowing was not unto repentance, because of the goodness of God; but it was rather the sorrowing of the damned, because the Lord would not always suffer them to take happiness in sin (Mormon 2:8, 12–13).[27]

The narrative in the Book of Mormon and the didactic commentary that accompanies it are presented in a setting of teaching later readers. The same can, of course, be said about the purpose for the historical narratives of the Hebrew Bible. The moralizing is added so that modern readers will understand the causes of the recorded events and be able to avoid the misfortunes experienced by the people in the narrative, while duplicating their successes. Note these comments of Moroni: "And this cometh unto you, O ye Gentiles, . . . that ye may repent, and not continue in your iniquities until the fulness come, that ye may not bring down the fulness of the wrath of God upon you as the inhabitants of the land have hitherto done" (Ether 2:11). The book maintains that its purpose is to teach distant generations. It does so using the same theology that underscores the deuteronomic history in the Hebrew Bible, as is evidenced in the following passage which is repeated at least a dozen times: "Inasmuch as ye shall keep the commandments of God ye shall prosper in the land; and inasmuch as ye will not keep the commandments of God ye shall be cut off from his presence" (Alma 38:1). This fundamental component of the Book of Mormon's theology is viewed by Latter-day Saints as being at the core of the book's message for readers in modern times.

The Book of Mormon teaches theology in a more direct manner also. Much of it consists of discourses and writings of the prophets who are the main characters in the narrative. These treatises constitute one of the most important sources of Latter-day Saint doctrine. Many of the beliefs that are considered uniquely LDS are found in the words of Book of Mormon prophets.

The Title Page states specifically that the book was written by divine command and, "by the spirit of prophecy and of revelation." Joseph Smith asserted that his role in bringing it forth was that of a translator, and that he was not responsible for its content. The book itself claims consistently that what it contains is revelation from God, received and recorded by prophets who were God's spokesmen. Mormons view the Book of Mormon as a book with a divine purpose, containing those things that God inspired someone to include in it. The Book of Mormon makes this claim in several places. A notable example is that of Lehi's son Nephi, whose record is found at the beginning of the book: "And after I had made these plates by way of commandment, I, Nephi, received a commandment that the ministry and the prophecies, the more plain and precious parts of them, should be written upon these plates; and that the things which were written should be kept for the instruction of my people" (1 Nephi 19:3). Thus God made known to him what he should include in his record—specifically mentioning "the ministry and the prophecies." Later Nephi writes, "Nevertheless, I do not write anything upon plates save it be that I think it be sacred" (1 Nephi 19:6).

Although the Book of Mormon maintains consistently that it contains the revealed word of God, it makes no claim to being either perfect or infallible. Moroni, while completing his father Mormon's record, laments, "Lord, the Gentiles will mock at these things, because of our weakness in writing; for Lord thou has made us mighty in word by faith, but thou has not made us mighty in writing" (Ether 12:23). He continues, "When we write we behold our weakness, and stumble because of the placing of our words; and I fear lest the Gentiles shall mock at our words" (Ether 12:25). In the last line of the Title Page he states, "And now, if there are faults they are the mistakes of men; wherefore, condemn not the things of God." Latter-day Saints believe that the Book of Mormon contains God's word, while at the same time they acknowledge its imperfection. They believe that anything placed in the stewardship of human hands—whether they be those of Mormon or Moroni, or of Joseph Smith and his successors—is suscep-tible to error. Yet they view the Book of Mormon as divine in origin, the effort of divinely commissioned and divinely inspired mortals to do the work of God.

It has been noted already that Latter-day Saints believe that Joseph Smith was a prophet called by God to restore to the world the Christianity of Jesus and the apostles, which had been lost from the earth after the time of the apostles. They believe that one of the most important parts of that restoration was the publication of the Book of Mormon, which took place at the very beginning of the movement—even prior to the organization of the Church of Jesus Christ of Latter-day Saints. Believers view the coming forth of the Book of Mormon as a means by which correct doctrines of Christianity were restored, as a foundation upon which the later works of restoration could rest. Joseph Smith referred to the book as "the key-stone of our religion." [28]

The Title Page tells us that the Book of Mormon was written for three groups of readers in a distant time: (a) The descendants of the Book of Mor-mon nations (called Lamanites—identified as the native people of the Western Hemisphere), (b) the Jews, and (c) the Gentiles, meaning everyone who is neither Lamanite nor Jew. The Book of Mormon writers specifically state that their words are directed not to people of their own day but to their distant descendants and others who would read it when God would cause it to be brought to light. Latter-day Saints see it as a voice from the past speaking to readers of the present. Many passages in it contain a kind of intimate personal counsel to anticipated readers, as do these words in the last chapter of the book:

> Now I, Moroni, write somewhat as seemeth me good; and I write unto my brethern, the Lamanites. . . . And I seal up these records, after I have spoken a few words by way of exhortation unto you. Behold, I would exhort you that when ye shall read these things, if it be wisdom in God that ye should read them, that ye would remember how merciful the Lord hath been unto the children of men, from the creation of Adam even down until the time that ye shall receive these things, and ponder it in your hearts. . . . Yea, come unto Christ, and be perfected in him, and deny yourselves of all ungodliness; and if ye shall deny yourselves of all ungodliness; and love God with all your might, mind and strength, then is his grace sufficient for you, that by his grace ye may be perfect in Christ . . . (Moroni 10:1–3, 32).

Phrases such as "I will show unto you" and "thus we see," occur regu-larly throughout the book and demonstrate its didactic nature (e.g., 1 Nephi 1:20; 16:29). As Latter-day Saints view the Book of Mormon as their book for this day, it is a major source of their theology, providing fundamental statements regarding many of the basics of their faith. They find in it a paradigm for behavior as well. The historical narrative presents both the positive and the negative in actions of nations and individuals. Believers view the events that are described in it as *types* for circumstances of the present as well as for anticipated events of the future. They believe that the book was brought to light to bless humankind in a time when the issues of life would be such that lessons learned from the past would provide the key to well-being in the present. The faithful of today recognize in their societies and in their personal lives the cycles of history that are presented in the Book of Mormon—in which individual and collective behavior is followed by divinely dispensed blessings or curses. Latter-day Saints see in the pages of their book God at work in human affairs.

A Second Witness for Jesus Christ

Perhaps the most basic assertion made by the Book of Mormon is that its purpose is to convince the world that Jesus is the Christ, as stated on its Title Page. Throughout the Book of Mormon (subtitled "Another Testament of Jesus Christ") this purpose is evident. The words of Nephi are typical of the emphasis placed by the Book of Mormon on Jesus: "For we labor diligently to write, to persuade our children, and also our brethren, to believe in Christ, and to be reconciled to God for we know that it is by grace that we are saved, after all that we can do. . . . And we talk of Christ, we rejoice in Christ, we preach of Christ, we prophesy of Christ, and we write according to our prophecies, that our children may know to what source they may look for a remission of their sins" (2 Nephi 25:23, 26).

According to the narrative, Lehi and his children saw visions and conversed with heavenly messengers, as early as 600 B.C.E. whereby they learned in detail concerning the future ministry of their Messiah, Jesus (1 Nephi 1:9–11; 2 Nephi 10:3, 11:13–14:30; 25:19). Jesus' ministry is the very core of the Book of Mormon and thus also of Latter-day Saint theology. All of the Book of Mormon prophets are depicted as testifying of Jesus—those prior to his life in anticipation of him and those afterward in remembrance of him.

The Book of Mormon's emphasis on Jesus goes far beyond purported predictions about his life. In its pages Latter-day Saints find the fullest expression of the doctrines of their Christian faith. It contains, couched in the words of its prophets, a theology of Christ that Mormons believe far excels in clarity and direction the doctrines preserved in the New Testament. The Book of Mormon justifies its own existence by asserting that the "fullness" of Christianity cannot be found in the Bible. It claims to be a second witness of Jesus alongside the New Testament; yet it claims to preserve Christianity more clearly and more fully than does its Old World counterpart. Specific areas in which Latter-day Saints find clearer statements of truth in the Book of Mormon than in the Bible include: the nature of Jesus and his relationship to God, the nature of humankind, the purpose for human existence, the nature of revelation and sacred writings, the fall of Adam, and the atoning sacrifice of Jesus Christ. The Book of Mormon's message is expressed clearly yet eloquently, making its teachings accessible to readers on any level of understanding or maturity. Because of this the Book of Mormon is used as the key book in teaching young Latter-day Saints their religion's essential doctrines, as it is used also by missionaries as the primary tool in their efforts to convert others to their faith.

THE DOCTRINE AND COVENANTS

Latter-day Saints acknowledge the Bible and the Book of Mormon as containing revelations from God to prophets of past ages. As Joseph Smith claimed that he was a prophet of equal status with those of antiquity, it should not be surprising that he claimed to have received revelations from God as well. Indeed he recorded many proclamations which are believed by Latter-day Saints to be the word of God delivered through his modern spokesman. These are collected in a volume called, in full, the Doctrine and Covenants of the Church of Jesus Christ of Latter-day Saints. The "Explanatory Introduction" from the most recent edition outlines the Latter-day Saint view of this volume of modern revelation:

> The Doctrine and Covenants is a collection of divine revelations and inspired declarations given for the establishment and regulation of the kingdom of God on earth in the last days. Although most of the sections are directed to members of the Church of Jesus Christ of Latter-day Saints, the messages, warnings, and exhortations are for the benefit of all mankind, and contain an invitation to all people everywhere to hear the voice of the Lord Jesus Christ, speaking to them for their temporal well-being and their everlasting salvation. . . . In the revelations the doctrines of the gospel are set forth with explanations about such fundamental matters as the nature of the Godhead, the origin of man, the reality of Satan, the purpose of mortality, the necessity for obedience, the need for repentance, the workings of the Holy Spirit, the ordinances and performances that pertain to salvation, the destiny of the earth, the future conditions of man after the resurrection and the judgment, the eternity of the marriage relationship, and the eternal nature of the family. Likewise the gradual unfolding of the administrative structure of the Church

is shown with the calling of bishops, the First Presidency, the Council of the Twelve [Apostles], and the Seventy, and the establishment of other presiding offices and quorums. Finally, the testimony that is given of Jesus Christ—his divinity, his majesty, his perfection, his love, and his redeeming power—makes this book of great value to the human family and of more worth than the riches of the whole earth.

The Doctrine and Covenants consists of 138 divisions called "sections" and two "Official Declarations." Sections 1–135 are revelations or official statements that came as part of the ministry of Joseph Smith. One section (no. 136) is considered to be a revelation to Brigham Young, Joseph Smith's successor in the leadership of the Church (1844–77), and another (no. 138) is to Joseph F. Smith, a nephew of the founding Prophet, and President of the Church, 1901–18. Official Declarations 1 and 2 are proclamations by Wilford Woodruff (President of the Church, 1889–98) and Spencer W. Kimball (President of the Church, 1973–84) respectively. Like all who have followed Joseph Smith in the presidency of the Church, these four men are viewed by Latter-day Saints as prophets, and their canonized statements are therefore considered to be the revelations of the mind of God.[29]

Most of Joseph Smith's revelations date from 1828 to 1833, a period of great activity in the establishment of the Church and its doctrines. In the early years of the Church, copies of the revelations circulated independently or in unofficial collections. In 1831 more than sixty were collected for publication in a book called the "Book of Commandments." After about two-thirds of the book had been typeset and printed, a mob of anti-Mormons attacked the printing office, destroying the press and its soon-to-be-published book.[30] Some of the scattered sheets were later placed together, and a few dozen copies of the Book of Commandments were bound, containing only those revelations that had been printed at the time the press was destroyed.[31]

In 1835 the first collection entitled "Doctrine and Covenants" was published in Kirtland, Ohio. It contained 102 sections.[32] Later editions were published as subsequent revelations were made known, including the 111-section edition of 1844 from Nauvoo, Illinois, where most of the Latter-day Saints had settled following their expulsion from their homes in Missouri. In 1876 in Salt Lake City a new edition was published containing additional sections, bringing the total to 136.[33] It was not until 1981 that new scriptural material was added to the collection of revelations: an 1836 revelation of Joseph Smith which had never been included previously (no. 137), and a 1918 revelation by Joseph F. Smith (no. 138). Also added was Official Declaration 2, a 1978 proclamation by Spencer W. Kimball.

THE PEARL OF GREAT PRICE

The shortest volume in the LDS canon is the Pearl of Great Price, which takes its name from the treasured jewel of Jesus' parable in Matt 13:45–46. Franklin D. Richards, the early Mormon apostle who compiled the book, wrote in its preface, "It is presumed, that true believers in the Divine mission of the Prophet JOSEPH SMITH will appreciate this little collection of precious truths as a *Pearl of Great Price. . . .*"[34] The book is a collection of some of the writings of Joseph Smith and is thus viewed by Latter-day Saints as revelatory in nature. It was first published in Liverpool in 1851. Richards, who was overseeing the work of the Church in Great Britain, viewed with regret the paucity of reading material for British Latter-day Saints, who already numbered over 30,000,[35] even though the first LDS missionaries had arrived there only twelve years previously.[36] He made a collection of several significant writings of Joseph Smith and published them in his book. The compilation contained a number of revelations that were added subsequently to the Doctrine and Covenants and are thus no longer included in the Pearl of Great Price.[37] Nonetheless, Latter-day Saints have Richards to credit for compiling the work, which later became part of their canon.

The first American edition was published in Salt Lake City in 1878. By then the collection had gained widespread popularity among leaders and laymen alike, and in a General Conference of the Church two years later it was canonized by the membership as scripture, officially making it one of the Church's Standard Works.[38] Though it originated in a semi-official manner and was not canonized until late in the nineteenth century, the Pearl of Great Price holds a position equal with the other Latter-day Saint scriptures.

The most recent edition (1981) includes the following titles: "Selections from the Book of Moses," "The Book of Abraham," "Joseph Smith—Matthew," "Joseph Smith—History," and "The Articles of Faith."

Selections from the Book of Moses

From 1830 to his death in 1844, Joseph Smith was involved intermittently in a project that he considered of extreme importance: a revision of the Bible.[39] He made changes in over 3,000 verses of the King James text.[40] The final product of his efforts, which was first published over two decades after his death, is called the "Joseph Smith Translation" (JST) or, sometimes, the "Inspired Version."

Joseph Smith believed that he was "a seer, a revelator, . . . and a prophet."[41] As God's spokesman, he believed that he had both the authority and the ability to make changes in the Bible as God directed. In doing so, he never claimed to have consulted any text other than his English Bible, but he made changes that interpreted, added to, took from, and clarified the King James text that he used. His calling, as he viewed it, was to restore lost biblical material, correct inadvertent or deliberate errors that had come into the text since its writing, and otherwise make revisions that he considered appropriate. He created a text that seemingly goes beyond the words of the Bible to capture what he felt were its authors' original intentions. The Joseph Smith Translation includes changes that range from small textual revisions, clarifying individual words or passages in the King James text, to vast additions of material found nowhere else in world literature. The "Selections from the Book of Moses" fall into both these categories.

Perhaps the most significant part of the Bible revision is the material contained in the first part of Genesis, which is included in the Pearl of Great Price. Here Joseph Smith departed substantially from his King James text and added a large amount of new material. The "Selections from the Book of Moses" consist of Joseph Smith's rendering of Gen 1:1–6:13. It is substantially longer than the corresponding biblical text of 151 verses; Joseph Smith's revision consists of 356 verses. Among other things, the "Book of Moses" adds to the biblical account a lengthy introduction, in which Moses speaks with God prior to seeing in vision the creation of the earth (chapter 1); an explanation of Satan's evil motives (4:1–4); an account of some experiences of Adam and Eve following their expulsion from Eden (5:1–16); an account of Cain's rebellion and the spiritual degeneration of Adam's decendants (5:17–59); and a record of the ministry of Enoch (6:22–7:69).

The Book of Abraham

The second selection in the Pearl of Great Price, entitled "The Book of Abraham," is believed to be a transcription of part of Abraham's record as revealed to Joseph Smith. This five-chapter composition deals with Abraham's life from his early days in Ur until his travels to Egypt. It includes an account of a vision of Abraham concerning the pre-earth existence of the human race and the creation of the earth. Joseph Smith's interest in Abraham resulted in part from his purchase of some Egyptian papyri in 1835.[42] Though the connection between the papyri and the "Book of Abraham" is unclear, it appears that Joseph Smith's possession of the Egyptian texts led to his bringing forth of the document concerning Abraham, which deals in part with things Egyptian. In 1842 it was published in serial form in the LDS newspaper, *Times and Seasons*, at Nauvoo, Illinois.

Together with the "Selections from the Book of Moses," the "Book of Abraham" makes major contributions to Latter-day Saint theology. They teach doctrines concerning the nature of God, the pre-earth existence of humankind, the creation, the fall of Adam, and the atonement of Christ, that are found nowhere else in the Bible or the other books of the LDS canon.

Joseph Smith—Matthew

A second Pearl of Great Price selection from Joseph Smith's Bible revision is "Joseph Smith—Matthew." [43] It is the Mormon prophet's revision of Matthew 24, Jesus' prophecy of future events regarding Jerusalem and the world. Joseph Smith's revision adds little new material to this chapter; for the most part, it is a rearrangement of the King James text. In Matthew 24, Jesus responds to his disciples' questions concerning the destruction of the temple and the events that would precede his future advent (Matt. 24:3). His discussion deals with both issues, which in Matthew's account are not well defined in the disciples' thinking. [44] "Joseph Smith—Matthew" reorganizes the text by dividing Jesus' words into two sections, the first dealing with calamities of the near future (destruction of the temple, false Christs and prophets, affliction and death of the apostles), and the second dealing with circumstances that would precede Jesus's return in glory.

Joseph Smith—History

The most significant events in Joseph Smith's career from about 1816 to 1829 are recorded in the "Joseph Smith—History." [45] The Mormon prophet dictated the account of his early activities to a scribe in 1838 but it was published first in 1842, when it appeared as part of a series in the *Times and Seasons*. [46] The 75-verse account is of tremendous importance to Latter-day Saints, as it records their Prophet's purported visitations by God and Jesus, the messenger Moroni, and John the Baptist (who restored the authority to baptize). The "Joseph Smith—History" gives them the personal account of the first prophet of their faith, whose testimony stands in it as a challenge to believer and nonbeliever alike: "I had seen a vision; I knew it, and I knew that God knew it, and I could not deny it." [47]

The Articles of Faith

In response to a request from a Chicago newspaper editor for information concerning the new religion, Joseph Smith compiled a list of some of the fundamental doctrines of the LDS faith. [48] They were published in the *Times and Seasons* on 1 March 1842 and now form the last section of the

Pearl of Great Price. The "Articles of Faith" consist of thirteen brief statements that summarize some of the basic doctrines believed by Latter-day Saints. They are not a formal creed or confession, but an informal overview of beliefs. Neither do they include all of Latter-day Saint theology; some of the most important doctrines of Mormonism are not mentioned at all in the "Articles." Nonetheless they are in a sense all encompassing, as the 9th Article summarizes: "We believe all that God has revealed, all that he does now reveal, and we believe that He will yet reveal many great and important things pertaining to the Kingdom of God." The "Articles of Faith" make a meaningful contribution to the faith of the Latter-day Saints, summarizing their position with regard to the nature of God, Jesus' atoning sacrifice, baptism, divine authority, church organization, spiritual gifts, scripture, revelation, and Christian behavior—to name a few of the doctrines mentioned.

SCRIPTURE IN MORMON LIFE

The sacred writings of the Latter-day Saints perform a *practical* function within that faith; they are not used in any kind of ritual situation. They are not used in chanting, reciting, or praying, or in any similar rite. They contain no saving powers nor powers to bless; nor is reading them a sacramental act. In Latter-day Saint theology the reading of scripture functions as a means to achieving an important end—education in the principles of the faith so that one can be in harmony with the will of God.

To Latter-day Saints the primary purpose for reading sacred writings is to learn about God. By examining the chronicles of his dealings with humankind and the divinely inspired theological statements recorded concerning him, one learns the will of God so one can direct one's life in accordance with it. Joseph Smith stated with regard to the Book of Mormon that one "would get nearer to God by abiding by its precepts than by any other book."[49] Believers view the Book of Mormon and their other Standard Works as paradigms for human behavior. In them, the rights and wrongs of human action are displayed, as are the consequences of humankind's power to choose. They believe that one cannot be saved in ignorance of the things of God,[50] making it necessary therefore to learn the laws of God and conform to them. Though not a saving ritual in and of itself, the reading of scripture contributes to one's salvation by teaching the divinely revealed principles, laws, and ordinances by means of which one is saved.

The reading of scripture plays an important role in bringing about communication with God, according to LDS belief, through a process of vicarious experience. Though the reader is not present at the events depicted in the sacred book, study brings those events to life and enables the reader to witness them indirectly and extract from them according to individual needs. An oft-repeated Book of Mormon passage relates the account of one prophet's study of a sacred text and his use of it for his own community: "I did liken all scriptures unto us, that it might be for our profit and learning" (1 Nephi 19:23). Latter-day Saints "liken" their scriptures to themselves, not in the sense of believing that the texts actually refer to them, but in the sense of applying parallel lessons from the past to parallel circumstances of today. This application of scriptural content is important in the faith as a means of bringing the things of God directly into the lives of believers. Daily exposure to sacred events—if only through reading—is constantly recommended among Latter-day Saints as a means by which they can learn to pattern their lives after the examples taught in their scriptures and thereby learn to do God's will.

Latter-day Saints believe in what they call "personal revelation." In their theology, communication between God and mortals is not restricted to prophets and apostles. While these are viewed as receiving revelation in behalf of the Church and the entire world, each individual church member claims the right to receive divine communication for his or her own needs, believing that in all areas of life where critical decisions must be made or where the will of God must be ascertained, prayers uttered in sincerity and faith will be answered. This is not a doctrine unknown elsewhere in Christianity (cf. James 1:5), but in Mormonism it is a fundamental belief (cf. Moroni 10:3–5). Study of scripture facilitates this process greatly by teaching faithful worshipers the will of God so they can dedicate their lives to comply with it and by creating an environment of thoughtful worship and reflection in which divine direction can be received. When one is immersed in a sacred record and in harmony with what is revealed, one can communicate with God.

Many of the religions of the world have in their formative periods a miraculous event that demonstrates to believers divine sanction. Judaism has the exodus from Egypt, and Islam has the revelation of the Qurʾan. In these, the perceived miraculous occurrences have exhibited enormous power in creating and sustaining the communities that are based upon them. In Mormonism such a miraculous event is the revelation of new scripture. Though the holy books are not the only features of the Latter-day Saint faith that claim to be miraculous, still they, more than anything else, are held up to believer and nonbeliever alike as the test of the assertions of Joseph Smith and the Church of Jesus Christ of Latter-day Saints. The religious movement that Joseph Smith set in motion early in the nineteenth century must stand or fall on its claim to modern revelation. The belief that God has spoken in modern times, and does so still in the Church, is central to the existence of that faith. This belief, possibly more than any other thing, defines the Latter-day Saint community among other religions and provides its sustaining identity.

NOTES

1. "Articles of Faith 9," *The Pearl of Great Price: A Selection from the Revelations, Translations, and Narrations of Joseph Smith* (Salt Lake City: The Church of Jesus Christ of Latter-day Saints, 1981) See "Pearl of Great Price," below. Since pagination is not consistent in different editions of the LDS scriptures, all references in this study will be cited by book, chapter, and verse numbers, rather than by page.
2. James E. Talmage, *The Articles of Faith* (Salt Lake City: The Church of Jesus Christ of Latter-day Saints, 1924), pp. 296–313.
3. "Joseph Smith—History" vv. 1–20, *Pearl of Great Price*; see below. See also Donna Hill, *Joseph Smith, the First Mormon* (Garden City, N.Y.: Doubleday, 1977), pp. 41–54.
4. Talmage, p. 236.
5. "Article of Faith 8," *The Pearl of Great Price*.
6. Joseph Fielding Smith, comp., *Teachings of the Prophet Joseph Smith* (Salt Lake City: Deseret Book, 1938), p. 56.
7. "Joseph Smith—History" vv. 1–10, *Pearl of Great Price*.
8. Andrew F. Ehat and Lyndon W. Cook, eds., *The Words of Joseph Smith* (Provo, Utah: Religious Studies Center, Brigham Young Univ., 1980), pp. 421–25.
9. John A. Widtsoe, ed., *Discourses of Brigham Young* (Salt Lake City: Deseret Book, 1971), p. 124.
10. Widtsoe, p. 125.
11. Brigham H. Roberts, *A Comprehensive History of the Church of Jesus Christ of Latter-day Saints* (Salt Lake City: Deseret News Press, 1930), I, 393–94; Milton V. Backman, Jr., *The Heavens Resound: A History of the Latter-day Saints in Ohio, 1830–1838* (Salt Lake City: Deseret Book, 1983), pp. 270–72.
12. Smith, p. 290.
13. Ehat and Cook, pp. 350–51, 358, 361.
14. Ehat and Cook, p. 351.
15. Smith, p. 327.
16. "Article of Faith 8," *Pearl of Great Price*.
17. Smith, p. 10.
18. Smith, p. 327.
19. *The Doctrine and Covenants of The Church of Jesus Christ of Latter-day*

Saints (Salt Lake City: The Church of Jesus Christ of Latter-day Saints, 1981), 20:9. See "Doctrine and Covenants," below.

20. Smith, p. 10.

21. Talmage, pp. 255–95. See also Noel B. Reynolds, ed., *Book of Mormon Authorship* (Provo, Utah: Religious Studies Center, Brigham Young Univ., 1982).

22. "Joseph Smith—History" v. 34, *Pearl of Great Price.*

23. "Joseph Smith—History" vv. 27–75, *Pearl of Great Price.*

24. Milton V. Backman, Jr., *Eyewitness Accounts of the Restoration* (Orem, Utah: Grandin Book Company, 1983), pp. 169–200.

25. Letter received from Jerry P. Cahill, Director of Public Affairs, The Church of Jesus Christ of Latter-day Saints, 4 August 1983.

26. See Hill, pp. 55–60, 70–89.

27. All Book of Mormon and Bible references will be cited in the text of this study, rather than in the notes.

28. Smith, p. 194.

29. See *Doctrine and Covenants* 68:4.

30. James B. Allen, Glenn M. Leonard, *The Story of the Latter-day Saints* (Salt Lake City, Utah: Deseret Book, 1976), pp. 68–69.

31. T. Edgar Lyon, *Introduction to the Doctrine and Covenants and the Pearl of Great Price* (Salt Lake City: Deseret News Press, 1948), p. 30. The most complete history of the Doctrine and Covenants is Robert J. Woodford, "The Historical Development of the Doctrine and Covenants," unpublished Ph.D. Dissertation, Brigham Young Univ., 1974; see also Robert J. Woodford, "The Doctrine and Covenants: A Historical Overview," in Robert L. Millet and Kent P. Jackson, eds., *Studies in the Doctrine and Covenants*, Studies in Scripture, vol. 1 (Salt Lake City: Randall Book Co., 1984).

32. Lyon, p. 32.

33. Lyon, p. 32–33.

34. Preface, 1st ed.; *Pearl of Great Price* (Liverpool: F. D. Richards, 1851) p. v, original punctuation and emphasis retained.

35. H. Don Peterson, "The Birth and Development of the Pearl of Great Price," in *Pearl of Great Price Symposium* (Provo, Utah: Brigham Young Univ., 1976), p. 5.

36. Roberts, II, 22–26.

37. Peterson, pp. 7–13.

38. Peterson, pp. 12–13.

39. See Robert J. Matthews, *"A Plainer Translation": Joseph Smith's Translation of the Bible* (Provo, Utah: Brigham Young Univ. Press, 1975), pp. 26–28.

40. Matthews, *Translation*, p. 425.

41. *Doctrine and Covenants* 107:92.

42. See Jay M. Todd, *The Saga of the Book of Abraham* (Salt Lake City: Deseret Book, 1969), pp. 151–69.

43. Titled "Joseph Smith 1" prior to the 1981 edition.

44. Cf. A. E. Harvey, *Companion to the New Testament* (Cambridge: Oxford Univ. Press and Cambridge Univ. Press, 1973), pp. 92– 93.
45. Titled "Joseph Smith 2" prior to the 1981 edition.
46. Milton V. Backman, Jr., *Joseph Smith's First Vision*, 2nd ed. (Salt Lake City: Bookcraft, 1980), p. 125.
47. "Joseph Smith—History" v. 25, *Pearl of Great Price.*
48. See Edward J. Brandt, "The Articles of Faith: Origin and Importance," in *Pearl of Great Price Symposium*, (Provo, Utah: Brigham Young Univ., 1976), pp. 69–71.
49. Smith, p. 194.
50. See *Doctrine and Covenants* 131:6.

☪ ISLAM: Qur'an and Hadith

Frederick M. Denny

THE REVELATION OF THE QUR'AN

Christianity was born with a holy scripture already available as a heritage from the Jewish past, but Islam came into being as a religion and a community inspired and regulated by a simultaneously emerging scripture. The Qur'an, meaning "recitation," was orally revealed to the Arabian Prophet Muhammad by the Archangel Gabriel, according to Islamic belief, and thus did not descend to earth in scriptural form strictly considered. But the Message itself claimed to be from a "heavenly book" preserved in the presence of God. The act of writing is set forth in the first verses to be revealed, when they proclaim that "Thy Lord is the Most Generous, who taught by the Pen, taught man that he knew not" (96: 4–5). Throughout the chronological periods of the Qur'an's revelation to Muhammad, it is self-consciously "scripture," as can be seen in this early Meccan passage: "No! I swear by the fallings of the stars (and that is indeed a mighty oath, did you but know it) it is surely a noble Qur'an in a hidden Book none but the purified shall touch, a sending down from the Lord of all Being" (56:78).[1] Later in the Meccan period, we read of the "Clear Book" (al-kitāb al-mubīn), that God has made it an "Arabic Recitation" (qur'ānan 'arabiyyan), so that the hearers would be able to understand it (and be without excuse, it is implied). The "Clear Book" is, in its original, heavenly form called the "Mother of the Book" (umm al-kitāb), "with Us; sublime indeed, wise" (all from 43:1–4).

Muhammad received his call to prophecy when he was about forty years old. Orphaned early, he grew up under the care of his grandfather and then an uncle, but he was poor and had to work hard first as a shepherd and later in the employ of a wealthy widow named Khadīja, with whom he later had a long, happy marriage.[2] His reliability and trustworthiness earned him the nickname Al-Amīn ("The Upright") in his youth and he seemed to have an unusual sensitivity and sympathy for

84

others, especially the weak and downtrodden. As he grew older he took to seasonal retreats to a cave in a mountain outside Mecca, as apparently other thoughtful Meccans also did. These people are called by the Qur᾽an *ḥanīfs*, which in that context means pure monotheists, neither Jew nor Christian, but patterned on the original faith of Abraham, who is called *ḥanīf* (e.g., in 2:135; 3:67).[3] One night when Muhammad was alone in meditation in his cave, the Archangel Gabriel is said to have come to him while he was sleeping.[4] Placing a brocaded coverlet over Muhammad he commanded him to "Recite!," whereupon the frightened Muhammad replied "I am not a reciter" (*mā anā biqāri᾽ in*). Gabriel pressed down the cover, causing Muhammad to fear for his life because of the force. The same exchange took place. Finally after a third command from Gabriel to "Recite!", Muhammad said "What shall I recite?" And then Gabriel revealed the first passage of the "Recitation":

> Recite: In the Name of thy Lord who created, created man of a blood-clot.
> Recite: And thy Lord is the Most Generous, who taught by the Pen, taught man that he knew not. (96:1– 5).

The revelation of these verses has been celebrated ever since during the final days of the holy month of Ramaḍān, when the Muslims fast each day from dawn to dark. The night when Muhammad received these first revelations is known as *Laylat al-Qadr*, "The Night of Power," which is "better than a thousand months; In it the angels and the Spirit descend, by the leave of their Lord, upon every command. Peace it is, till the rising of dawn" (97:3–5).

Some authorities interpret the first word, *iqra᾽*, as meaning "read" rather than "recite," and that is a possible rendering.[5] The response of Muhammad would then be "I am not a reader," that is "I am illiterate." This has been used to prove Muhammad's inability to have composed the Qur᾽an himself and thus safeguards its divine provenance and inimitability. But it is more likely that *iqra᾽* means "recite," or even "speak out," without specific reference to the matter of literacy or illiteracy. (Interestingly, the ambiguous Arabic construction *mā anā biqāri᾽in* can mean either "I am not a reciter" or "What shall I recite?", because *mā* is either a negative particle or the interrogative pronoun "what.")

After a hiatus in the revelation, when Muhammad was afraid he was going mad and became severely depressed and doubtful, the recitations started coming again. The process of revelation is called in Arabic *waḥy*, which means the same as the English "revelation" but carries also the sense of verbal inspiration through the mind or, as the Qur'an itself expresses it, the "heart."

> Truly it is the revelation [tanzīl—"something sent down"] of the Lord of all Being, brought down by the Faithful Spirit [traditionally identified as Gabriel] upon thy heart, that thou mayest be one of the warners, in a clear, Arabic tongue. (26:193–195)

There are vivid descriptions of the process of revelation. ʿĀʾisha, the principal wife of Muhammad after Khadīja's passing, reported him as declaring that the inspiration "comes to me at times like the clanging of a bell, and that is the type which is most severe for me; it then leaves me, I have retained of it what the angel said. At times the angel appears to me in human form and speaks to me, and I retain what he says."[6] Sometimes the revelation came as "from behind a veil" (42:51). ʿĀʾisha also reported that she saw her husband sweating when the inspiration came, even on cold days. Once when Muhammad was in this state, the heavenly words came to him saying:

> O thou shrouded in thy mantle, arise, and warn! Thy Lord magnify, thy robes purify and defilement flee! (74:1– 5)

Those words are considered to be the second revelation, closely following the "recite" summons that had been received in the cave. From the first, Muhammad's revelations were "like the true vision in sleep, and every vision . . . like the bright gleam of dawn." The second revelation descended after Muhammad, through sheer terror, had had Khadīja wrap him up tightly. A later Meccan passage, after the troubling period of silence when the revelations ceased, reads:

> O thou enwrapped in thy robes, keep vigil the night, except a little (a half of it, or diminish a little, or add a little), and chant the Qur'an very distinctly. (73:1–4)

Chronology of the Qur'an

The reader will doubtless notice by now that the chronology of the revelation bears no relation to the numbers of the chapters in which they occur in the canonical text. The Muslims have, from the time the Qur'an was collected after Muhammad's death, recognized a chronological as well as a canonical ordering of the chapters, called "Suras." Each Sura contains a certain number of verses, known as āya (pl. āyāt), which also means "sign." The verses are also known as qur'āns, "recitations," and so the Qur'an as complete book is simply a collection of a great number of sepa-

rate recitations revealed to Muhammad over the entire course of his prophetic career, first in Mecca and later in Medina. The Meccan period was
when Muhammad was first preaching the ethical monotheism of the Message, a preaching very similar to that of the Bible, especially Moses and the
Prophets. There is a strong emphasis, particularly in the early Meccan period, on the coming judgment of God and the need to repent and be purified. Oaths and vivid imagery are frequently used, as in the following
typical passage:

> No! I swear by the Day of Resurrection. No! I swear by the reproachful soul.
> What, does man reckon We shall not gather his bones? Yes indeed; We are
> able to shape again his fingers. Nay, but man desires to continue on as a liber-
> tine, asking, "When shall be the Day of Resurrection?" But when the sight is
> dazed and the moon is eclipsed, and the sun and the moon are brought to-
> gether, upon that day man shall say, "Whither to flee?" No indeed; not a ref-
> uge. Upon that day the recourse shall be to thy Lord. Upon that day man shall
> be told his former deeds and his latter; nay, man shall be a clear proof against
> himself, even though he offer his excuses. (75:1–15)

ARABIC POETRY AND THE QUR'AN

The pre-Islamic Arabs of the Jāhiliyya, the "Age of Ignorance," de-
lighted in poetry, which was their supreme art form.[7] It had a sacred character to it, for poetic utterance was the ecstatic, yet ritualized bringing
forth of verses inspired by a jinnī. The word for poet in Arabic is shā'ir,
which literally means "one who knows," in the sense of perceiving what
others cannot see. The poetry of the Arabs focused on such subjects as
manly honor and courage, wine drinking and the joys of intoxication, satis-
faction of sexual desire, the fine points of beloved pieces of property like
horses and camels, war and the martial arts, the wonders and beauties of
nature, and the excellence and dignity of patrons of poetry. Poetry also was
used for boasting, invective, insult, and cursing, and a gifted practitioner
could strike terror in the hearts of his enemies, or the opponents of his
patron. The oral memory of the generally illiterate Arabs was able to retain
large quantities of verse and revel in the reciting of it. There were bardic
contests, such as at the great annual fair of 'Ukāz, not far from Mecca.
Poets from many regions of Hejaz (West Central Arabia) would gather and
compete for honors by means of odes composed according to a fairly strict
model. To say an old thing in an utterly fresh and arresting way, and in the
process bring honor to one's tribe and patron, was the mark of the superior
poet. The language used was understood by all and is that which came to

be known as al-Fuṣḥā, "the purest" Arabic. It was a sort of koiné that transcended the many dialects of the tribes scattered here and there across a vast territory. How it came into being before there was a developed form of writing is a mystery.[8]

The recitations delivered by Muhammad fell on ears finely tuned to the turnings and nuances of speech. The Qurʾan gradually won over the hearts, minds, and loyalties of the Arabs by its sheer rhetorical excellence and power, which was from the beginning regarded as proof of its divine origin. Muhammad was thought by some to be a poet, or a sort of shamanic seer—called a kāhin—or perhaps just mad, possessed by a jinnī (spirit) (52:29–30). But the Qurʾan boldly asserts that he is none of these; rather he is a "noble Messenger" (rasūl) of God. It was not insulting to regard someone as a poet, or a kāhin, or even one possessed, for each had a recognized and honored niche in Arabian society as traffickers in the sacred. But Muhammad, the Qurʾan insisted, was not to be fitted into the old religious and cultural categories of Arabian thought. He was a breakthrough, because of the coming upon him of the Qurʾan. Muhammad absolutely refused to take credit for the Qurʾan and those who came to join him in the Islamic movement then and since have all insisted that it is purely and entirely God's message. The Qurʾan is highly self-conscious about its own virtues and qualities and sets forth boldly its superiority to all other writings. In a late Meccan Sura we read:

> God has sent down the fairest discourse as a Book, consistent in its oft-repeated [admonitions], whereat shiver the skins of those who fear their Lord; then their skins and their hearts soften to the remembrance of God. (38:23)

THE QURʾAN AND THE RELIGION OF ABRAHAM

If the early Meccan period[9] is characterized by oaths and striking imagery, before long we begin to read of prophets and other figures of the past and the ways in which history bears on the present, especially as warning and example. There are numerous parallels with the Old Testament, although the materials were not apparently taken from it. There were Jews in Arabia and their traditions and legends were fairly widely known, even beyond their community. Abraham had always been considered to be father of the Arabs, too, and stories connected with him and his progeny were well known.[10] The Sura of Joseph, which comprises the single longest narrative in the Qurʾan, comes from the Meccan period, probably toward the end of it. The laconic nature of the Qurʾanic version of the legend suggests that the hearers knew the story and so did not require the kind of detail that one who was reared on the Biblical version (Genesis 37, 39–50) expects. Joseph in the Qur'an is the model of prophethood and uprightness, but the story is not told primarily in order to communicate information about him, but to proclaim God's great works. During the Meccan period God is referred to frequently as *al-Raḥmān*, the "Merciful," a name for God that was used by the Jews in South Arabia. Another name is *rabb*, "Lord," that appears frequently in the Meccan period, as well, and is often used in relation to matter pertaining to Jews and Christians. Allah is the most common name for God throughout the Qur'an.[11] But it was an old Arabian name and did not have any exclusive connection with the strict monotheism that Muhammad was preaching by means of the Qur'an. The Qur'an advises people to "Call upon God (*Allāh*), or call upon the Merciful (*al-Raḥmān*); whichsoever you call upon, to Him belong the Names Most Beautiful" (17:110).

The Qur'an brought about a revolution in the ways Arabs thought about life and, especially death. Typical of pre-Islamic belief and worldview was a sort of fatalism.[12] The Qur'an itself characterizes the Arabs of old, who say: "There is nothing but our present life; we die, and we live, and nothing but Time destroys us" (45:24). Then the Qur'an proceeds to reveal the message of warning and good news that there will be a day of resurrection and judgment, followed by eternal reward in heaven or damnation in hell. In all of this the Qur'an claims to be repeating the true revelations of former prophets.

> Say you: 'We believe in God, and in that which has been sent down on us and sent down on Abraham, Ishmael, Isaac and Jacob, and the Tribes, and that which was given to Moses and Jesus and the Prophets, of their Lord; we make no division between any of them, and to Him we surrender. (2:136)

The complete message and means of salvation were made known and followed through the career of Abraham, who for Muslims as well as for Jews and Christians—"People of the Book," as the Qur'an calls them—is the "Father of Faith."

> No: Abraham in truth was not a Jew, neither a Christian; but he was a Muslim and one pure of faith; certainly he was never of the idolaters. Surely the people standing closest to Abraham are those who followed him, and this Prophet [i.e., Muhammad], and those who believe; and God is the Protector of the believers. (3:67–68)

The word "Muslim" in this passage, and in every place, means "submitted" to God and should not be taken in the sense of Muslim as a member of the Islamic Ummah founded by Muhammad at Medina. That is, all sincere monotheists are in some manner muslims in the generic sense, in that they have surrendered to God. In the foregoing passage, it seems that the Qur³an is not claiming Abraham as one of Muhammad's own, or the new religion's own, so much as that Muhammad and the new Muslims belong to the original creed of Abraham, and are thus rightly guided. The sequence of prophetic messengers to various peoples has been completed with Muhammad, who restores the pure religion of Abraham. Muhammad is referred to in the Qur³an as the "Seal of the Prophets" (33:40), which means both the last one and the authenticator of what had been truly proclaimed before.

Scripture and Literacy

The Arabs were to be the last people to receive a prophet and through them the Qur³anic message would spread to all peoples. Muhammad is referred to as *al-nabī al-ummī* in the Qur³an (7:157−158), a title that has traditionally been thought to mean "the illiterate Prophet." (Muhammad's supposed inability to read or write has already been mentioned in connection with the call to prophesy, in reference to Sura 96:1 and the possible rendering of the exchange between Gabriel and Muhammad as "Read!" "I cannot read.") Modern analysis of the title suggests an additional meaning, while not necessarily denying the traditional one or replacing it entirely.[13] *Ummī* may mean "unscriptured," in the sense of Gentile.[14] The occurrence of the human plural, *ummīyūn*, makes this even more likely. In 62:2 we read:

> It is He who has raised up from among the *ummīyūn* a Messenger from among them, to recite His signs to them and to purify them, and to teach them the Book and the Wisdom, though before that they were in manifest error, and others of them who have not yet joined them.

Arberry translates the key word "common people," while Pickthall hedges with "unlettered ones," which can be taken to mean "illiterate" or "scriptureless." The Arabic word for "recite" in this passage is *yatlū*, which can mean either that or "read," just as with the q-r-' root, which gives us "recitation," "reading," "Qur³an," and so forth. It is not necessary to be literate in order "to teach them the Book and the Wisdom." The Muslims have always insisted on the priority of memorization of the Qur³an by heart and the multitude of blind reciters down through the ages testifies to the possibility as well as the importance of this. So, interestingly, we see in a passage like this one a suggestion that, while it is essential to have a book, it is not essential to be able to read it, in the sense of possessing the capacity to read writing. Of course, the Muslims have always worked hard to spread literacy and calligraphy became the central sacred art form. But the primary responsibility is to have the Message by heart and to follow it. Mere literacy will not accomplish this.

A few lines after the ones quoted above, we read the famous gibe at the Jews:

> The likeness of those who have been loaded with the Torah, then they have not carried it, is as the likeness of an ass carrying books. (62:5)

Woe unto those who read but do not obey. *Ummīyūn*, like *ummī*, most likely means "unscriptured," or, more awkwardly, "unmessaged," and in that sense "common folk" (as opposed to chosen peoples). The Arabs as a whole were not illiterate, but that meaning is also included, probably. But mere literacy is neither a necessary nor sufficient condition for the act of *islām* or the gift of faith. If it were so, what would have become of Muhammad, who, the Muslims insist, was illiterate?

The Medinan period of the Qur²an's revelation, that is, after Muhammad and his small band of Muslims had made the fateful *hijra* or "emigration" from hostile, idolatrous Mecca to the oasis town of Medina, is characterized by quite different content than the Meccan revelations. Although warning of judgment and announcing of good news of God's guidance still can be heard clearly, there is also a great deal of more practical, mundane matter. This is because in Medina Muhammad became a political and military leader, as well as continuing to serve as Prophet. The Medinan Suras contain much in the way of legal and ritual detail, although not in a systematic, codified form. In the early Medinan Sura known as "The Cow" (no. 2), the longest chapter in the Qur²an, can be reviewed virtually all of the contents that had been revealed to date. It is sometimes called, for this reason, "The Qur²an in Miniature." It enjoys priority of position in the canon, coming right after the first Sura, which is a prayer and, like the Lord's Prayer of the Christians, the paradigm of prayer.

THE COLLECTION OF THE QUR²AN

Although there is some circumstantial evidence to suggest that Muhammad was engaged in the collecting and arranging of the Qur²an before his death, probably with the help of his last amanuensis Zayd ibn Thābit, the task was not definitely accomplished until the time of the third Caliph, ʿUthmān.[15] By that time, the Arab-Islamic empire had grown to vast proportions and there were armies stationed in remote places. When different groups came into contact with each other and discerned that there were differences in the way certain Qur'anic passages were recited, for example in the prayer services, there was heated debate and disagreement. Consequently, ᶜUthmān sought to achieve a canonical recension to avoid major dissension. But long before this, according to a well-known tradition, the first Caliph, Abū Bakr, is said to have ordered a collection of the Qur'an after a large number of reciters had been killed in the Battle of Yamāma. Zayd is said to have done this and then handed the manuscript over to ᶜUmar, who, according to one source, had suggested the project to Abū Bakr in the first place. After ᶜUmar's death the recension is said to have been passed on to his daughter Hafsa. Later, according to this story, it formed the basis of the definitive recension completed under ᶜUthmān.

Whatever the truth of the matter, and there are reasons for grave doubt,[16] the recension we now have certainly dates back to the Qur'an of ᶜUthmān in all essentials. As modern critical scholars have insisted, this is certainly not a critical text in the scientific sense. It is, rather, a *textus receptus*, with the absolute authority of the consensus of the Muslims that it is indeed the true Qur'an in all respects. To suggest looking behind and beyond it is both blasphemous and unnecessary in the Muslim view.

There were other codices of the Qur'an, or parts of it, circulating from even before the death of the Prophet, and many knew the text by heart. The different tribal groups in the various military outposts under ᶜUthmān each had their own codices, and that was what was at the heart of the problem. No single codex was universally regarded as the standard, original Qur'an. When the ᶜUthmānic codex had been completed, a decree was published that all others were immediately to be destroyed and replaced by the new, official one. Several copies were made of the new recension and sent out from Medina to a number of provincial capitals and probably also to Mecca, the ritual center of the new religion. According to the evidence, the scholarly task headed up by Zayd was exceedingly carefully executed, with exhaustive searches for Qur'anic material in whatever form it had been preserved: written down on a variety of materials or kept in the memories of the Companions. Exacting comparisons were made between codices and informants and dialectal peculiarities were also gone into, with the result that the Quraysh dialect (the Prophet's own) would be preferred in all cases of doubt or disagreement.

But although the ᶜUthmānic recension was official, other codices were still known to be in use,[17] even in public worship, as late as three centuries after Muhammad's death. But a consensus had been achieved to the effect that use of any recension but the ᶜUthmānic one was illegal. One individual was threatened with execution in Baghdad if he persisted in introducing "rare and singular readings" into the public prayer service. His name was Ibn Shanabūdh (d. 328/939), and he was an accomplished expert in recitation.[18] But it was one thing to know the history of the text, and its variants, and another to employ them in worship. There are acceptable variant readings of the Qur'an, the most widely acknowledged being a list of seven, although there are three beyond that recognized by some and even four more beyond those, for a total of fourteen.[19] These variant readings (qirā'āt) are not the same thing as the old separate codices. And these are not different Qur'ans or even different "versions" of the same Qur'an. They are all descended from the ʿUthmānic recension and simply display minor variants in the readings of the standard text, readings that were early associated with the specific cities in the early Islamic world and their Qur'an schools: Mecca, Medina, Damascus, Basra, and Kufa. Today, although all muqri's, "masters of readings and recitation," know the seven readings and beyond thoroughly, there is for all practical purposes only one in nearly universal favor, that of Ḥafs (d. 802), named after the person who received the reading from ʿĀsim (d. 744), a Kufan master and one of the original seven.[20] The number seven is traced back to a ḥadīth of Muhammad that told of his having received the Qur'an in seven different "readings," as the Arabic word aḥruf (lit. "letters", pl. of ḥarf) was interpreted to mean.

The achievement of a standard exemplar of the Qur'an text was a slow process because of the incomplete system of writing Arabic at the time of the Prophet and for some time afterwards. This is where the oral transmission of the text was so important, safeguarding it in a direct human linkage from master to students and so on down through the generations. It was not until almost three centuries had elapsed until a completely voweled and "pointed" Qur'an text was available, from which authentic copies could then be made. This development parallels that of the Jews in their long labors to produce a Masoretic text of the Hebrew Bible. Both Aramaic and Hebrew, on the one hand, and Arabic, on the other, are based on a consonantal alphabet that, in writing down, requires augmentation with vowel markings in order to be precise about pronunciation and grammar. In early Islamic times, even some of the consonants were not clearly distinguished from each other, so that markings in addition to vowels had to be added.

FORM AND CONTENT OF THE QUR'AN

The ʿUthmānic recension was deficient as to writing system, but in its essentials, as was already mentioned, it is the Qur'an we now have, with regard to the arrangement of Suras, their number and content, and the bare consonantal text. The numbering of the verses and the names of the Suras were added later. The so-called "Mysterious Letters" that open certain of the Suras were already in the ʿUthmānic recension. There are 114 Suras in the Qurʾan, arranged roughly in order of length, beginning (with the exception of the *Fātiḥa*, the short prayer that "opens" the Qurʾan) with the longest and proceeding on down to the very brief last Suras, the final two of which are in the form of "charms" against witchcraft and evil magic. The whole text is approximately equivalent in length to the New Testament. But there is no real similarity between the Qurʾan and the Bible overall, whether in form or style.

As for content, there is no doubt upon reading the Qurʾan for the first time that it belongs to the Abrahamic traditions and breathes the same air as Moses, Gideon, Elijah, Amos, Job, John the Baptist, and Jesus. Although the Qurʾan is heavily oracular, apocalyptic, and in its own way quite poetic, with little in the way of narrative historical matter, it is also fundamentally concerned with God's utter sovereignty and justice, tempered by mercy and compassion.[21] There are numerous references to past peoples who had been reached by God through his messengers, and whose responses to God serve as continuing reminders, whether of warning or example, for those to whom the Qurʾan is addressed.

Western critics have, at least in the past, insensitively pointed out what to them were dull repetitions and opaque constructions of the Qurʾan, without seeking to appreciate what there is about the Book that totally captivates those who surrender to it as God's true Message. The very repetitions and frequent recurrences of fundamental themes are regarded as signs of its miraculous provenance and its merciful insistence on being heard and obeyed. It is fair to predict that if one takes any random section, say of twenty-five or thirty verses, one will have a cross-section of "Guidance" (*hudan*) sufficient unto salvation. This is because of the moral urgency of the Message at each point of its progress, inviting people to the good and prohibiting the bad, as the Qurʾan in turn bids its followers to do in the governance of human affairs as God's vicegerents (*khalīfa*, pl. *khulafāʾ* = "Caliphs") on earth.

THE ROLE OF THE QURʾAN IN THE LIFE OF THE MUSLIMS

There are two main areas in which the Qurʾan provides fundamental authority and guidance for the Muslims. One is as the primary source of law and doctrine. The other is as the "prayer-book" of the Islamic commu-

nity. These two roles are complementary and together form the comprehensive and integral range of belief and expression that is the symbol and
action system of Islam.[22] The Qurʾan provides both the norms for faith and
behavior as well as the dynamic for fulfilling them. It is both the source of
truth for the Muslims and the means of realizing that truth in action. Before the Qurʾan had been revealed in any large quantities it had already, in
closest cooperation with the remarkable career of Muhammad, established
its place at the center of Muslim faith and order, not in a static sense, but as
a forceful, living, intending, future-directed presence. As prayer-book
from the very beginning, the Qurʾan instructed and informed its followers
at the same time that it strengthened and sensitized them.[23]

Learning the Qurʾan involves both the mastery of its content, so as to
be able to understand and apply its factual and conceptual matter, and the
mastery of its proper recitation, for purposes of devotion to God and personal and communal spiritual nurture.

Exegesis

The first task centers in exegesis, called *tafsīr* in Arabic. From the
time of Muhammad, the Muslims turned to the difficult task of trying
to understand fully what the Message was saying. In the process, they
reached out to the sacred writings and lore of other traditions, most notably Judaism and Christianity, as well as the intellectual and cultural past
of the Arabs, particularly in the realm of language.

Over the centuries three main types of exegesis were developed.[24] The
first, and at all times the most authoritative and "orthodox" is known as
"commentary handed down" (*tafsīr maʾthūr*). It emphasizes the accessible
and plain meanings of the passages and gathers together sober, scholarly
opinions and positions, complete with their sources, scrupulously cited.
This type of exegesis often runs to great length and reached its peak of
development around the beginning of the fourth Islamic century under
Al-Ṭabarī (d. 923), whose great work runs to thirty volumes in a modern
edition.

A second type of exegesis is what can loosely be translated as "rational commentary" (*tafsīr bi al-raʾy*). This type has had a somewhat controversial history, because it emphasizes theological issues in an often
speculative manner, something that has never found fertile soil in Islam,
which is more devoted to issues of law and "orthopraxy" than to correct
doctrine in the theologically abstract sense. The great Muʿtazilite "rationalist" scholar al-Zamakhsharī (d. 1144) wrote a profound commentary,
but his Sunnī readers, at least, to this day have been warned to pay attention only to the penetrating philological and grammatical explanations
and to leave the tainted speculative interpretations alone. The great syn-

thesizer of law, theology and mysticism al-Ghazālī (d. 1111) had disdain for *tafsīr maʾthūr*, "traditional exegesis," and championed the rational type, too. But he never produced a full *tafsīr*. The final main type of commentary is called in Arabic *taʾwīl*, a term which in the Qurʾan means the same thing as *tafsīr*. But it later came to mean "symbolic" or "allegorical" exegesis, penetrating into the hidden and deeper meanings of the text, beneath the surface. This type of exegesis has been pursued especially by the Sufis, the mystics of Islam, as well as the Shīʿites, that powerful and influential minority that focused on the Prophet's descendants, through ʿAlī and Fāṭima, as the true guides (Imāms) of the community. *Taʾwīl* is both highly speculative and imaginative, and thus deeply satisfying and suggestive at the level of spirituality.

All three major types of Qurʾan commentary: traditional, rational, and allegorical have their places in the total life of the Muslim community. And although there have been and continue to be honest disagreements over them, there is at the same time a high level of tolerance of them. In a sense, the traditional type stands at the bottom as a sort of foundation of commentary. Above this stands the rational approach, which seeks to exhaust the conceptual level through disciplined reflection. Then at the top stands the symbolic or allegorical type, which operates not primarily to explain, at least in response to a desire for mere information, but aims for enlightenment, or gnosis, and ecstatic union with God.

Recitation

Exegesis of the Qurʾan is essential for purposes of law and governance, and in those two activities the traditional type prevails, for obvious reasons. But the other side of the Qurʾan's role in the Islamic community is just as important, and far more wide-reaching and penetrating in the lives of the believers. That is because, although relatively few ever reach the level of scholarly ability necessary for acceptable exegetical activity of an original sort, practically every Muslim can master the fundamentals of recitation.

Islamic education from the earliest times has been dedicated to teaching the Qurʾan and its proper recitation, beginning at an early age. The *kuttāb*, "Qurʾan school," was the institution that was developed for this. Even today, when public education in Islamic countries centers in those universally acknowledged subjects that are necessary for success in the modern world, there still is training in the Qurʾan, if not always during the regular class day, then after school at the local mosque or some other place. Children, in most cases boys together in one place and girls in another, are seated in neat rows, each with a slate or paper tablet, while the teacher writes the Arabic letters and words and phrases on the blackboard and goes over them in a rhythmic oral manner which helps memorization. The

Qur'anic ear is trained at the same time as the Qur'anic eye, and these two together remain with the Muslim all of his or her life, as an ingrained system of guidance and values. If the appreciation of the Qur'an is an acquired taste, it is acquired very early by Muslims, who then nurture and preserve it throughout their lives, not only in prayer and the celebrations that feature chanting, but also in the visual realm, because the calligraphy of the Qur'anic Arabic has provided the fundamental aesthetic of Islamic art and decoration.

Most Muslims do not speak or read Arabic, because the Arabs comprise only a substantial minority of the Ummah, or Community. But the recitation of the Arabic Qur'an is cultivated throughout the Islamic world and the five daily prayers require Arabic, too, although there are prayers and phrases that can also be offered up in the vernacular of the worshippers. It would be too much to say that typical Muslims in non-Arabic-speaking locales fully understand what they are reciting or hearing, but they try to, and often the shaykh of a community, who usually knows a fair amount of Arabic, provides translations and paraphrases as well. The use of Arabic in non-Arabophone regions is based on the conviction that it is indeed a sacred, and not just a liturgical language. There is something about the Qur'anic Arabic that puts people in touch with God as nothing else can. Therefore, reciting the Qur'an in a proper manner is akin to what Christians would call a "sacrament," although that term is neither used by nor is congenial to Muslims. But when the Qur'an is recited, God's Sakīnah, "Tranquility," "Security," descends, bringing with it comfort and power. (It is interesting to compare this with the Hebrew *Shekhinah*.) As has often been observed in modern comparative studies of Islam and Christianity, when attempting to discern parallels between the two traditions, the Qur'an in Islam is most nearly akin, both structurally and functionally, to Christ in the Christian tradition. Both are considered to be God's "Word," and both have come down into the world for the guidance and salvation of humankind. Each provides both doctrine and power for these ends and the comforting presence that heals and sustains people through the most difficult and tragic experiences to which life exposes them. Both Qur'an and Christ have given to their respective traditions their central visual-symbolic forms: the calligraphic arabesque in aniconic Islam, and the face of the Savior in Christianity, whether on icon or crucifix.

THE PROPHETIC SUNNAH AS ENSHRINED IN THE HADĪTH

A discussion of scripture in Islam would be incomplete without a consideration of an additional collection of sources on authentic Islamic belief and practice. The Shahāda, that short formula which serves as the basic creed of Islam, reads: There is no god but God. Muhammad is the Messenger of God." (Lā ilāha illā Allāh. Muhammad rasūl Allāh.) Saying this at least once with belief makes one a Muslim. The first shahāda, or "witnessing," concerns the unity of God, whose nature and purposes have been revealed in the Qurʾan, "in a clear Arabic speech." But the second shahāda focuses on the human agency chosen by God to fulfill his purposes of warning and guidance. Muhammad is, thus, inextricably bound up in the basic structure of the religion. He came to be, for his Ummah, the exemplary human being, upon whom all others should pattern their lives, from proper faith and devotional practices all the way to the homelier aspects of mundane existence. Islam from the beginning has been considered to be a total way of life, with no separation between religious and secular realms. From a combination of the Qurʾan and the life and habits of Muhammad, the Muslims have developed a unified and integrated vision of what authentic human life should be.

Muhammad as Exemplary Human

Lest the second shahāda be considered idolatrous, it must be added immediately that Muhammad is considered to be completely human, with no dimension of divinity in him. It is utterly against orthodox belief and practice to raise him to an exalted level through adoration or prayer to him. But his example is trustworthy, and is in fact attested in the Qurʾan itself, which gave rise to the veneration of the Prophet who transmitted it, and who was so intimately identified with it.

> You have a good example in God's Messenger for whosoever hopes for God and the Last Day, and remembers God oft. When the believers saw the Confederates [i.e., unbelievers] they said, "This is what God and His Messenger promised us, and God and His Messenger have spoken truly." (33:21)

> God and His angels bless the Prophet. O believers, do you also bless him, and pray him peace. Those who hurt God and His Messenger—them God has cursed in the present world and the world to come, and has prepared for them a humbling chastisement. (33:56)

> My chastisement—I smite with it whom I will; and My mercy embraces all things, and I shall prescribe it for those who are godfearing and pay the alms, and those who indeed believe in Our signs, those who follow the Messenger, the Prophet of the common folk [al-nabī al-ummī], whom they found written down with them in the Torah and the Gospel, bidding them to honour, and forbidding them dishonour, making lawful for them the good things and making unlawful for them the corrupt things, and relieving them of their loads, and the fetters that were upon them. Those who believe in him and succour

him and help him, and follow the light that has been sent down with him—
they are the prosperers. (7:156–157)

These and numerous other passages from all periods of the Qur³an's revelation add up to a most powerful endorsement of Muhammad as the true
guide on the human plane, and made so by God's special decree. The idea
of a "Muhammadan Light" is introduced in the last passage quoted, and
this notion has persisted as a deep conviction among the Muslims. The
Shī ᶜites, who follow the line of Imāms descended from the prophet through
Fātima and ᶜAlī, as was noted above, regard the Light as being perpetuated
in that noble line. All Muslims believe that God's guidance continues to
animate the Community by means of the Prophet's Sunnah, which is the
total of his "custom," or life and habits, as set forth in a peculiar literary
form known as hadīth, to which we now turn in conclusion of this examination of scripture in Islam.

From the beginning of Muhammad's prophetic mission, which began
with the command to "Recite!", both he and his companions clearly distinguished between his own speech and that of God. But as time passed,
even Muhammad's historically conditioned utterances came to exert considerable influence, which is not surprising in light of his momentous mission and the growing number of people who were being attracted to it as a
divinely ordained matter. By the time of the founding and development of
the Medinan Ummah, with its political, military, and judicial, as well as
ritual and doctrinal dimensions, Muhammad's words and example were
definitive, although still considered to be his and not God's. After Muhammad's death, the recollection of his own sayings and actions and habits
came over the generations to be second only to the Qur³an in authority.
Thus it was that the Qur³an, God's Speech, and the Sunnah, his Prophet's
"Custom," were institutionalized as the fundamental sources of Islamic jurisprudence. The two were inseparable, with the Prophet being regarded
as the best of interpreters of the holy book.

HADITH: CONTENT, FORM AND FUNCTION

People preserved Muhammad's words and his contemporaries' descriptions of his actions in the form of reports, known in Arabic as hadīth
(pl. ahādīth), a term which contains the sense of "new," "coming to pass,"
and "occurrence." [25] It came to mean a "tradition" in the form of a brief report. What the hadīths, taken together, do is to provide a literary form for
the preservation of that Sunnah of Muhammad which had come to be so
prestigious and which provided a model for the Muslims to follow, as has

been said above. *Sunnah*, "custom," was an old Arabian concept that contained the idea of the way things are done, and had been done. There is a sense that a *sunnah* is a "beaten path," by means of which people maintain a proper direction in life, with correct procedures for coping with the challenges and accidents of fortune. The Qurʾan itself uses the term in the sense of God's "method" or "way" of dealing with his creatures, especially of old (e.g., 33:62).

The *hadīths* range in content and character from quite sober and simple declarations of Muhammad's views and judgments on a great variety of subjects, to exalted, almost theological discourses, to frankly hagiographical rhapsodies proclaiming the Prophet's incomparable virtues and achievements.[26] There is a great amount of valuable historical information in them, but there is also a significant amount of questionable content, and no small amount of outright forgery.[27] The more discerning Muslim scholars fairly early turned their attention to the question of authenticity of the *hadīth* materials, which increased steadily as the years passed. A special science of tradition was developed, which had as one of its main subdisciplines a fascinating and exacting field known as "the Science of Men" (ʿilm al-rijāl). If, after a century or two, a *hadīth* had been in circulation and widely accepted, it stood a good chance of being included among those traditions that were considered reliable.

But the scholars put all *hadīths* to severe tests, centering in the chain of attesters that had transmitted it from the Prophet's time down to the present. A report on this or that, like saying prayers while riding a camel, may be quite plausible-sounding on the face of it. After all, Muhammad prayed, and he rode camels, and sometimes he did both at the same time. Even so, it is not sufficient to have a plausible report. There needs to be authentication by reliable transmitters, who form a "chain," known technically as an *isnād* (lit. "supports," sing. *sanad*). The experts scrutinized each link in the chain and then determined what sort of "grade" to assign the *hadīth*, ranging from "sound" (*ṣaḥīḥ*) to "acceptable" (*ḥasan*) through a number of intermediate grades to "weak" (*daʿīf*), which is the lowest acceptable category, to a number of other types that should be rejected in most cases, because of missing links in the *isnād*, or oddities, and other circumstances. Widely attested *hadīths*, with a variety of *isnāds*, are generally considered to be sound, because it would have been impossible to have forged them and gained such universal attestation. The individual links in the chain of attestation were of course real people. Vast amounts of biographical information were gathered by the *hadīth* experts in order to pass judgment on their reliability, honesty, intelligence, memory power, knowledge of Arabic, movements during life, relationships with those with whom they were linked, and other matters. It is notable how significant the actual community was in the assembling of the authentic record of their Prophet's Sunnah. Consensus of the Ummah has, especially for the Sunnī majority, been one of the sources of jurisprudence, coming after Qurʾan and Sunnah. Interestingly, it is in turn based partly on a fateful utterance attributed to Muhammad, namely, that "My people shall never agree together on an error."

The following is an example of a "sound" *hadīth*, together with its *isnād*, as reported in the Ṣaḥīḥ (i.e., "sound" [collection]) of al-Bukhārī (d. 870), generally acknowledged to have been the greatest of all *hadīth* experts, who made the most reliable collection.

> Ḥajjāj bin Minhāl reported to us: 'Shaʿba related to us:' He said: ʾAlqama bin Marthad told me: "I heard Saʿd bin ʿUbayda [who got it] from Abū ʿAbd al-Raḥmān al-Sulami [who got it] from ʿUthmān, may God be pleased with him, from the Prophet, God bless him and grant him salvation. He said: 'The Best among you is the one who learns and teaches the Qurʾan.'"[28]

The *isnād* comes first and the *matn*, or "text," afterwards. The casual reader is naturally interested only in the *matn*, but the pious Muslim seeking guidance from the Prophet's Sunnah looks closely at the *isnād* before deciding on the *hadīth's* authority. It is difficult for the non-Muslim scholar who has not been trained in the traditional methodology of *hadīth* criticism, which has included vast amounts of memorization, to use many traditional sources. This is because they often do not have subject indexes but rather indices of *isnāds* and individual transmitters. A few years ago a long-term project jointly shared in by Muslim and non-Muslim Western scholars was completed: a vast concordance of the *hadīth* literature.[29] When I showed it to one of my students, a Lebanese Muslim, after leafing through the elephant folios and examining a number of extensive entries, turned to me and declared: "With this one does not need a shaykh!" Whatever the final truth of that judgment, it remains true that in order to study traditional sources one still either has to have a shaykh, or be one.

In a sense, the *hadīth* scholars are the Talmudists of Islam. In addition to six highly revered collections of Ḥadīth within the Sunnī tradition,[30] as well as others among the Shīʿites, there are yet others of value, as well as very many extensive commentaries and special sub-collections made from the original collections. The *hadīths* have been utilized very widely in jurisprudence, which requires special training and techniques in addition to *hadīth* science. The Sunnah of the Prophet is never studied from motives of idle curiosity, although it contains a universe of fascinating information and arcane lore. As with the Qurᵓan, it is studied for purposes of guidance and regulation of the life of the Ummah before all else. But study and discussion of these two types of Islamic "scripture," the one from God and the other from and about his Prophet, are themselves centrally important ways of being religious within the Islamic scheme of things.

The Ḥadīth are never recited or used in worship; only the Qurᵓan may be used for those activities. However, the rubrics of worship and other devotional duties are found in the Ḥadīth, and there is much information about Muhammad's devotional life and ideas. But the Ḥadīth are very frequently cited by Muslims, either in official contexts, or among ordinary folk, either as edifying discourse or to prove a point by adducing a text. Once a man was with some fellow Muslims during the animal sacrifices of the Great Feast. After slaughtering his sheep, this person jumped over it in an odd little motion. One of the others immediately asked him why he did this, suspecting "innovation," that euphemism which means "heresy." "What is your authority?" the observer asked. Hearing no answer, he pressed the issue by asking whether there was a ḥadīth about jumping over the victim. "No," was the reply. "Then is it from the Qurᵓan?" "No." "Then where did you get authority for this practice?" "From Allah," was the final reply, followed by a scornful silence after which the matter was dropped. Islam does not countenance free-lancing in doctrinal elaboration or ritual observance. It has its unassailable textual sources of guidance in both spheres, as well as in every other.

Ḥadīth Qudsī: "Divine Saying"

There is a third type of definitive utterance in Islam that lies between the Qurᵓanic revelation and the speech of Muhammad. It is a special category of ḥadīth known as the "Divine Saying" (ḥadīth qudsī), containing the words of God but distinguished from the Qurᵓan and transmitted through the Prophet in a manner similar to other weighty pronouncements. That is, most scholars consider the exact wording of such ḥadīths to be Muhammad's, but solidly based on divine revelation as to the meaning. So this genre of saying falls between verbal divine revelation and the divinely informed reliability of the Prophet, even when speaking out by himself.[31] The ḥadīth qudsī is often particularly meaningful for the spiritual life and has generally no connection with jurisprudence. Two examples of ḥadīth qudsīs (matns only) will give some idea of their quality.

> Where are those who love one another through My glory? Today I shall give them shade in My shade, it being a day when there is no shade but My shade. (Related by al-Bukhārī)[32]

When Allah decreed Creation He pledged Himself by writing in His book which is laid down with Him: My mercy prevails over My wrath. (Related by Muslim and others)[33]

The Sufis especially search the "Divine Sayings" for special, hidden meanings by which they will be enabled to draw nearer to God. One of the most poignant for them is the saying: "I was a Hidden Treasure and I wished to be known, and so I created the world."[34] This type of saying proliferated greatly, often being more a kind of ecstatic utterance of individual mystics than reliably authenticated ḥadīths that found a home in such unimpeachable collections as those of al-Bukhārī and his nearly equally great contemporary Muslim. Nevertheless, shaky examples purporting to be of the ḥadīth qudsī genre do provide information on religious attitudes as well as practices. While they are almost always lofty in speech and subject matter, occasionally they go to such an extreme as this famous one: "The love of cats is a part of faith."[35] This is not as droll as it may sound on first reading, because one of the most beloved of Muhammad's Companions was Abū Hurayra, who transmitted the greatest number of ḥadīths and was so exceedingly fond of the little pet he was often seen holding that he was given the nickname just mentioned: "Father of the Kitten."

CONCLUDING REMARKS

Islamic scripture, both that revealed as the Qurʾan and that which emerged from the life of Muhammad and its devoted cultivation by the community, serves to unify and regulate the Muslims in a manner perhaps unmatched by any other sacred writing. The Qurʾan teaches the faithful what to believe, and in the process assures them of the efficacy of their faithfulness by means of its mysterious powers. Anyone who reads the Qurʾan with a serious and respectful, even if not reverent attitude, is likely to start suspecting that the Qurʾan is also "reading" him. This is particularly the case when the original Arabic is being read aloud. Added to this uncanny aura surrounding the Qurʾan and its reader is the highly sensuous character of the words and phrases as they charm people's hearing and seeing by means of chanting and calligraphy. These lift the believers far above the merely informational level of the Scripture's content. So important is the ritual performance dimension that a well-attested ḥadīth of the Prophet declares: "He is not one of us who does not recite the Qurʾan beautifully." (al-Bukhārī)[36] Exegesis, as was observed, is a critically important enterprise, for purposes of doctrinal exposition and especially for jurisprudence. But it is at the level of devotional behavior where the Qurʾan displays its greatest power and bestows its peculiar grace and blessings. There is something essentially democratic about Qur'an recitation, as well as the preservation of the text, to which the believers have exerted themselves mightily by means of individual and group memory. The *ḥāfiẓ al-Qur'ān*, "Guardian of the Qur'an," in the sense of having the text by heart, has been in all ages a most treasured asset and a proof of God's continuing guidance of his obedient servants.

There are important differences between the Qur'an and Ḥadīth, both as to their provenance and roles, as well as their form and style. This essay, by characterizing both of them as "scripture" is not suggesting that Qur'an and Ḥadīth are of equal value within the Islamic scheme of things. The Qur'an beckons its hearers to enter into the world of God's essential nature. The recollection, by means of *dhikr*, a mantra-like repetition of Qur'anic verses that became a highly sophisticated spiritual discipline of Sufism, is testimony to the Muslims' strong sense of the yearning of God and his creatures for fellowship with each other. The "friends" (*awliyā'*) of God, who is himself proclaimed by the Qur'an as the greatest "Friend" (*walī*), find, at the level of mundane existence, their perfect model in Muhammad. The Sunnah does not circulate among the Muslims primarily as writing, nor is it recited. It provides, rather, the ideal pattern for human life and complements the Qur'an's role of sustaining spiritual power and means of contact with God. The Sunnah of Muhammad completes the Qur'an, in a real sense, as the definitive commentary on the Revelation, enshrined in the Ḥadīth literature and, even more, in the lives of Muhammad's people.

NOTES

1. Muslims believe that the Qur'an can neither be imitated nor translated. Yet many attempts at translation, or rather interpretation, have been made since earliest times by both Muslims and others. There are several adequate English versions of the text. My preference, used in this article, is A. J. Arberry, *The Koran Interpreted* (New York: Macmillan, 1955).

   The contents of the Qur'an are arranged in chapter-like divisions called *sūras*. They number 114 in all and vary greatly in length. Taken together they comprise a volume roughly equivalent to the New Testament in length. The basic division of the contents of the Qur'an is according to whether the materials were revealed during the Meccan period of Muhammad's prophetic career (610–622 c.e.) or in the period following the Hijra, or "emigration" to Medina, where a theocratic community was established, known as the Ummah. Various chronologies of the Qur'an have been advanced, both in traditional Islamic scholarship and in modern critical studies. The most widely accepted of the latter was advanced by the German semitologist Theodor

Nöldeke (1836–1930) in his prize-winning essay of 1860, *Geschichte des Qorans*, which has been extensively revised and expanded over the years by the author and his collaborators. The final and definitive edition is by Nöldeke, Friedrich Schwally, Gotthelf Bergsträsser and Otto Pretzl, in 3 volumes (Leipzig: Dieterich'sche Verlagsbuchhandlung, 1909–1938; reprinted Hildesheim: Georg Olms Verlag, 1970). This monumental work is available only in German.

An excellent English language reference on the Qur³an is W. Montgomery Watt, *Bell's Introduction to the Qur³ān* (Edinburgh: Edinburgh University Press, 1970). It is based on an earlier work by the Scottish scholar Richard Bell. Watt's revision contains a useful "Table of Suras" with comparisons of four different chronological schemes, including both the standard Muslim one (known as the "Egyptian") and Nöldeke's. Finally, there is the thorough survey of Qur³anic scholarship by Alford T. Welch, "Al-Ḳur³ān," in *The Encyclopedia of Islam*, new edition (Leiden: E. J. Brill, 1960), Vol. V. pp. 400–429.

2. There are many biographies of Muhammad, perhaps the most important being that of Ibn Isḥāq, (d. *ca.* 767 C.E.), known as the Sīra ("life"). It is available in an English translation by Alfred Guillaume under the title *The Life of Muhammad* (Oxford: Oxford University Press, 1955). The best recent studies are W. Montgomery Watt's *Muhammad at Mecca* (Oxford: Clarendon Press, 1953) and *Muhammad at Medina* (Oxford: Clarendon Press, 1956). They have been abridged in *Muhammad: Prophet and Statesman* (Oxford: University Press, 1961). A sensitive and accessible modern Muslim treatment is that of Martin Lings, *Muhammad: His Life Based on the Earliest Sources* (New York: Inner Traditions International, 1983).

3. This term is discussed, with reference to modern critical theories, by Frederick M. Denny, in "Some Religio-Communal Terms and Concepts in the Qur³an," *Numen*, Vol. XXIV, Fasc. 1 (February, 1977), pp. 26–34.

4. There exist differing versions of this story. I have based my retelling on Ibn Isḥāq's *Sīra*, pp. 104–7 of the Guillaume translation, cited in n. 2.

5. Guillaume renders it "read," p. 106.

6. Reported in traditions collected by both al-Bukhārī and Muslim. *Mishkāt al-Masābīḥ*, a collection of Prophetic traditions (ḥadīth) made by al-Baghawī and al-Khaṭīb al-Tibrīzī, translated by James Robson (Lahore: Sh. Muhammad Ashraf, 1966), Vol. 4, p. 1254.

7. A detailed and absorbing survey is "Pre-Islamic Poetry," by Abdulla el-Tayyib, in A. F. L. Beeston, T. M. Johnstone, R. B. Serjeant and G. R. Smith, eds., *Arabic Literature to the End of the Umayyad Period* (Cambridge: Cambridge University Press, 1983), pp. 27–109. Also, see A. J. Arberry, *The Seven Odes: The First Chapter in Arabic Literature* (London: Allen & Unwin, 1957), which includes superb translations of the most famous ancient Arabic odes.

8. See A. F. L. Beeston's observations concerning the evolution of Arabic in the opening chapter of *Arabic Literature*, especially pp. 5–6. For technical and

bibliographic detail, see Chaim Rabin's section of the article "ʿArabiyya" in The *Encyclopedia of Islam*, new edition (Leiden: E. J. Brill, 1960), Vol. I, pp. 564–67.

9. Theodor Nöldeke's chronology divides the Meccan period into early, middle and late, based primarily on a progressive change of style. See W. Montgomery Watt's summary analysis in *Bell's Introduction to the Qurʾan*, pp. 109–12.

10. See Y. Moubarac, *Abraham dans le Coran* (Paris, J. Vrin, 1958).

11. See "Allāh," by Louis Gardet, *Encyclopedia of Islam*, new edition, Vol. I, pp. 406–9.

12. A detailed examination, with many illustrations from poetry, is Helmer Ringgren, *Studies in Arabian Fatalism* (Uppsala: A.-B. Lundequistika Bokhandeln, 1955).

13. Joseph Horovitz, "Jewish Proper Names and Derivatives in the Koran," *Hebrew Union College Annual*, Volume II (1925), reprinted Hildesheim: Georg Olms Verlag, 1964, pp. 190–91, argues that ummī in the Qurʾan is an adaptation of the Hebrew ummōt ha-ʿōlām ("nations of the earth") and thus carries the meaning "non-Jewish," Gentile.

14. The interpretation "unscriptured," in the sense of belonging to the common, uneducated people (*laikos*), was first suggested by Abraham Geiger in *Was hat Mohammed aus den Judenthume aufgenommen?* (Bonn: F. Baaden, 1833), p. 28.

15. A reliable review is that of A. Jones, in *Arabic Literature to the End of the Umayyad Period*, pp. 235–41. John Burton, in *The Collection of the Qurʾān* (Cambridge: Cambridge University Press, 1977), argues that the text which we now have was complete in all essentials by the time of Muhammad's death. This view is not widely accepted.

16. See Jones, op. cit., pp. 236–37, for a review of the evidence.

17. A technical study, including variant readings, is Arthur Jeffery, *Materials for the History of the Text of the Qurʾan* (Leiden: E. J. Brill, 1937).

18. The story is told in *Ibn Khallikān's Biographical Dictionary*, translated by M. G. de Slane (1868), reprinted New York, 1961, Vol. 3, pp. 16–18.

19. The variant readings of the Qurʾan and related issues are surveyed in Frederick M. Denny, "Exegesis and Recitation: Their Development as Classical Forms of Qurʾānic Piety," in *Transitions and Transformations in the History of Religions: Essays in Honor of Joseph M. Kitagawa*, Frank E. Reynolds and Theodore M. Ludwig, eds. (Leiden: E. J. Brill, 1980), pp. 91–123, especially 113–16.

20. A detailed treatment of the readings, with charts showing the readers' interrelations with each other, is Labib as-Said, *The Recited Koran*, translated and adapted by Bernard Weiss, M. A. Rauf, and Morroe Berger (Princeton, N.J., The Darwin Press, 1975), especially chapters 1–4.

21. A penetrating analysis of the Qurʾan's content is Fazlur Rahman, *Major Themes of the Qurʾān* (Minneapolis and Chicago: Bibliotheca Islamica, 1980). See

also the insightful appreciations by Kenneth Gragg, *The Event of the Qur'ān: Islam in Its Scripture* (London: Allen & Unwin, 1971) and *The Mind of the Qur'an: Chapters in Reflection* (London: Allen & Unwin, 1973).

22. For a discussion of these two aspects and their mutual relationship, see Denny, "Exegesis and Recitation."

23. Of course, the Qur'an was not a book in the sense of a collected codex during the time in which it was being revealed to and appropriated by Muhammad and his Companions.

24. A rich exampling of *tafsīr* materials in translation is Helmut Gätje, *The Qur'ān and Its Exegesis: Selected Texts with Classical and Modern Muslim Interpretations*, translated by Alford T. Welch (London: Routledge & Kegan Paul, 1976). There is very little Qur'anic exegesis translated into English. One of the reasons for this is because much of it is concerned with Arabic grammar, which requires a knowledge of Arabic to understand, even in another language. But there is much in Qur'anic commentary that is translatable and there is increasing interest among scholars to make it available.

25. A good introduction to the subject is M. M. Azami, *Studies in Hadīth Methodology and Literature* (Indianapolis: American Trust Publications, 1977). A more detailed and demanding work is G. H. A. Juynboll, *Muslim Traditon: Studies in Chronology, Provenance and Authorship of Early Ḥadīth* (Cambridge: Cambridge University Press, 1983).

26. *Mishkāt al-Masābīḥ*, cited above in n. 6, provides a full range.

27. The classic Western orientalist study, which is very skeptical, is Ignaz Goldziher's book-length "On the Development of the Hadīth," in the author's *Muslim Studies*, 2 vols., a translation of *Muhammedanische Studien* (1889–90) by C. R. Barber and S. M. Stern (London: Allen & Unwin, 1967, 1971), Vol. 2, pp. 17–251.

28. Ṣaḥīḥ al-Bukhārī, 9 vols. (Cairo: Dār al-Shaʿb, n.d.), vol. 6, p. 236.

29. A. J. Wensinck, J. P. Mensing, J. B. Brugman, M. F. ʿAbd al-Bāqī et al., *Concordance et indices de la tradition musulmane*, 7 vols. (Leiden: E. J. Brill, 1933–1969). In Arabic. A useful one-volume English tool is A. J. Wensinck, *A Handbook of Early Muhammadan Tradition Alphabetically Arranged* (Leiden: E. J. Brill, 1927 and reprinted).

30. The most prestigious collections are those of the two third Islamic century contemporaries al-Bukhārī and Muslim ibn al-Ḥajjāj. Fortunately, both collections are now available in English translation, and other collections promise to appear in English over the next few years.

31. The best introduction, together with many translated examples of *ḥadīth qudsī*, is William A. Graham, *Divine Word and Prophetic Word in Early Islam* (The Hague and Paris: Mouton, 1977).

32. *Forty Hadith Qudsi*, selected and translated by Ezzeddin Ibrahim and Denys Johnson-Davies (Beirut and Damascus: Dar al-Koran al -Kareem, 1980), p. 100.

33. Ibid., p. 40.

34. As quoted in Martin Lings, *What Is Sufism?* (Berkeley and Los Angeles: University of California Press, 1975), p. 23.
35. Quoted in Graham, *Divine Word and Prophetic Word*, p. 72.
36. Many *ḥadīths* concerning the "excellent qualities" of the Qurʾan are collected in *Mishkāt*, Vol. II, pp. 446–70.

ZOROASTRIANISM:
Avestan Scripture and Rite

James W. Boyd

Different views of the meaning and role of the sacred Avesta distinguish orthodox from reform Zoroastrians today. Although the terms
"reform" and "orthodox" each encompass a wide variety of beliefs and
practices and are probably arbitrary categories when applied to any particular individual, they are useful in delineating two fundamentally different
approaches to the Avestan scriptures. Briefly stated, the reform view characteristically assumes the Avestan writings to be a holy book which is the
source of specific Zoroastrian doctrines and beliefs. The orthodox position, on contrast, does not initially think of the Avesta as a text to be read
for its doctrinal content, but rather as a transcript of the language spoken
in Zoroastrian holy rites. The implications of these two orientations are
far-reaching, affecting not only daily life and practice but also basic conceptions of the nature of religious truth.

This essay will begin with a brief description of the Avestan literature
in order to establish a proper basis for the discussion comparing reform
and orthodox views. Certain popular views of Zoroaster as the prophet
who received the Avesta also will be noted in order to help explain what
the reform movement is responding to. The orthodox position, which is to
be distinguished from both popular and reform Zoroastrian views, will
then be discussed. In explaining the orthodox position, we will be using
some interpretive categories unfamiliar to the orthodox themselves, but
which we hope will be true to the orthodox position and understandable
to both Western readers and reform Zoroastrians. A major purpose of this
interpretive discussion, beyond indicating to interested western readers
some aspects of contemporary Zoroastrian thought and practice, is to argue that the orthodox Zoroastrian view of the Avesta has something important to say both to reform Zoroastrians and to students of religion seeking
to understand the meaning of scripture in religion.

109

BACKGROUND: THE AVESTAN LITERATURE

There are three main Zoroastrian sources written in the Avestan language: the Yasna, Yashts, and Venidad.[1] The Venidad is largely concerned with various spiritual powers. The Yashts consist of twenty-four hymns to various spiritual powers. The Yasna of seventy-two chapters is often seen as the heart of the Avestan literature and contains five metrical groupings of hymns which are in an older dialect than the rest of the Avesta.[2] These hymns are called the Gathas, and are thought to have been composed by Zoroaster himself, possibly as early as 1500–1000 B.C.E. (Boyce, 1975:3ff.; 1982:1ff.) The remainder of the Avesta is called the "Younger Avesta" by Western scholars.

Scholars are not certain when the Avesta was written down, but it is generally held to be in the Sasanian period of Persian history, perhaps as late as the sixth century C.E. It is likely that Christian and Manichaean proselytizing, together with their stress on the value of the written word, led to the writing of the Avestan oral tradition. The Avesta at that time apparently consisted of twenty-one divisions (nasks) of which the extant Avesta is only a small part.[3] It contained liturgical texts and works on cosmogony, eschatology, law, medicine, astronomy, natural history, the life of Zoroaster and the history of man (Boyce, 1968:34). It is not likely that many manuscripts of the whole Avesta ever existed, and it is estimated that over the course of their long history as much as three-fourths of the entire Zoroastrian Avesta was lost.[4] In large part, it is the liturgical material that survives. Commentaries on the Avesta are written in the Middle Persian language called Pahlavi. Many of them date from the 9th century C.E.[5]

THE AVESTA AS HOLY DOCTRINE: THE REFORM VIEW

As a way of characterizing what we are calling the reform view it is useful to begin with a sketch of a few popular beliefs about Zoroaster as prophet and then note how the reformists repond to them.[6] The *Zardusht Nameh* [The Book of Zoroaster], a Persian text written in 1278 C.E., is the principal source of the popular tradition.[7] Three incidents in this biography of Zoroaster highlight his role as bringer of the Avesta as a revealed book of teachings.

The first concerns a dream Zoroaster's mother Dugdav had when she was in her sixth month of pregnancy. In the dream vicious animals attack her, tear open her womb and grab the unborn child (Zoroaster). Dugdav cries out in fear but the unborn Zoroaster speaks to her and counsels calm. Then a youth appears (possibly the heavenly twin of Zoroaster)[8] holding in one hand a luminescent branch and in the other the book of the creator. The youth throws the book at the animals, and all but three scatter. He strikes those three with the luminous branch and its fire consumes them. The youth then takes the baby Zoroaster and replaces him in the womb of his mother, calms her fear and announces that her son will be a great prophet.

The second event which highlights the theme of the holy book occurs when Zoroaster is thirty years of age. At this important time Zoroaster encounters the Divine. Led by the spiritual power, the Good Mind (*Vohuman*), Zoroaster makes a heavenly journey and arrives at the assembly of Ahura Mazda, the Lord of Wisdom, who is surrounded by the Bountiful Immortals (*Amesha Spentas*). There, among other events, Zoroaster receives the Zend Avesta (the Avesta with "interpretation"). Returning to his dwelling, Zoroaster begins to preach, but meets with little success.

In the third event Zoroaster succeeds in converting King Vishtasp, who becomes Zoroaster's royal patron. During the conversion episode Zoroaster presents the Avesta to the king and recites some of it, explaining that God has given him this book and has delegated him to bring it to all his creatures. He proclaims the Avesta to be the guide for all human action, which when followed leads to heaven. When it is not followed one is on the path to hell.

Two of the three episodes, the revelation of the Zend Avesta, and the conversion of Vishtasp, emphasize the importance of the Avesta as a holy book of teachings to be preached and followed. The reform view, while accepting the basic concept that the Avesta is the source of Zoroastrian doctrine, "demythologizes" most of the above narrative. It discounts the supernatural and mythological tone of the dream and heavenly journey stories, and claims only the historicity of the prophet Zoroaster, the Avestan hymns he composed, and the fact that he succeeded in convincing a king named Vishtasp that the Avesta should furnish the norms for one's life. The reformists argue further that only those portions of the Avestan writings which Zoroaster himself composed are authentic, namely, the Gathas. These lyrical hymns of the prophet define the essentials of the Zoroastrian faith. The remainder of the "Younger Avesta" is considered by the reformists to be doctrinally authentic only in those areas where it agrees with the Gathas.

Thus the reform view is based on the premise that Zoroastrians possess a holy written scripture, the Avesta, brought by the prophet Zoroaster. Only the oldest and most original portions of this text, however, should serve as the norm for what the tradition teaches and believes. Reformist efforts to interpret the suggestive but succinct Gathic hymns without the perspective of the whole of the extant Avesta and the Pahlavi commentaries have resulted in a variety of views. Some reformists find in the Gathas a pure, refined monotheistic faith in Ahura Mazda, the Lord of Wisdom, the sole creator of the world. The theological dualism of the later Pahlavi writings, which posits a principle of evil co-eternal with God, is considered a corruption of the true teachings of the tradition.[9] Other reformists have found the teachings of the Gathas to have close affinities with Hindu beliefs. Irach Taraporewala, for example, in his work *The Divine Songs of Zarathushtra* (1951:xi) seeks to show "how all the great ideas I had so highly admired in Sanskrit Scriptures were also discoverable in the Avesta."

Of even greater consequence for the life of the Zoroastrian community is the reformist view of ritual. Since the Gathas contain no explicit directives for ritual observance (a preoccupation of the Avestan Vendidad and the later Pahlavi writings) some reformists argue that Zoroaster must not have considered ritual an important aspect of the religion.[10] On this view, the rituals which form the basis of orthodox Zoroastrian worship should not be considered essential to the faith and are in need of radical change. For many reformists what is essential to the faith is the moral teaching of Zoroaster.[11] The Lord of Wisdom, Ahura Mazda, revealed to the prophet Zoroaster a way of life based on good thoughts, words, and deeds. Myth and ritual are to be interpreted allegorically in order to arrive at their implicit rational and ethical teachings.

For an early reformist of this century, C. M. Madan, it was the rationality of Zoroaster's Avestan teachings and not their prophetic origin that certified their authority. In most of life, he wrote, a reasoned position is better than one imposed from above by a higher authority. Zoroastrianism never claimed that the authentic Avestan scriptures were revealed. In Madan's words, " . . . there can be no room in its [Zoroastrian] propaganda for belief in a divinely inspired revelation" (cf. Hinnells, 1980:135). Madan's rationalist, liberal approach to the Avestan scriptures does not typify the reform Zoroastrian position, but it does highlight a major presupposition of the reform view, namely, that the heart of the Zoroastrian religion has to do with rational, cognitive matters. By the term "cognitive," we refer to those concepts and statements that can be said to be either true or false and which make up the content of religious belief claims. The reform view assumes a dominantly cognitive approach to their religious tradition. Rituals, which largely consist of recitations in an Avestan language not understood by laymen and priests alike, are unessential for they are noncognitive. Prayers, they claim, should be said in the vernacular (not in the dead language of Avestan, as is the orthodox custom) so that they can be understood and thus be meaningful to the worshipper (Hinnells, 1981:67).

This cognitive orientation is also the basis for reform views on two contemporary issues being debated in the Zoroastrian community: conversion and intermarriage. With regard to conversion, reformists argue that those persons not born Zoroastrian who sincerely wish to adhere to the teachings of Zoroaster and adopt the Zoroastrian moral life style, including prayerful worship in the fire temples, should be allowed to convert to Zoroastrianism. Since the religion has essentially to do with the teachings of the tradition, adherence to those teachings warrants acceptance into the community. Likewise, marriage with non-Zoroastrians, provided the faith is adhered to and taught to the children, should also be allowed, if not encouraged, to swell the dwindling numbers of the Zoroastrian community.[12]

THE AVESTA AS HOLY RITE: THE ORTHODOX POSITION
The Orthodox Response

Like the reformists, the orthodox too are members of a community that has inherited the Avestan scriptures. What they have not inherited is a certain view of the holy book which treats the Avesta as principally a doctrinal text whose purpose is to convey cognitive meanings to the reader or speaker involved. A holy book, considered as a doctrinal text, "allows entry into the world of ideas" (Wheelock:49).[13] The orthodox, in contrast, initially approach the Avesta as holy words to be uttered in a liturgical or ritual context, not principally as a text meant for reflective-critical thinking.

A different configuration of meaning results when the Avesta is understood as holy rite rather than holy doctrine. Though orthodox Zoroastrians treat the Gathas as having special significance, the whole of the Avesta is considered authentic, for it is all essential to the tradition's ancient liturgies. The validity of this assertion is tied to the orthodox claim that ritual holds a central place in Zoroastrian life and practice. The orthodox note that though one may refer to Zoroaster as a proclaimer of holy doctrines, the Gathas themselves portray him principally as a reformer of holy rituals. The Gathic terms for Zoroaster are *manthran* (one who produces sacred utterances [*manthra*]) and *zoatar* (a priest, one who conducts the rituals which actualize and preserve these inspired utterances). In other words, Zoroaster is characterized more as a priest than as a prophet. The orthodox also observe that Gathas themselves are not "works of instruction" which clearly define doctrines; they are more like liturgical utterances intended to be said aloud and proclaimed. The term "Avesta" itself probably means "authoritative utterance" (Boyce, 1979:3), suggesting that there is an approach to the scriptural language which is not initially cognitive but auditory.

The orthodox response to the popular portrayal of Zoroaster in the *Zardusht Nameh* focuses less on the need to demythologize it and more on the need to correct it.[14] As has just been noted, the ancient and therefore more authentic writings of the Zoroastrian tradition portray Zoroaster as a *manthran* and priest.[15] Orthodox scholars are aware that the model of the prophet as the bringer of the holy book appears only in this thirteenth-century Persian text and not in other Avestan and Pahlavi biographies of Zoroaster. The *Zardusht Nameh* was composed in the Islamic period when the concept of a holy book delivered by a divinely appointed prophet was highly valued (Darrow:175).

Furthermore, what needs to be noted about the history of the Avesta itself, the orthodox emphasize, is its long oral tradition and the nature of the books that now survive. The Avesta may have been preserved in oral tradition for as much as two thousand years, and though the written Avesta originally contained materials with clear cognitive import (law, medicine, etc.), the surviving remnants are largely the liturgical portions.[16] This is due not simply to historical accident (the priests knew this material most thoroughly) but underscores the primacy of those portions of the whole Avesta which were used as holy words to be uttered in the rituals. The Avestan Yasna of seventy-two chapters, for example, is and has been throughout its history principally a form of articulated speech, not a written text. This oral history and liturgical purpose of the extant Avesta support the claim, the orthodox assert, that religious meaning is not only or even primarily the property of words as conveyers of ideas. Religious meaning fundamentally resides in actions, specifically speech acts intimately related to ritual gestures. For the orthodox, ritual is the heart of the Zoroastrian tradition.

An Interpretation of the Orthodox Position

The assertion that ritual involves a mode of meaning which is distinguishable from cognitive meaning requires considerable elaboration. To sympathetically understand the orthodox claim may even require a deliberate "suspension of disbelief" on the part of many, for as the American philosopher Charles Frankel has noted about contemporary attitudes, there is "a curious unwillingness to grant value to any aspects of human life unless they can be shown to have a cognitive function" (Frankel:38).

Our initial response to the orthodox assertion that there is a mode of meaning intrinsic to ritual speech acts and gestures may be a case in point.

It should be acknowledged that any religious ritual can become inauthentic and reduced to a "repository of sanctimonious foolishness" (Frankel:182). Several dangers are inherent in the repetitive and patterned nature of ritual activity: the suppression of creative spontaneity, degeneration into empty form, and the hypnotic effect of monotonous sounds resulting in mere boredom. Any liturgy may become too stylized and static, its recitations and cryptic gestures becoming, over time, opaque to any creative meaning. This problem seems especially pressing for people who see rituals as mere vehicles for beliefs because rituals are often ineffective in clearly communicating beliefs.

From an orthodox position, however, Zoroastrian rituals are not simply prescribed gestures and utterances which accompany, augment, or even enact the tradition's belief (cf. e.g., Eliade, 1959). To so conceive of ritual is to give primary rather than secondary value to the cognitive function and involves the unwarranted assumption that ritual language functions in the same way ordinary informative language does. A close look at the use of the Avesta in Zoroastrian rituals does not support this assumption. In fact, the Avestan Yasna of seventy-two chapters, which is the basis for the most important high liturgy conducted daily in Zoroastrian fire temples, violates all kinds of rules and norms of ordinary language usage.

In ordinary language, whether written or spoken, the standard assumption is that a major use of words is to convey information. Although information is certainly contained in the Avestan Yasna, one finds a strangely fragmented "text" if it is judged on the basis of the primary function of conveying information. Conceptually, the Yasna as a whole lacks even a simple cohesiveness. There is no logical movement of ideas according to topics, and it lacks coherent argument or even a semblance of a connected story. Individual sections may meet some of these criteria, but the Avesta Yasna as such is not a tightly knit set of ideas characteristic of a prose narrative or a treatise. This suggests that we are dealing with a different style of organization and internal coherence (Wheelock:50), and that all efforts which approach the Yasna as being primarily a repository of doctrines are misdirected.

Furthermore, when a Zoroastrian priest recites the entire Yasna by memory, the general conditions of communication in ordinary language do not pertain. Normally if communication is to be successful one says only as much as is necessary. If too much is said, the listener stops paying attention. Other basic rules of good communication, such as maintaining relevance to the topic or situation at hand and being as clear as possible with regard to the information being conveyed, do not characterize the ritual language of the Yasna liturgy.

The Avestan language, even if translated in the vernacular, contains little or no new information for the Zoroastrian participant. Rather, numerous formulae based on a fixed "text" are repeated. Memorized sets of utterances, which must be said in a prescribed way and pattern, characterize the ritual. The actual uttering of the Avestan words, in fact, appears redundant, superfluous, and ineffective if judged by the norms of ordinary communication. Yet the Yasna liturgy continues to be performed daily and apparently has conveyed some form of meaning for centuries. All this suggests that there must be a different pattern of relevance, a different noetic function embodied in this ritual activity.

In rituals, the speech acts themselves (the priest articulating the Avestan Yasna) together with nonverbal systems of expression (ritual gestures, movements, specific consecrated objects in patterned arrangements) create a meaningful situation in which the speaker and sympathetic listener participate. To use Wheelocks' terms, ritual language is to be primarily understood as "situating" rather than "informing" speech (Wheelock:59ff.).[17]

An example of "situating" speech is found in drama. Many people enjoy attending such dramas as *Hamlet* that are already well known to them. They attend the play in order to fully participate in the situation the drama presents. The actors' lines, in the context of the stage set, create a situation in which both the actors and the audience participate. Each actor is not reflecting upon his or her own ideas in a spontaneous way but in voicing a prescribed "text" which, when properly uttered, effects or creates the situation intended.

An authentic religious ritual is analogous to such a dramatic performance. The priest knows the fixed "text" by heart and the intent of the voicing of the words is to create a specific situation for the participants involved. Ritual performances, like dramas, are primarily event-situations in which one can participate (Grimes:57). Ritual language, the speech articulated by the priest, is a major means of effecting the situation, an event that is newly created at each presentation. And like dramatic language, the Avesta of the Yasna only secondarily resides in a written text; it is a living, situating language only when spoken.

But what is the nature of these situating ritual events? Because the Yasna is a daily ritual we must first understand that its major significance lies not in an occasional dramatic performance but in its regularity. Rather than a momentary experiential participation in a "dramatic" event, the Yasna ritual effects a more on-going situational stance in life. The daily performance of the Yasna can influence the quality and character of a person's whole mode of life. The difficulty is that any effort to describe in cognitive terms a mode of life which claims to go beyond the merely conceptual can only be suggestive at best.

Earlier it was mentioned that rituals suffer the danger of becoming repetitive and monotonous. We have seen that the basis of this criticism rested on the assumption that the language of ritual functioned like most ordinary language does, to convey new information. From the perspective of situating speech, however, a number of positive things can occur when a person listens to or recites well-known words in a repetitive way. When that is done, our thirst for the new and the interesting is slowed; our senses are lulled. In consequence, we cease to be trapped for the time being "within the labyrinth of words and all the inherited ideas that fester there" (Barrett: 301–302). We begin to become more receptive, in a way not dominated by delineating concepts, to the situation we are in. We begin to open up, ceasing to measure and separate everything in strict definitional terms. A sense of wholeness rather than separateness can be awakened. The dramatic (not conceptual) flow of the ritual becomes creative and transformative for the participant. In Victor Turner's words, the ritual can provide "a limited area of transparency on the otherwise opaque surface of regular, uneventful social life" (Turner:93).

A musical event may furnish a proper analogy at this point. There are dimensions of experience that go beyond the cognitive in a deep musical experience. The performing musician and the sympathetic listener during a significant musical event can be transformed by a deeper sense of awareness which elevates the human spirit and is conducive to creative perspectives not easily delineated in cognitive terms. Musical sensitivity is something acquired over time through repeated exposure to fine performances. Ritual sensitivity, a receptivity at the vital depths of our being, allows for an openness to a mode of meaning not confinable to the cognitive and is acquired over time. When one participates in a ritual on a daily basis, the character and quality of one's entire life can be made more transparent to encompassing meaning. In light of this fact, issues such as conversion and intermarriage are serious concerns for the orthodox. One does not simply come to know the true center of the Zoroastrian tradition through acceptance of a belief system. Deafness to the articulate power of ritual is not easily overcome.

Ritual utterances may convey limited kinds of information, but more importantly, they *do* something. The act of ritual speech effects a situation in which sympathetic humans creatively participate. The Avestan term used most often to describe the character of Avestan ritual utterance is *spenta*, an adjective which appears to mean "possessing power" (Boyce, 1975:196). At the very least it can be agreed that Avestan speech possesses a linguistic "power" which has the potential for structuring human experience. The orthodox claim is that spoken language in an appropriate context does have a structuring force to it.

Questions remain, however. Even if one grants that rituals can structure meaningful human experience and perspectives, what is the function of the information content of the ritual language itself? In the Yasna, for example, the priest repeatedly utters the phrase *ashem vohū* ["righteousness is good"], frequently praises good thoughts, words and deeds, and professes the Zoroastrian confession of faith (the *Fravarāne*) several times, portions of which, translated, mean:

> I profess myself a Mazda-worshipper, a Zoroastrian . . . accepting the Ahuric teaching. . . . To Ahura Mazda, the good, rich in treasures, I ascribe all things good. . . . (Yasna 12.1)

These are only a few examples of the types of utterances contained in the Avestan Yasna. Some statements are expressive of attitudes, others of intentions, still others are assertive or directive. But our concern at the moment is that these sample phrases and sentences clearly have cognitive import and express basic elements of traditional Zoroastrian beliefs. Is it not likely that this information content is also essential to the Yasna ritual's efficacy?

To press the question in terms of the drama analogy, certainly it is the case that part of the appeal in attending a play which one knows well lies not only in being involved in the dramatic situation once again, but also in mentally engaging in and pondering the ideas being presented. The story of *Hamlet* has universal meaning and cogency. Do not the ideas conveyed in the Avestan recitation of the Yasna function similarly, playing a critical role in the efficacy of the ritual?

The orthodox answer is yes, of course, but not in a manner one might suppose given our automatic cognitive orientation toward language. In Avestan the ritual language itself is called *manthra* (Sanskrit *mantra*), a term meaning something like an "instrument of thought," from the base *man*, "think" (Boyce: 1957:8). As instruments of thought Avestan *manthras* clearly possess cognitive meanings which can and should be understood.

As an orthodox priest, F. M. Kotwal, states, the Avesta conveys meanings "which can be cogent to the mind and compelling to the heart" (Kotwal and Boyd, 1982:50, n. 54).

But having said this, we must also be reminded that for the orthodox the *primary* function of the language of the Yasna is situating and not informing. When the Zoroastrian priest declares *ashem vohū* ("righteousness is good"), praises good thoughts, words and deeds, and professes the Zoroastrian confession of faith, he is not simply "talking about" the ideas of righteousness and good conduct, or explaining to himself and others that he is a Zoroastrian. He is seeking to bring about the actual situation of personal and social righteousness, to take an ethical stance then and there. His assertion that he is a Zoroastrian helps him to *be* one. As we stated previously, the language does more than convey information, it is the *doing* of something. *Manthras* are active agents when invoked.[18] Invocation is essential here. For the performative power to be effective, the language must be articulated verbally. The Avestan Yasna, in so far as it remains written or unuttered, i.e., simply as a text to be read and mentally pondered, is not *manthra* (Kotwal, 1977:37). The Avestan language "possesses power" (*spenta*) and is an "instrument of thought" (*manthra*) only in the verbal act of ritual utterance by a qualified person.

Because the ideational aspect of ritual utterances is not the dominant characteristic of Avestan liturgical speech, the conceptual meanings of the words are not in the forefront of the speaker's thought. In the Yasna recitation, the priest's total concentration is on the proper voicing of the word-sounds themselves. This differs from the situating mode of dramatic language. In a drama communication follows the mode of ordinary discourse. Both the speakers and listeners are aware of the meanings of the spoken words. The participants think about what is being said in at least two different ways. Much of the time there is an immediacy of comprehension as the information-bearing words are spoken; at other times the listener steps back from the situation, and in a detached mood considers more critically the meanings conveyed.

In Avestan ritual utterance, however, neither the mode of immediate comprehension nor the reflective-critical mental stance is dominant. Rather, ritual speech involves a certain mental surrender to the speech act itself.[19] The focus of mental concentration is on the act of speaking the word-sounds as such. When this occurs, the participants are not bounded by information-bearing words. The Avestan sounds themselves become the vehicle of "meaning." Through this mode of self-surrender, conceptual distinctions which predetermine ordinary experience are transcended.

For example, distinctions between subject and object tend to disappear. Any form of critical-analytical mental detachment is abandoned in favor of a total engagement in the act of voicing the ritual language.

From an informational point of view this does not appear to be a mode of communication, for no accustomed meanings are conveyed via a sequence of logically connected ideas. Ritual language, in fact, "appears to be used in ways that violate the communication function" (Tambiah:179). This is due to the fact that in the situating power of ritual utterance, separate meanings of words are transcended or fused into a concentrated wholeness. Confining mental categories are transposed into an openness and deep receptivity to the total situation in which one is immersed. A form of knowing occurs which is not reducible to conceptual distinctions. *Manthra* has a noetic function peculiar to itself; it is *sui generis*. One might say that its chief characteristic is that of consecrating rather than communicating.

But again, this is not to dismiss ritual language as totally noncognitive, i.e., as unrelated to claims of truth or falsity. There are tests of adequacy applicable to ritual language just as there are to ordinary informative language, though in a transposed mode applicable to the unique nature of ritual meaning. For example, coherence and correspondence tests of adequacy are applicable to ritual (Jennings:118–19). With regard to coherence, one can ask, is there an inner appropriateness to all the actions and words of the ritual itself? Does the Avestan Yasna have a dramatic-liturgical internal coherence? A close study of the ritual suggests that it does.[20] In terms of the correspondence test of adequacy, ritual action can be judged valid if it corresponds to a world of significant actions. Ritual is falsified when it no longer serves as a paradigm for significant action outside the ritual context itself. A definite type of significant action characterizes the Zoroastrian Yasna liturgy. The proper performance requires a disciplined and focused personality. The priest must acquire an alert sensitivity to the sounds and actions of the immediate situation of the whole ritual content and its context. In Zoroastrian terms, he must become righteous (an *ashavan*), i.e., become rightly aligned with life; he must come to know the order and rhythm of things as they are. An authentic ritual act must be "fully-minded"; the priest must be mindful of all that transpires in that situation. The orthodox would claim this to be an essential quality for any significant action within or without a ritual context.

Thus ritual is a way of gaining knowledge; its noetic function involves a unique mode of inquiry and discovery. Through ritual, persons can not only begin to discover who they are in the world but "how it is" with the world in which they live (Jennings:113). They can come to know a sense of the order (*asha*) that surrounds them. But it is a coming to know which is acquired not by detached analysis, but by total engagement with a specific situation. Ritual engagement can teach us to see and act differently, not in the sense of acquiring new reflective information but through the very *praxis*, the actual doing or participating in the event. It is a specific kind of seeing and doing which can become a model for all important actions in one's life.[21]

One final issue needs to be mentioned regarding the validity of ritual. The issue concerns orthodox metaphysical claims about the cosmic efficacy of ritual observance. When the Zoroastrian priest seeks to produce the condition of righteousness by uttering the word-sounds *ashem vohū*, for example, the orthodox claim that there is more occurring here than a mere structuring of individual and social experience and perspective. The ritual brings about a cosmic ordering (*asha*) as well, in which spiritual powers bring increase and bounty (*spenta*) to the whole of creation. This is a wide-ranging metaphysical claim. Is it a valid one?

In terms of the topics discussed in this essay, no position has been taken in response to this question. Before one denies or assents to this type of metaphysical claim, it is important to underline the basic distinction between the "situating" efficacy of ritual language and any claim of cosmic efficacy (cf. also Wheelock:61). In the preceding discussion we have attempted to suggest the plausibility of the claim for linguistic efficacy. We have noted that unlike the reform view which treats the Avesta as a holy text allowing entry into the world of ideas, the orthodox understand themselves as a community which possesses a holy, spoken, ritual tradition, the presentation of which has situating power. That cosmic righteousness (*asha*) is established through the performance of the Yasna is yet another claim. Indeed, it is clearly an interpretive claim with far-reaching conceptual implications. The validity of such a cognitive claim about the power of ritual language must be argued in the arena of rational discourse. Such a claim will be subject to much debate, with positions taken depending largely on prior commitments to certain metaphysical and linguistic views.

Most reform denials of orthodox metaphysical claims appear to be due to a kind of positivistic outlook which denies the name "reality" to anything but the empirical and the tangible, together with the prevalent assumption that all language follows the rules of ordinary information discourse. Most reformists have not taken seriously the orthodox claim of the power of situating speech, *spenta manthra*, because they have confused the orthodox ontological claims (which they reject) with the rituals' linguistic, situating claim (of which they are largely unaware).

Similarly, the orthodox have failed to make basic distinctions regarding their own view of the holy Avesta. One early orthodox spokesman, R. E.

Sanjana, attempted to argue in 1924 the orthodox position but did so by unknowingly assuming reformist premises. He claimed that Zoroaster was free from all sin and error and received perfect, single-minded inspiration (Sanjana:85). He therefore pronounced the Avesta more authoritative than either the Bible or the Qur'an (Sanjana:131ff.). Sanjana's attempted defense of the authenticity of the whole of the Avesta (not just the Gathas) was meant to establish the doctrinal unity of the Avesta. His underlying assumption was that the real coherence of the Avesta lay primarily in conceptual and doctrinal matters and not with liturgical, situating events. Sanjana's defense misrepresents and is inadequate to the real center of orthodox concerns, namely the preservation of transforming Avestan ritual which seeks to reach beyond the limits of doctrinal thought to larger more expansive meanings.

Perhaps by clearly distinguishing between two views of the Avesta, one "situating" and the other "informing," and by noting that the ritual's situating power can be distinguished from ontological interpretations of that power, a basis can be established whereby reform and orthodox Zoroastrians can begin to engage in creative discussion with each other. These two views of the Avesta are not necessarily incompatible. On the contrary, when the integrity of each position is properly understood and respected, the possibility that each will enhance the other is truly promising.

ACKNOWLEDGMENT

I wish to thank my colleagues at Colorado State University, Professor William Darrow of Williams College, and Dr. Firoze M. Kotwal, Dastur of the Wadia Atash Bahram in Bombay, India, for their helpful comments on this essay.

NOTES

1. There is also a group of minor texts named the *Khorda Avesta* (Small Avesta) assembled for ritual purposes. Middle Persian translations survive of the Gathas (see below), Yasna, a few Yashts, the Vendidad and the Nirangistan, a priestly text devoted to ritual regulations.
2. Martin Haug, a famous nineteenth-century German philologist, made the discovery that the Gathas were linguistically older than the rest of the Avesta.
3. Of the complete Avesta (as it existed in the nineteenth century), only one *nask* has been preserved in its entirety—the Vendidad [*Vidēvdād*]. The remainder of the extant Avesta is made up of fragments from other books assembled for liturgical purposes.
4. This circumstance was due to many factors, two of which are the long depen-

dence on oral tradition resulting in the possession of few written copies and a history of invasions and the literary changes they brought about, beginning with Alexander, followed by the Arabs, and finally the annihilation wrought by the Turkish Mongol invasions. See Boyce, 1979.

5. For a survey of Pahlavi literature, see Boyce, 1968, 31–66. For a survey of the history of Iranian studies dealing with Avestan and Pahlavi works, see Dresden, 1968, 168–90.

6. The reform view of the Avesta can more accurately be characterized in two stages: earlier nineteenth century and contemporary. The earlier reformists for the most part emphasized the role of Zoroaster as a prophet who received the holy doctrine. The contemporary reformists are more directly influenced by Western scholarly views of the Avesta and stress the central importance of the Avestan Gathas as the sole source of Zoroastrian belief and practice. For our purposes, however, it will be enough to treat these as two aspects of the "reform view."

7. The *Zardusht Nameh* was composed in verse by Zardusht Bahram Pazdu. For the most part it is a paraphrase of Book 7 of the *Dēnkard* ["Acts of the Religion"], an encyclopedic work on Zoroastrianism compiled in the ninth and tenth centuries C.E. The Persian paraphrase was translated into old Gujarati (*Prākrit*) verse by Mobed Rustam Peshotan Jamjiar, a poet-priest of Surat, India, in the seventeenth century C.E. An English translation appears in Wilson (1843:477–522).

8. For a thorough discussion of the Zoroaster legend, see William R. Darrow's unpublished doctoral dissertation, "The Zoroaster Legend: Its Historical and Religious Significance," Harvard University, April, 1981.

9. Many "orthodox" Zoroastrians also find some aversion to the theological dualism of the Pahlavi writings, but on theological grounds rather than on the basis of the writings being later and inauthentic. See, e.g., Kotwal and Boyd, 1982: chapters 1, 21.

10. Martin Haug's influence on reformist views is direct, in this instance. Gathic silence about rituals and the divine beings associated with them meant, for Haug, that Zoroaster "neither believed in them, nor thought them to be an essential part of religion." See Haug, 259–60.

11. J. J. Modi (1962), e.g., sees the Zoroastrian religion as almost exclusively a matter of ethics, i.e., Good Thoughts, Words and Deeds. See also Hinnells, 1980: 138.

12. See, e.g., the article "US Jews Open Their Arms to Converts," reported in the Zoroastrian magazine *Parsiana*, vol. 4, no. 6 (December, 1981), p. 7.

13. Much of the following discussion is deeply indebted to the recent articles by Wade T. Wheelock (1982), Theodore Jennings (1982) and the book by Ronald L. Grimes (1982).

14. That a literalistic approach to the Avesta and other writings of the tradition is not an essential aspect of "orthodox" thought is evident in Dastur F. M. Kotwal's remarks (1982: ch. 2).

15. For a discussion of the various texts considered authentic by an orthodox Zoroastrian priest, see Kotwal's commentary and Appendix I in the same work (1982).

16. It could be objected that of the three major parts of the Avesta, the Vendidad is not usefully characterized as liturgical. The orthodox response, not totally satisfactory to some, is that the Vendidad is a high liturgical service which starts at midnight and lasts about seven hours.

17. Avestan ritual language is our main concern; the meaning of ritual gesture is a separate topic.

18. A characteristic epithet for the spiritual being Srōsh (Sraosha), Ahura Mazda's vice regent on earth, is tanu manthro, "having manthra for body." This concept of manthra as an active personal agent is very similar to the notion of "prayer as person" discussed by Sam Gill in his article on Navajo Prayer Acts (Gill, 1977).

19. Perhaps the phrase "mental surrender" is overstating the matter. As Professor William Darrow has helpfully pointed out to me, it could be argued that an important aspect of the priest's attitude toward ritual language is the conviction that manthra has a metaphysical status, i.e., is part of the structure of creation itself. Thus what appears to be a surrendering of mental concerns is in fact based on a preliminary metaphysical concept. This raises the whole issue of the role of prior cognitive commitments in the efficacy of ritual. For our immediate purposes, however, it seems appropriate to say that any reflective-critical mental stance is not the dominant mode of experience in authentic Avestan ritual utterance.

20. Several essays exist which summarize the basic format of the Yasna ritual, e.g., Haug: 403–7. A more thorough description and interpretation of the details of the Yasna ritual is now in progress, a collaborative effort between Dastur Firoze M. Kotwal and myself.

21. Jennings (117) states that ritual action does not primarily teach us to see differently but to act differently—ritual provides us a pattern of doing rather than a point of view. In the sense that ritual does not primarily teach us new reflective information, we would agree—we do not see differently because we have acquired new information. But ritual does alter our seeing in the sense of changing our orientation toward on-going situations. In that respect ritual does teach us to "see" and act differently.

WORKS CONSULTED

Austin, John, 1962. *How to Do Things with Words.* Ed. J. Rumson. New York: Oxford University Press.

Barrett, William, 1979. *The Illusion of Technique.* Garden City, N.Y.: Anchor Press.

Boyce, Mary, 1968. "Middle Persian Literature." *Iranistik: Literatur.* Leiden/Köln: E. J. Brill, 31–66.

———, 1970. "Zoroaster the priest," *Bulletin of the School of Oriental and African Studies.* XXXIII/1, xx, 22–38.

————, 1975, 1982. *A History of Zoroastrianism.* Vols. I & II. Leiden/Köln: E. J. Brill.

————, 1979. *Zoroastrians: Their Religious Beliefs and Practices.* London: Routledge and Kegan Paul.

Darrow, W. R., 1981. "The Zoroaster Legend: Its Historical and Religious Significance," unpublished Ph.D. dissertation, Harvard University, April, 1981.

Dresden, M. J., 1968. "Survey of the History of Iranian Studies." *Iranistik: Literatur.* Leiden/Köln: E. J. Brill, 168–90.

Eliade, M., 1959. *Cosmos and History.* Trans. W. Trask. New York: Harper Torchbooks.

Frankel, Charles, 1951. *The Love of Anxiety.* New York: Harper and Row.

Gill, Sam D., 1977. "Prayer as Person: The Performative Force in Navajo Prayer Acts." *History of Religions.* 17/2, 143–57.

Grimes, Ronald L., 1982. *Beginnings in Ritual Studies.* Washington, D.C.: University Press of America.

Haug, M., 1878. *Essays on the Sacred Language, Writings and Religion of the Parsis,* 2nd ed., Boston: Houghton, Osgood & Co.

Hinnells, John R., 1980. "The Parsis: a bibliographical survey (1)," *Journal of Mithraic Studies.* III:1/2, 100–149.

————, 1981. *Zoroastrianism and the Parsis.* London: Ward Lock Educational.

Jennings, Theodore W., 1982. "On Ritual Knowledge." *The Journal of Religion.* 62/2, 111–27.

Kotwal, F. M. and Boyd, J. W., 1977. "The Zoroastrian paragṇā ritual," *Journal of Mithraic Studies.* 2/1, 18–52.

————, 1982. *A Guide to the Zoroastrian Religion: A Nineteenth Century Catechism with Modern Commentary.* Chico: Scholars Press (in press).

Masani, Rustom P., 1962. *Zoroastrianism: The Religion of the Good Life.* New York: Collier Books.

Modi, J. J., 1937. *The Religious Ceremonies and Customs of the Parsees.* 2nd ed., Bombay.

————, 1962. *A Catechism of the Zoroastrian Religion.* Bombay.

Sanjana, R. E., 1924. *The Parsi Book of Books: The Zend Avesta.* Bombay.

Stahl, Fritz, 1979. "The Meaninglessness of Ritual." *Numen* XXVI, Facs. 1, 2–22.

Tambiah, Stanley, 1968. "The Magical Power of Words." *Man* n.s. 3/2:175–208.

Taraporewala, I. J. S., 1951. *The Divine Songs of Zarathushtra.* Bombay.

Turner, Victor, 1957. *Schism and Continuity in an African Society: A Study of Ndembu Village Life.* Manchester: Manchester University.

Wheelock, Wade T., 1982. "The Problem of Ritual Language: From Information to Situation." *Journal of the American Academy of Religion.* L:1, 49–71.

Whitehurst, James Emerson, 1969. "The Zoroastrian Response to Westernization: A Case Study of the Parsis of Bombay." *Journal of the American Academy of Religion.* XXXVII/3:224–36.

Wilson, J., 1843. *The Parsi Religion.* Bombay: American Mission Press.

𑀑 HINDUISM:
Veda and Sacred Texts

Robert C. Lester

In 1981, a large part of South India experienced severe drought. While several government agencies worked, sinking deep wells and transporting water from outside the area, learned scholars and priests publicly offered prayers for rain. The scholars and priests chanted verses, in Sanskrit, from a 3,500-year-old revelation called *Veda*.

Addressing the 13th All India Vedic Convention that same year, the governor of the state of Tamilnadu remarked that, "The Vedas contain what we need in this life and what we aspire for beyond this life. It is gratifying that attempts are being made to discover the scientific basis of the Vedic traditions and the truths enshrined therein and reinterpret them to the modern world."[1] The governor urged that public education in India should follow the example of personal, one-to-one impartation of knowledge set by those who have transmitted Veda.

Veda, "knowledge," "that which is known, in truth," is the revelation which inspires the diverse belief systems and lifestyles that constitute Hinduism. Hinduism holds much in common with other religions having their roots in India: Buddhism, Jainism and Sikhism; its distinguishing mark is reverence for Veda. Self-styled,[2] the Hindu calls himself a *Vaidika*, "one who adheres to Veda" or a *Sanatani*, "one who believes in the eternal" as revealed by Veda.

ORAL TRANSMISSION

Veda consists of prayers, interpretations of their meaning, and instructions for their ritual use. It was first received by ancient sages (*rishi*, "seer", "knower") who "saw" or inwardly heard it in a state of heated receptivity, intense concentration fostered by rigorous discipline (*tapas*), of mind and

126

body. ". . . a rishi is so called as he has obtained a vision of truth (*rsir-darsanat*); the fountain of self-existent knowledge flowed towards them when they were engaged in *tapas*."³ The rishis resonated with root-vibrations; the fundamental sounds of life welled-up within them and burst forth in powerful speech, speech offered to the gods through fire-rituals (*yajna*, lit. "sacrifice").

> O Lord of Holy Word! That was the first beginning of the Word when the Seers fell to naming each object. That which was best and purest, deeply hidden within their hearts, they revealed by the power of their love.
>
> They (friends) followed by sacrifice the path of the Word and found her (the Word) entered in among the Seers. They (the Seers) led her forth and distributed her among many. In unison the seven Singers chant her.
>
> Yet certain ones, though seeing, may not see her, and other ones, though hearing, may not hear her. But to some the Word reveals herself quite freely, like fair-robed bride surrendering to her husband.⁴

With meticulous care, the rishis passed on what they saw/heard to their disciples, by word of mouth. The disciples, in turn, passed it on, orally, to their disciples. Those who chanted prayers for rain in 1981 drew these prayers from memory, having received them orally from a teacher who himself had mastered Veda by hearing it from his teacher; and so on, in an unbroken line back to the second millenium B.C.E. Hinduism is unique among the world's great religions, being founded on a revelation which is *orally* transmitted. Veda is truth and power only when spoken; it is not scripture; it is *Sruti*, "that which is heard"; *heard* by the rishis and *heard* by those to whom the rishis articulated it, passed down from master to disciple, generation to generation, for more than 3,500 years. This is the more amazing when we see that in written form it would constitute several large volumes and that it is transmitted precisely as it was first heard, with care for intonation and rhythm as well as syllable and word.

THE ETERNAL WORD

Every morning, just at dawn, the devout high caste Hindu, having prepared himself by bathing the body and purifying and concentrating the mind, recites a prayer (*mantra*), beckoning and saluting the rising sun, the stimulator of life, the illuminator of mind, the brilliant symbol of the Supreme Reality, Brahman:

> OM. Bhuh, Bhuvah, Svah.
> tat savitur varenyam,

bhargo devasya dhimahi,
dhiyo yo nah pracodayat.[5]

OM. Earth, Atmosphere, Sky.
We meditate upon the glorious splendor
     of the vivifier divine.
May he himself illumine our minds.

The portion of the mantra beginning, "We meditate" is called the *Gayatri*, "The Protector of the Singer," or the *Savitri*, "The Stimulator"; it is the supreme prayer:

> Verily, the Gayatri is everything here that has come to be, whatsoever there is here. Verily, the Gayatri is speech. Verily, speech both sings of (*gayati*) and protects (*trayate*) everything here that has come to be.[6]

Recited morning and evening, at twilight, the junctures (*samdhya*) of night and day, it dispels the darkness, destroys the effects of bad deeds[7] and harmonizes body, mind and spirit with the physical worlds and the primal, universal forces. The Gayatri is the touchstone of Veda, ". . . the boon-giving mother of Veda,"[8] the first words of Veda transmitted by the teacher who initiates a young man into study of Veda. Together with "OM" and the utterances (*vyahriti*) identifying the three realms—earth, atmosphere and sky—it is the concentrated essence of Veda, the gateway to the Supreme:

> The Lord of Creatures milked out (as it were) from the three Vedas the sounds A, U, and M,[9] and Bhuh (earth), Bhuvah (atmosphere), Svah (sky). Moreover from the three Vedas . . . (He) milked out that Rig (Rigveda)-verse, sacred to Savitri, which begins with the word *tad*,[10] one foot from each.

> Know that the three imperishable great utterances, preceded by the syllable OM, and (followed) by the three-footed Savitri are the portal of the Veda and the gate leading (to union with) Brahman.[11]

A mantra (lit. "thought-instrument") is an extraordinary prayer, ". . . words arising from the depths,"[12] the breath of the Supreme,[13] words which are the sound-essences of that which they name, words which embody essential reality in human speech. The sound is more important than the meaning of the words; it harmonizes the speaker with basal, universal forces, evokes and draws on the life-force of that which is named. Mantra sounds energize, integrate and protect the speaker. The power of mantra depends upon its being received orally, in private, from a master, who, like the rishis, resonates with the Supreme (*Brahman*).

OM is the imperishable syllable,[14] *The Sound* (*pranava*), the primordial Word, all reality concentrated in the simplicity of one syllable:

The Brahman created Brahma, the creator seated on the lotus; having been created, Brahma began to think, "By which single syllable may I be able to enjoy all the desires, all the worlds, all the gods, all the Vedas, all the sacrifices, all the sounds, all the rewards, all the beings, stationary and moving." He practiced self-control (*tapas*) and saw OM, . . . the all-pervading, omnipresent, the eternally potent Brahman, . . . [15]

OM—This syllable is this whole world. The past, the present, the future—everything is just the syllable OM. And whatever else that transcends threefold time—that too, is just the syllable OM. For truly, everything here is Brahman.[16]

This syllable, indeed, is imperishable Brahman; this syllable, indeed, is the end supreme. The one who knows this selfsame syllable will surely obtain whatever he desires.[17]

OM is Brahman, the one, single essence which "bursts forth"[18] manifesting and pervading all beings and things; it is Brahman manifest; it reveals Brahman, unmanifest, the supreme silence:

There are verily two Brahmans to be meditated upon, sound and non-sound; by sound alone is the non-sound revealed.[19]

OM is the supremely integrating sound, the sound-essence of reality, the bow by which the self (*atman*) is shot to the target, Brahman.[20]

The sounds, "*bhuh*" (earth), "*bhuvah*" (atmosphere), "*svah*" (sky) are the world-creating utterances, the sound-essences of the three realms. Uttered, they are the head, navel and feet of the Lord of creation, the eye of whom is the sun:

From his navel issued the Air;
from his head unfurled the Sky,
the Earth from his feet, from his ear
    the four directions.
Thus have the worlds been organized.[21]

Now (in the beginning) this (world) was, verily, unuttered (*a-vyahrtam*). When he, the Real, the Lord of Creation, performed austerity, he uttered *bhuh, bhuvah, svah*; this, indeed, is the Lord of Creation's coarse form . . . Therefore one should reverence earth, atmosphere and sky; for thereby the Lord of Creation, the soul of all, the eye of all, becomes reverenced . . . [22]

MANTRA AND RITUAL

The power of Veda is actualized in ritual performance, the performance of fire-rituals (*yajna*, lit. "sacrifice"). Veda is received and transmitted in four lines: Rig Veda, Sama Veda, Yajur Veda and Atharva Veda, in accordance with priestly function in the rituals. Each line consists of two layers: a basic Collection (*samhita*) of mantras and one or more, interpretive visions or hearings called *Brahmanas*. The mantras of the Rig Veda are verses (*rc*[23]) to be recited by the *hotṛ* ("invoker") priest. These verses, numbering 10,850, gathered in 1,028 poems, address the fire (*Agni*), personified, and through the fire others of the gods and goddesses (powers) whose activities are deemed appropriate to the occasion. Thus, Rig Veda 1.1:

> I magnify Agni, the priest, the divine ministrant of the sacrifice, the Hotri priest, the greatest bestower of treasures. Agni, worthy to be magnified by the ancient sages and by the present ones—may he conduct the gods hither. May one obtain through Agni wealth and welfare day by day, which may bring glory and high bliss of valiant offspring. Agni, whatever sacrifice and worship thou encompassest on every side, that indeed goes to the gods.
>
> Thee, O Agni, we approach day by day, O (god) who shinest in the darkness; with our prayer, bringing adoration to thee—
>
> Thus, O Agni, be easy of access to us, as a father is to his son. Stay with us for our happiness.[24]

The power of the Hotṛ's recitation depends not only upon time and place, and syllable and word order, but meticulous care as to intonation and rhythm. A syllable may have raised, low or mixed accent, significantly determining the meaning of a word or phrase. Bráhman signifies the prayer (and, the Supreme Reality) while brahmán, the pray-er, the priest.[25]

The Sama Veda (1,875 mantras) and Yajur Veda (1,975 mantras) are based upon Rig Veda:

> One man with utmost care creates the verses; another sings a song in chanted meters. A third, the Brahman, tells forth the wisdom of being, while yet a fourth prescribes the rules of sacrifice.[26]

The mantras of the Sama ("music") Veda, most of which are identical to ones found in Rig Veda, are to be sung by the *Udgatṛ* ("singer") priest. While the Hotṛ recites and the Udgatṛ sings, the *Adhvaryu* ("sacrificer") priest performs the manual acts of the ritual, sounding the sacrificial formulae (*yajus*) which include Rig Vedic mantras and make up the mantra-collection of the Yajur Veda.

> I will think only sweet things; I will produce only sweet things; I will bear only sweet things; I will speak only sweet things; May I utter forth words sweet to the gods and words which men love to hear; may the gods therefore

protect me so that I may embellish (the occasions with the beauty of my speech), and may our forebears also applaud me (for my speech).[27]

The mantras of the fire-priest (*atharvan*)—spells, charms and incantations to promote general well-being, avert calamities and expiate wrongdoings—were originally part of ancient popular lore. They are recited by the Brahman priest, the supervisor or overseer of the ritual, in order to "cover" and "check" errors or lapses in the performance.

Peaceful be earth, peaceful ether, peaceful heaven, peaceful waters, peaceful herbs, peaceful trees; may All-gods bring me peace; may there be peace through these invocations of peace; with these invocations of peace which appease everything, I render peaceful whatever here is terrible, whatever here is cruel, whatever here is sinful; let it become auspicious; let everything be weal to us.[28]

THE BRAHMANAS

The *Brahmanas*, "that which pertains to the brahmán (the priest)" or "that which pertains to Bráhman (the Word, the Supreme)," the second layer of each of the four Vedas, consist of injunctions and instructions on the manner of performing the rituals, together with explanations of their meaning. They are lengthy, complex and highly technical, detailing the measurements of the sacrificial ground, the construction of fire-altars, the vessels of offering, the substances to be offered, the mantras to be employed.

The Brahmanas speak of the Vedic mantras as the breath of the Supreme:

It is—as, from a fire laid with damp fuel, clouds of smoke separately issue forth, so, lo, verily, from this great Being has been breathed forth that which is Rig Veda, Yajur Veda, Sama Veda, Hymns of the Atharavans . . .[29]

the offspring of imperishable Speech:

Speech, the imperishable, is the first-form of Truth, mother of the Vedas, the hub of immortality; may She, in happiness, come to us, in the sacrifice; our protecting Goddess, may She be easy of invocation for us.[30]

the purifying, immortal fruit, given through the rishis:

May the mantras which are purifying and which lead one to well-being . . . may the essence that the Seers (rishis) had stored accrue to us; may that immortal fruit deposited with the custodians of the Veda be secured for us . . . the divine mantras that the gods have gathered for us . . .[31]

The rishis are the "life-breaths",[32] "the first-born Brahman",[33] they who spin out the thread of the sacrifice.[34] The Brahmanas praise the power of the Gayatri and address the Supreme Lord as manifest in the sun, "the three Vedas blazing":

> That Supreme Lord is (the Sun), this disc that burns; those Rik hymns are there in it, the disc is fashioned by the Riks; . . . the light that shines therein, that is the Samans, . . . the Being in that disc and light,—He is the Yajus; . . . This is verily the three Vedas blazing, this the golden Being who is within the Sun . . . He is Brahman, the waters, the fire within the waters, the essence, the Immortal Brahman, the three worlds, the syllable OM.[35]

By means of Veda, the Lord of Beings, the Brahman in personal form, brought forth the three layered world and human speech:

> The Lord of Beings verily controlled this universe by means of the threefold Veda . . . He considered . . . let me take the sap (*rasa*) of the threefold Veda. Saying 'bhuh,' he took the sap of the Rigveda. That became this earth. The sap of it which streamed forth became fire (agni), the sap of the sap. Saying 'bhuvah,' he took the sap of the Yajurveda. That became this atmosphere. The sap of it which streamed forth became wind (vayu), the sap of the sap. Saying 'svah,' he took the sap of the Samaveda. That became yonder sky. The sap of it which streamed forth became the sun, the sap of the sap. Now of one syllable he was not able to take the sap: of OM, just of that. That became this speech . . .[36]

The Brahmanas interpret sacrifice on two different levels: objective and subjective. The former is concerned with sacrifice as outward ritual act (*adhi-yajna*) and the latter presents sacrifice as a meditation on the inner self (*adhi-atman*). The *Satapatha Brahmana* of the Yajur veda defines the five great sacrifices to be performed daily:

> Five in number are the Great Sacrifices; they are the great continuous sacrifices; the propitiation of all things created, of human beings, of the fathers, of the gods, and of the sacred lore. One should make daily offerings to all creatures; thereby one achieves the propitiation of all creatures, every day one should offer gifts, even if it be only with a cup of water; thus one achieves the propitiation of human beings; every day one should, even if it be only with a cup of water, make offerings to the fathers; thus one achieves the propitiation of the fathers; every day one should make offerings to the gods, even if it be only with sacred twigs (in fire); thus one achieves propitiation of the gods. Then the propitiation of sacred lore; learning one's own Veda is that propitiation; speech, mind, and intellect are the various utensils of this sacrifice; Truth is the final purificatory ceremony; heaven is the end; he who

understands this and every day does his sacred duty, gains three times the world that is gained by one who fills the whole world with wealth and gifts it away . . .[37]

The last of the five, learning one's Veda, is the key to the other four as they depend upon the recitation of Vedic word.

The subjective interpretation presents sacrifice as a meditation on the inner self (*adhi-atman*). This interpretation is offered particularly in the sections of the Brahmanas called *Aranyaka* ("forest-related") and *Upanishad* ("secret instruction"):

> That which for the ancients was a building up (of sacrificial fires) was, verily, a sacrifice to *Brahma*. Therefore with the building of these sacrificial fires the sacrificer should meditate upon the *ātman*. So, verily, indeed, does the sacrifice become really complete and indeficient. (1.1)[38]

"Verily, a person is a sacrifice."[39] The eye is the sun, the mind is the moon, the breath, the wind, speech, the fire.[40] These two levels of interpretation are the inspiration for two distinct traditions of Vedic exegesis which will be discussed below.

EARLY COMMENTARY: THE VEDANGA

Early transmitters of Veda recorded the names of the sages who first heard the Word, but nothing of their time, place or personal characteristics. Hindu classical literature and the great majority of present-day Hindus simply affirm that the eternal Veda, fourfold, mantras and brahmanas, was heard shortly after creation—at the beginning of the present cycle of time the rishis recaptured knowledge that was lost (to man) in the great dissolution ending the previous cycle. Historical-critical scholarship argues that Veda developed over a period of from 1,300 to 1,500 years, the earliest portions, Rig Veda mantras, being composed *c.* 1800 B.C.E. and the latest portions of the brahmanas *c.* 300–500 B.C.E. Veda itself gives surface evidence of a layered development in the fact that the Brahmanas do not present themselves as Veda and some portions of the brahmanas refer to Veda as only three-fold (Rk, Saman, Yajus).

Veda inspires an extensive literature, beginning *c.* 700 B.C.E. Out of concern to preserve the purity and intelligibility of the revealed Word, masters of Veda set forth works on etymology, grammar, phonetics, meter, astronomy/astrology, and ritual performance. These come to be known, collectively, as the *Vedanga* ("Veda-branches"). Yaska's *Nirukta* ("Etymology"), c. 600 B.C.E., for example, is a commentary on the meanings of 1,709 Vedic words. "Without this, there can be no understanding of the mantras."[41] Yaska sifts and collates existing word-lists:

> Former rishis had direct intuitive insight into dharma ("law"), and brahman made itself manifest to them. They handed down by oral instruction (upadesa) the hymns to later generations who were destitute of direct intuitive insight. The later generations, declining in powers of upadesa, compiled this work (the existing word-lists) in order to comprehend the meaning.[42]

The Vedanga writings set apart Sanskrit as the language of revelation, "the breath of the Supreme." Panini's Astadhyayi ("Eight Chapters") c. 500 B.C.E. is a definitive grammar of the Sanskrit language.[43] It is as a consequence of Panini's work that the language becomes distinguished as sam-skrita, "refined," "perfectly structured," in contrast to popular dialects (prakrita, "unrefined"). After Panini, Sanskrit becomes the preserve of an elite—the priesthood and officials of the court. Panini's commentators refer to him as "a perfected one" (siddham), divinely inspired. Hsüan Tsang (602–664 C.E.), a Chinese scholar and traveler in India, records that he visited the birthplace of Panini, there found a statue of the sage and was told the story of how the Supreme Being himself, having first arranged the letters of the alphabet, assisted Panini in his work.[44]

The Vedangas on phonetics and meter are intended to insure the precise articulation of Veda; those on astronomy/astrology, the proper time for ritual performance. The Manu Smriti ("Traditions according to Manu") c. 200 B.C.E., one of the numerous Vedangas on ritual performance collectively known as the Kalpa Sutras,[45] sets forth Vedic truth as dharma ("law", "that which is established"). Manu defines the duties and privileges of the various classes of men according to their level of birth (varna) and their stage of life (ashrama). Beginning with creation, he records how the self-existent Lord, Himself created the classes of gods and men by the words of Veda and assigned to each his role ". . . for the sake of the prosperity of the worlds."[46] He defines the sacraments, the special responsibilities of priests and kings, the duties of women, and civil and criminal law, together with the types of punishment.

Manu distinguishes Veda as sruti, "that which is heard," the unauthored revelation, from smriti, "that which is remembered," that which is called to mind and authored by those who have heard Veda and have reflected deeply upon it.

> By Sruti is meant Veda, and by Smriti, the institutes of sacred law (dharma); those two must not be called into question in any matter, since from those two the dharma shines forth.

Whatever law has been ordained for any person by Manu, that has been fully declared in Veda: for that sage was omniscient.

Veda is the eternal eye of the manes, gods, and men; the Veda-ordinance is both beyond the sphere of human power and beyond the sphere of human comprehension; that is a certain fact.

All those smriti and all those despicable systems of philosophy, which are not based on Veda, produce no reward after death; for they are declared to be founded on darkness.

All those (doctrines) differing from Veda, which spring up and perish, are worthless and false, because they are of modern date.[47]

Manu restricts the knowledge and use of Veda to the higher classes of men.[48] According to Veda[49] the society which adheres to dharma is divided fourfold: the priests (brahman) are the head of the social body, the warriors (kshatriya), the chest and arms; businessmen and farmers (vaishya), the abdomen and thighs, and laborers (sudra), the feet. It is the dharma of male members of the first three classes to learn, study, and recite Veda. Each by family tradition, belongs to a particular Veda. Vaishyas and Kshatriyas are permitted use of Veda only in their private, familial rites; Brahmans only are permitted to teach Veda and perform rituals for others. Women (even the high born) and sudras are excluded from study of Veda;[50] the latter, also from participation in Vedic rites.

Of created beings the most excellent are said to be those which are animated; of the animated, those which subsist by intelligence; of the intelligent, mankind; and of men, the Brahmans.

The very birth of a Brahman is an eternal incarnation of the dharma; for he is born to fulfill the dharma, and becomes one with Brahman (the Supreme Reality).[51]

Brahmans, Kshatriyas, and Vaishyas are initiated into Veda through the rite of upanayana ("approaching a teacher") and are thereafter considered to be "twice-born" (dvija)—born once physically, born again, spiritually, through initiation into Veda. Ideally, this initiation should occur between the ages of eight and twelve years. The first mantra spoken to the boy by his teacher is the Gayatri, "the mother of Veda." Thereafter, the boy should take up residence with the teacher and learn by heart, from hearing, the whole of the Veda belonging to his family line.[52] In addition, he should learn the Vedangas appropriate to his Veda, and, of course, the rituals through which Veda is actualized. Rote learning of Veda is only the foundation of the student's final goal—the practice of dharma in everyday life:

Even forgetful students of Veda are more distinguished than the ignorant, those who remember them surpass the forgetful students, those who possess a knowledge of the meaning are more distinguished than those who only re-member the words; men who follow the teaching surpass those who merely know the meaning.[53]

Yaska remarks that one who simply memorizes Veda without knowing its meaning suffers a curse.[54]

The Vedangas strongly condemn those who write down Veda or who study Veda from a written text.[55] They also condemn the Brahman who teaches Veda to those who are not qualified or who are unprepared; those who acquire Veda apart from ritually approaching a teacher are condemned to hell:

Even in times of dire distress a teacher of Veda should rather die with his knowledge than sow it in barren soil.

Sacred Learning approached a Brahman and said to him: "I am thy treasure, preserve me, deliver me not to a scorner; so (preserved) I shall become su-premely strong. But deliver me, as to the keeper of thy treasure, to a Brahman whom thou shalt know to be pure, of subdued senses, chaste and attentive."

He who acquires without permission the Veda from one who recites it, in-curs the guilt of stealing Veda, and shall sink into hell.[56]

The Vedanga texts come to be viewed as the first layer of Smriti, "the institutes of dharma." Smriti also includes an epic literature and numer-ous collections of "ancient lore" (purana), the epics dating contemporary to the Vedanga and the Puranas c. 400–900 C.E. We shall speak of these below.

VEDIC EXEGESIS: DARSANA

Vedanga begins an exegesis of Veda which is brought to fruition sys-tematically by two schools of thought (darsana, "viewpoint") or traditions of teachers (sampradaya), known as the Karma-mimamsa and the Ve-danta. The Karma-mimamsa ("Investigation of Ritual Action") tradition follows the Brahmanas' objective interpretation of sacrifice and exegetes Veda as essentially injunction to ritual action. The Vedanta ("end of Veda," i.e., giving precedence to the Upanishads, the last portion of the Brah-manas)[57] follows the Brahmanas' subjective interpretation and exegetes Veda as essentially knowledge of Brahman/atman. The foundational texts of the two schools, Jaimini's Mimamsa Sutra and Badarayana's Brahma Sutra, (both c. 400 C.E.) are in conflict at several points, but their com-mentators reconcile the views, portraying them as essentially complementary. According to the commentators, the *Karma-mimamsa* is the "former" or "prior" investigation (*purva-mimamsa*)—inquiry into ritual action (*karma*); the Vedanta is the "latter" or "after" investigation (*uttara-mimamsa*)—inquiry into knowledge (*jnana*). Together, these *sampradayas* set forth the classical view of the authority of Veda.

Medieval Hinduism recognizes six schools of thought which accept the authority of Veda: *Nyaya*, *Vaiseshika*, *Samkhya* and *Yoga*, in addition to *Karma-mimamsa* and *Vedanta*. All recognize *sabda*, "word," "verbal testimony," as a valid source of knowledge (*pramana*); but the Nyaya, Vaiseshika, Samkhya, and Yoga give precedence to sense-perception (*pratyaksha*) and inference (logical reasoning, *anumana*) and admit as authoritative word, the testimony of great teachers as well as the words of Veda. Karma-mimamsa and Vedanta give precedence to *sabda* and *sabda* as Vedic word only. These two schools are, indeed, schools of exegesis rather than philosophy.

Sankara, the most famous commentator (*bhashyakara*) on the *Brahma Sutra*, remarks, characteristically:

> Brahman, as being devoid of form and so on, cannot become an object of perception; and as there are in its case no characteristic marks (on which conclusions, etc., might be based), inference also and the other means of proof do not apply to it; but, like religious duty (*dharma*, the prime concern of the Karma-mimamsa) it is to be known solely on the ground of Veda . . . if it has been maintained above that the Word enjoining thought (on Brahman) in addition to mere hearing (of the Word treating of Brahman) shows that reasoning also is to be allowed its place, we reply that the Word must not deceitfully be taken as enjoining bare independent ratiocination, but must be understood to represent reasoning as a subordinate auxiliary of intuitional knowledge.[58]

> In matters to be known from *sabda* mere reasoning is not to be relied on . . . As the thoughts of man are altogether unfettered, reasoning which disregards the sacred word and rests on individual opinion only has no proper foundation. We see how arguments, which some clever men had excogitated with great pains are shown, by people still more ingenious, to be fallacious, and how the arguments of the latter again are refuted in their turn by other men; so, on account of the diversity of men's opinions, it is impossible to accept mere reasoning as having a sure foundation.[59]

Jaimini begins his *Mimamsa Sutra*:

1.1.1: Now, the enquiry into dharma.

1.1.2: Dharma is that which is indicated by means of Veda as conducive to the highest good.[60]

In order to establish the authority of dharma, Jaimini must first establish the authority of Veda. He begins with words, words in general.[61] As can be seen from common experience, words are always present in our consciousness; the speaker manifests the words, he does not produce them; they are eternal.[62] Further, the relationship between words and their denotations is eternal—the potency for denotation is in the letters which make up a word:

> 1.1.5: The relation of the word with its denotation is inborn.[63]

While it is true that the inherent meaning of words can be vitiated by the speaker, the words of Veda are not vitiated because they are authorless. We see that indeed no author is indicated for Veda—only those persons important in its transmission are mentioned; given the importance of Veda, had there been an author, he certainly would have been remembered, as is the case with Valmiki, author of Ramayana and Vyasa, author of the Mahabharata.[64] Further, we see that Veda is transmitted in an unbroken, continuous chain of masters from the creation to the present time—there is no indication of human origin. Finally, Jaimini affirms that Veda is authoritative because it is the only source of knowledge of dharma (as, with Sankara, Veda is the only source of knowledge of Brahman), and it is not contradicted by any other source of knowledge—its authority is self-evident.

> 1.1.5: (Veda is) infallible regarding all that is imperceptible; it is a valid means of knowledge, as it is independent, according to Badarayana.[65]

Here, Jaimini refers to Badarayana's *Brahma Sutra* 1.3.28 and 29:

> 28: If it be said (that a contradiction will result) in respect of the word; we refute this objection on the ground that (the world) originates from the word, as is shown by perception and inference.
>
> 29: And from this very reason there follows the eternity of Veda.[66]

The general point of the objection that Badarayana is refuting is that since the world and the gods are seen to be subject to birth and death, the words connected with world and gods must also come to an end—the word is not eternal. Sankara, commenting on Badarayana, refers to Jaimini to the effect that the relationship between word and its denotation is eternal. Further, says Sankara, a word in its eternal denotation refers to a species (world, god) not individuals of that species (a particular world, god). Finally, he argues, both *sruti* and *smriti* (Badarayana's "perception and inference") indicate that the Word is prior to the world and the gods as they originate from it—he quotes from the *Brahmanas* and the *Manu Smriti*.[67] Commenting on *Brahma Sutra* 1.3.29, he concludes:

As the eternity of the Veda is founded on the absence of the remembrance of an agent only, a doubt with regard to it had been raised owing to the doctrine that the gods and other individuals have sprung from it. That doubt has been refuted in the preceding sutra. The present sutra now confirms the, already established, eternity of Veda. The eternity of the word of Veda has to be assumed for this very reason, that the world with its definite (external) species, such as gods and so on, originates from it. A mantra also (Rig Veda x.71.3, quoted above) shows that the speech found (by the rishis) was permanent. On this point Vedavyasa also speaks as follows: "Formerly the great rishis, being allowed to do so by Svayambhu (the Self-born), obtained, through their penance, the Vedas together with the *itihasas* (see below), which had been hidden at the end of the *yuga* (cycle)."[68]

Having established the authority of Veda, Jaimini recognizes the place of *smriti*, essentially echoing Manu:

1.3.1: (Objection)—Inasmuch as dharma is based upon Veda, what is not Veda should be disregarded.

1.3.2: (True view)—But (smriti) is trustworthy, as there would be inference (assumption, of the basis in Veda) from the fact of the agent being the same. (i.e., those who have written smriti are those who have been inspired by Veda and act according to Veda).

1.3.3: Where there is conflict (between Veda and Smriti), the smriti should be disregarded; because it is only when there is no such conflict that there is an assumption (of Vedic support).[69]

With respect to *smriti*, Jaimini and his commentators are interested only in those texts which have ritual action as their chief concern, principally the *Vedanga*. Sankara, on the other hand, does not shy from quoting the popular epic, *Mahabharata*, and the *Puranas*, classical texts in which Vedic ritualism has only a minor role. Indeed, Sankara writes a separate commentary on the *Bhagavadgita*, a portion of *Mahabharata*, along with commentaries on the major *Upanishads* and the *Brahma Sutras*, which purport to summarize the teachings of the *Upanishads*.

EPIC AND ANCIENT LORE

Smriti is essentially defined by the fact of its human authorship and its recognition of the authority of Veda. Each tradition of teachers defines what is, in fact, consistent with Veda. Some traditions recognize the whole Sanskrit literature which purports to be inspired by Veda: the texts of the six *Darsanas*, sectarian manuals (*Agama* and *Tantra*), devotional poetry, texts on dance-drama and music, etc. It is commonly accepted that Smriti is composed of Vedanga, Itihasa and Purana. This definition is confused by the claim of some that Itihasa and Purana are Veda or at least equal to Veda.

Itihasa ("So, indeed, it was"), epic, identifies the Mahabharata and the Ramayana, stories of the heroes of dharma. The central story of the Mahabharata ("The Great Descendents of Bharata"), c. 500 B.C.E. is a story of struggle for kingdom between the five sons of Pandu (the Pandavas) and the one hundred sons of Dhritarashtra (the Kauravas). The struggle exemplifies dharma and adharma ("anti-dharma"). Yudhisthira, the eldest of the Pandavas is called the Son of Dharma—he and his brothers triumph in the battle, but not before thousands are slain, including the brothers' immediate off-spring. The most revered portion of the epic, the Bhagavadgita, is a battlefield discourse between Arjuna, the third son of Pandu, and Krishna. Krishna is not mere man, but an incarnation of the Supreme Lord (Vishnu/Brahman in personal form) who takes birth among men to uphold the dharma and disperse the forces of adharma. Krishna's word to Arjuna urges adherence to the "institutes of dharma," but downplays ritualism in favor of simple devotion to the Supreme, personal Lord.

According to the epic itself, the story of the Bharatas was first related by one Krishna Dvaipayana, ". . . the great seer, whose puissance is boundless and whose fame is spread in all three worlds."[70] "The son of Satyavati composed this holy History after he had arranged the Eternal Veda by the power of his austerities and continence."[71]

Krishna Dvaipayana is also known as Veda-vyasa, "Veda-divider," as he mastered Veda and Vedanga and divided Veda fourfold:

> . . . hardly had he been born before he, by his sheer will, forced his body into full maturity; whereupon the famous sage mastered the Vedas and their branches, along with the histories (Mahabharata and the Puranas); and no one was to surpass him in austerities, in the study of Veda, in the observance of vows and fasts, in progeny, or in temper. Greatest of the scholars of the Veda, he divided the One Veda into four parts.[72]

The characteristics of Krishna Dvaipayana are the same as those attributed to the rishis who heard Veda. The sage is also credited with having compiled the eighteen Puranas. Vishnu Purana records that Veda-vyasa was Vishnu, Himself, having taken human form.[73]

It is commonly said that the Mahabharata is the Fifth Veda. It recognizes Veda and the rishis in much the same terms as the Manu Smriti:

> At the outset the Self-born caused those excellent Vedic sounds, that are embodiments of knowledge and that have neither beginning nor end to (spring

up and) flow on (from preceptor to disciple). From those sounds have sprung all kinds of actions. The names of the Rishis, all things that have been created, the varieties of form seen in existent things, and the course of actions, have their origin in Veda. Indeed, the Supreme Master of all beings, in the beginning, created all things from the words of Veda.[74]

However, elsewhere it speaks of itself, along with Veda as having been received by the rishis:

> Formerly the great rishis, being allowed to do so by Svayambhu (the Self-born), obtained, through their penance, the Vedas together with the itihasas, which had been hidden at the end of the yuga (cycle).[75]

The *Brihad-aranyaka Upanishad* of the Yajur Veda, includes both *itihasa* and *purana*, along with Veda, as part of what was "breathed forth" at creation.[76] The introductory story-summary, now accepted as part of the epic, records that:

> In this book Krishna Dvaipayana has uttered a holy Upanishad . . . Once the divine seers foregathered, and on one scale they hung the four Vedas in the balance, and on the other scale The Bharata; and both in size and in weight it was the heavier. Therefore . . . it is called the Mahabharata ("Great Bharata") . . . A brahman who knows the four Vedas with their branches and Upanishads, but does not know this epic, has no learning at all . . . No story is found on earth that does not rest on this epic—nobody endures without living off its food . . . If a man learns The Bharata as it is recited, as it once fell from the lips of Dvaipayana, immeasurable, sanctifying, purifying, atoning, and blessing—what need has he of ablutions in the waters of Pushkara? (a particularly sacred place of pilgrimage) . . . this Krishna (Dvaipayana) Veda . . . is a supreme means of sanctification equal to the Vedas . . . [77]

One who hears the Bharata and gives good gifts to the reciter and to brahmans is cleansed of all sins; indeed, he attains the highest goal, freedom from rebirth (*moksha*):

> The Bharata is worshipped by the very gods. The Bharata is the highest goal . . . the foremost of all scriptures. One attains Emancipation through the Bharata . . . He that listens with devotion to this Bharata from the beginning becomes cleansed of every sin even if he be guilty of Brahmanicide . . . or even if he be born in the Chandala (sudra) order.[78]

The *Ramayana* ("The Deeds of Rama") c. 200 B.C.E. is the work of the poet, Valmiki, and is considered to be the first and classic poem (*kavya*). It is the story of Rama, his beloved wife, Sita, his brothers—Bharata and Lakshmana, Hanuman, the monkey-warrior, in their struggle with and conquest of evil (*adharma*) represented by Ravana, the thousand-headed lord of the demons. Rama is portrayed as the ideal man, his rule (ram-rajya), the rule of dharma; Sita is the ideal woman; Hanuman, the arche-type of fidelity and devotion. In the course of time, Valmiki's original story is altered, making Rama, like Krishna (of the *Bhagavadgita*), an incarnation of the Supreme Lord, Vishnu, and Sita, his divine consort. The relationships between Rama and Sita and other characters of the drama become archetypes of the desirable relationship between God and man. The epic concludes with:

> This is the Epic Ramayana, adored by God Brahma himself, in which is established Lord Vishnu whose personality pervades the entire static and mobile universe, the Epic which destroys all sins, confers all fortune and is indeed equal to the Vedas. Even a quarter of a verse of it, nay even a word, brings salvation.[79]

The particular word that has power is the name, *Rama*. In devotional Hinduism, the chanting of the name of the Supreme Lord takes the place of Vedic mantras. The devotee may chant "Rama" with the same effect as chanting "OM."

Unlike Veda, the original form of which is inviolable, the *Mahabharata* and *Ramayana* have been translated into all of the fourteen vernacular languages of India. The story of Rama has been retold in several of these vernaculars, most importantly, in Tulsidas' Hindi, *Ramcaritmanas*, and Kamban's Tamil, *Ramayanan*. These vernacular versions have become more popular than the original.

Although classified as Smriti, the epics enjoy a very special status in this category; they consider themselves the equal of Veda, in effect Veda itself, manifest in story. They record, not only the word of man, but the word of God through His incarnations; they are scripture. The Sruti/Smriti line was drawn from the point of view of ritualistic, high-caste religion. The Vedanga is a highly technical literature, defining the religious life as a life of meticulous ritualism and restricting this life to members of the twice-born classes. Excluding the sudra, it excludes the great majority of the people. The *Mahabharata* and *Ramayana*, stories anciently told around the campfire after battle or narrated at the court on public occasions, stories of brahmans and kings, respecting the prescriptions of the institutes of dharma, but giving prominence to simple devotion and divine grace rather than ritualism, open Hinduism to the common man. Manu, the Karma-mimamsa and the Vedanta appeal directly to the content of

Veda. When the epics appeal to Veda they appeal, not to the content of mantras and brahmanas, but to Veda, simply as the indicator of Truth. This appears to be the case with most of the diverse sectarian traditions which arise in Hinduism, claiming authority for their special texts.

The Purana ("Ancient Lore") texts, composed between 400 and 1000 C.E., are, like the epics, essentially story. Beginning with creation, they set forth the genealogies of gods, sages and kings, relate the awe-inspiring feats of gods and sages and their effect upon the affairs of men, enumerate sacred places and the benefits derived from pilgrimage thereto, and define a variety of spiritual disciplines. They are veritable encyclopedias of popular Hinduism; their emphasis is essentially devotional. Tradition recognizes eighteen major puranas (*Maha-purana*) and numerous minor narrations (*upa-purana*) each of which is dedicated to a particular form of the Supreme Reality—Vishnu, Shiva, Agni, Krishna, and the like. The Puranas add very little to our understanding of Veda and Smriti. They are much quoted, but do not enjoy the high status of the epics.

CONCLUDING REMARKS

I have tried to present here the middle ground of a broad gamut of perspectives on Veda and sacred texts taken by Hindu sectarians. On one extreme, Arya Samaj ("Society of Aryas") Hindus, inspired by the life and teachings of Swami Dayananda Sarasvati (1824–1883), respect only the mantra portions of Veda as Sruti, classify the Brahmanas with Smriti, reject the Puranas and consider the Mahabharata and Ramayana to be, in certain portions, erroneous.[80]

On the other extreme, we may place the Sri-Vaishnavas ("Devotees of Vishnu, together with the Goddess") who believe that the vernacular (Tamil) poetry of twelve devotees of Vishnu, known as the *Alvars* ("those immersed in God"), *c.* 500–900 C.E., is Veda, in Tamil. The original vernacular text is seen to be, not Smriti, not a translation or re-telling of Smriti nor a translation of Veda, but Veda revealed once again in Tamil. Equally radical is the fact that the core of this revelation was received, not by a brahman or even a twice-born Hindu, but by Nammalvar, a sudra.[81]

The great sacrifices prescribed by Veda are today seldom performed. There are many fewer who pursue Vedic learning today than in ancient times, but it is pursued and with the same exactitude as aforetime. Max Müller, the famous Indologist who spearheaded the editing and translating of Veda into Western languages, effectively remarks on this phenomenon:

[It] . . . is a fact that can easily be ascertained by anybody who doubts it—at the present moment, if every Ms. of the Rg-Veda were lost, we should be able to recover the whole of it from the memory of the Srotriyas in India. These native students learn the Veda by heart and they learn it from the mouth of their Guru, never from a Ms., still less from my printed edition,—and after a time they teach it again to their pupils. I have had such students in my room at Oxford, who not only could repeat these hymns, but who repeated them with the proper accents (for the Vedic Sanskrit has accents like Greek) nay who, when looking through my printed edition of the Rg-Veda could point out a misprint without the slightest hesitation.[82]

Twice-born Hindus daily chant Vedic mantras in the morning and evening offerings to the sun and in their mid-morning domestic worship. Vedic mantras are chanted in the rites of the life cycle—rites of birth, initiation into Veda, marriage and death—prescribed by the *Kalpa Sutras* (Vedanga). Groups of brahmans chant Veda in unison at many temple festivals, as invocation at public meetings and on special occasions such as the recent drought in South India.

All India Radio, a government-controlled medium, regularly broadcasts recitation of Veda and lessons in the Sanskrit language. Sanskrit colleges, established for the purpose of Vedic studies, enjoy government support; Sanskrit-studies are encouraged in public education and scholars of Veda regularly receive national honors along side of noteworthy scientists, businessmen and artists.

The epics and puranas are much in evidence in Hindu life. The old tradition of the court bard is carried on by *kathakas* ("story-tellers," "reciters") who travel from place to place giving public recitations in the temples, enlivening festivals and pilgrimages. Individuals, especially women, commonly read portions of *Ramayana* daily, for the welfare of the family; to read the entire epic in daily segments over a period of several weeks is considered especially meritorious. Episodes from *Mahabharata* and *Ramayana*, are publicly performed in dance-drama; vocalists sing the stories in public concert. Once a year in many parts of India, the triumph of Rama over Ravana, *Ram-lila* ("the sport of Rama"), is publicly performed with human actors and papier-mâché figures. The "sports of Krishna" (*Ras-lila*, lit. "the sport of finest-essence"), narrated in the *Bhagavata Purana*, are publicly enjoyed in annual dramatic productions.

NOTES

1. *The Hindu*, Madras, February 8, 1983. The governor made reference to recent experiments carried out by an American psychologist in collaboration with

Indian scholars and priests, showing that the *Agnihotra*, a fire ritual pre-scribed by Veda, has the power to cure epilepsy and improve I.Q. Previous to these experiments, Indian scientists had reported *Agnihotra* effective against maladies such as migraine headache, herpes, hay fever, ringworm and diarrhea. *Indian Express*, February 7, 1983.

2. The term "Hindu" originates with outsiders as simply a reference to the people inhabiting the Indus (from Sanskrit, *sindhu*) River area of the Indian subcontinent.

3. Yaska, *Nirukta*, II.11, quoted in *Cultural Heritage of India*, S. K. Chatterji, et al., eds., Vol. I, p. 300 (Calcutta, Sri Gouranga Press, 1958). The *Nirukta* is discussed below.

4. *Rig Veda* 10.71.1, 3–4, from R. Panikkar, *The Vedic Experience* (Berkeley and Los Angeles, University of California Press, 1977), p. 94.

5. *Rig Veda* 3.62.10, ibid., p. 38.

6. *Sama Veda, Chandogya Upanishad* 3.12.1, from R. E. Hume, trans., *The Thirteen Principal Upanishads* (London: Oxford University Press, 1971), p. 207.

7. *Manu Smriti* II.101–102, from G. Buhler, trans., *The Laws of Manu* (Oxford: Clarendon Press, 1886), p. 48.

8. *Atharva Veda* 19.71.1, from W. D. Whitney, trans., *Atharva-Veda-Samhita* (Delhi: Motilal Banarsidass, 1971).

9. *OM* is made up of three sounds.

10. The *Gayatri Mantra* consists of three feet of eight syllables each; this, then becomes the standard for what is called the Gayatri meter.

11. *Manu Smriti* II.76,77,81, Buhler, pp. 44– 45.

12. *Rig Veda* 4.3.16, from R. T. H. Griffith, trans., *The Hymns of the Rgveda* (Delhi: Motilal Banarsidass, 1973).

13. *Yajur Veda, Brihad-aranyaka Upanishad* 4.5.11, Hume, p. 146.

14. The Sanskrit, *aksharam*, means both "imperishable" and "syllable."

15. *Atharva Veda, Gopatha Brahmana* I.16, from V. Raghavan, trans., *The Indian Heritage* (Bangalore: The Indian Institute of World Culture, 1956).

16. *Atharva Veda, Mandukya Upanishad* 1.1, Hume, p. 391.

17. *Yajur Veda, Katha Upanishad* 2.16, Hume, p. 349.

18. The literal meaning of *brahman*, "that which bursts forth."

19. *Yajur Veda, Maitri Upanishad* 6.22, Hume, p. 437.

20. *Atharva Veda, Mundaka Upanishad* 2.2.4, Hume, p. 372.

21. *Rig Veda* 10.90, Panikkar, p. 76.

22. *Yajor Veda, Maitri Upanishad* 6.6, Hume, p. 427.

23. This becomes, rg or rig, in combination with *veda*.

24. From S. Radhakrishnan and C. A. Moore, *A Source Book in Indian Philosophy* (Princeton: Princeton University Press, 1957), pp. 7–8.

25. *Yajur Veda, Satapatha Brahmana* 1.6.3.8 tells the story of Tvastr who by misplacement of accent extinguished the sacrificial fire rather than making it blaze up. The key word in this recitation, *indrasatru*, when given raised accent on the last syllable, means "the destroyer of Indra" (god of storm); when

given raised accent on the second syllable, it means, "he whose destroyer is Indra." J. Eggeling, trans., *The Satapatha-Brahmana* (Oxford: Clarendon Press, 1900).

26. The hotr, udgatr, brahman and adhvaryu, respectively; *Rig Veda* 10.71.1– 4, 11, Panikkar, pp. 94–95.

27. *Yajur Veda* III.iii.2, Raghavan, pp. 19– 20.

28. *Atharva Veda* 19.9, Raghavan, p. 33.

29. *Yajur Veda, Brihad-aranyaka Upanishad* 2.4.10, Hume, p. 100.

30. *Yajur Veda, Taittiriya Brahmana* II.viii.8.5, Raghavan, p. 35.

31. Ibid., I.iv.8, Raghavan, p. 34.

32. *Yajur Veda, Satapatha Brahmana* VIII.6.I.5, Eggeling, Part IV, p. 100.

33. Ibid.

34. Ibid., p. 124.

35. *Yajur Veda, Taittiriya Aranyaka* X.xiii–xv, Raghavan, p. 40.

36. *Sama Veda, Jaiminiya Upanishad Brahmana* 1.1.1, from Hanns Oertel, trans., *Jaiminiya Upanishad Brahmana* (New Haven: American Oriental Society, 1894).

37. *Yajur Veda, Satapatha Brahmana* XI.iii.7.5.6.1–3, Raghavan, p. 44.

38. *Yajur Veda, Maitri Upanishad* 1.1, Hume, p. 412.

39. *Sama Veda, Chandogya Upanishad* 3.16.1, Hume, p. 211.

40. *Yajur Veda, Brihad-aranyaka Upanishad* 2.5, Hume, p. 102f.

41. *Nirukta* I.15, quoted in *The Cultural Heritage of India*, Vol. I, p. 275.

42. *Nirukta* I.20, *The Cultural Heritage* . . ., Vol. I, pp. 294– 95.

43. According to A. L. Basham, *The Wonder That Was India* (London: Sidgwick and Jackson, 1956), p. 388, ". . . the most detailed and scientific grammar composed before the 19th century in any part of the world."

44. J. F. Staal, *A Reader on the Sanskrit Grammarians* (Cambridge, Mass.: MIT Press, 1972), pp. 4–5.

45. sutra, "thread," "clue," "aphorism," a statement of the essential point or truth, with an economy of words, facilitating memorization. The *Kalpa Sutras* elaborate dharma for one great cycle of time (*kalpa*).

46. I.21,31, Buhler, pp. 12– 14.

47. II.7, 10; XII.94–96, Buhler.

48. *Manu Smriti* II.

49. *Rig Veda* 10.90.

50. *Manu Smriti* II.

51. *Manu Smriti* I.96,98, Buhler, p. 25.

52. *Manu Smriti* II.

53. Ibid., XII.103, Buhler, pp. 507– 8.

54. *Nirukta* I.18, from L. Renou, *The Destiny of the Veda* (Delhi: Motilal Banarsidass, 1965), p. 25.

55. P. V. Kane, *History of Dharmasastra* (Poona: Bhandarkar Oriental Research Institute, 1962), Vol. II, Pt. I, pp. 347– 49.

56. *Manu Smriti* II.113–116, Buhler, p. 51.

57. *Vedanta* also has the meaning of, "the final, authoritative view of Veda."
58. G. Thibaut, trans., *The Vedanta Sutras of Badarayana with the commentary by Sankara* (New York: Dover Publications, Inc., 1962), Pt. I, pp. 306–7.
59. Ibid., Sutra 2.1.11, pp. 314–15.
60. Radhakrishnan and Moore, *Sourcebook*, p. 487.
61. Hereafter, I follow the commentaries as well as Jaimini.
62. *Mimamsa Sutra* 1.1.12–18, *Sourcebook*, pp. 489-90.
63. Ibid., p. 487.
64. *Cultural History of India*, Vol. III, p. 152.
65. *Sourcebook*, p. 487.
66. Thibaut, *Vedanta Sutras*, pp. 201, 211.
67. *Brihad-aranyaka Upanishad* I.2.4, "He, with his mind united himself with speech . . ."; *Taittiriya Brahmana* II.2.4.2, ". . . uttering *bhur* he created the earth . . ."; *Manu Smriti* I.21, "The several names, actions, and conditions of all things he shaped in the beginning from the words of Veda."
68. Thibaut, *Vedanta Sutras*, Pt. I, p. 211.
69. Radhakrishnan and Moore, *Sourcebook*, pp. 495–96.
70. J. A. B. van Buitenen, *The Mahabharata* (Chicago: University of Chicago Press, 1973), Vol. I, p. 129.
71. Ibid., p. 22.
72. Ibid., pp. 125–26.
73. M. N. Dutt, trans., *Vishnupuranam* (Varanasi: Chowkhamba Sanskrit Series Office, 1972), Pt. III, section III, p. 178f.
74. K. M. Ganguli, trans., *The Mahabharata* (New Delhi: Munshiram Manoharlal, 1976), Vol. IX, Santi Parva 232, p. 159.
75. As found in Thibaut, *Vedanta Sutras*, Pt. I, p. 211.
76. 2.5.10 and 4.5.11.
77. van Buitenen, Vol. I, pp. 30, 31, 43–44.
78. Ganguli, Svargarohanika Parva VI, Vol. XII, pp. 12–18.
79. Raghavan, *Heritage*, p. 292.
80. See J. T. F. Jordens, *Dayananda Sarasvati, His Life and Ideas* (Delhi: Oxford University Press, 1978).
81. See G. Damodaran, *Acarya Hrdayam* (Tirupati: Tirumala Tirupati Devas-thanams, 1976).
82. M. Müller, *India—What can it teach us?*, Collected Works, Vol. XIII, pp. 208-9.

 # BUDDHISM:
Sacred Text Written and Realized

Reginald A. Ray

Throughout its history, Buddhist tradition has maintained a paradoxical attitude toward its sacred texts. On the one hand, those texts have themselves been the objects of the utmost veneration; and life, limb, and more have been sacrificed to ensure their unaltered preservation and correct understanding. At the same time, Buddhism avers that the sacred text has, in and of itself, no particular value. Its worth depends entirely on what is done with it, and at best, the sacred text is never more than an aid that must be abandoned by each individual at a certain point on his journey toward the Buddhist goal of enlightenment. Thus in Buddhism, the sacred text is an answer to spiritual longing, and also no answer at all, or rather an "answer" in the way it points beyond and, in fact, away from itself.

The paradox of how Buddhism views its sacred texts is expressed in the "Discourse on the Great Decease" (*Mahāparinibbāna Sutta*),[2] an early *sutta* describing the events surrounding the death of the Buddha. As the Buddha's death approaches, his beloved attendant and disciple, Ānanda, is beside himself with grief. How, he asks, can the Blessed One, counselor, guide and friend for so many years, leave his disciples? Who will look after them, who will teach them and lead them henceforth? Ānanda's implication is perhaps that the Buddha set up some person or some institution in his place to act as final authority and arbiter in matters of dispute. But this the Buddha explicitly rejects. Instead, he says "henceforth, be ye lamps unto yourselves and be ye refuges unto yourselves, seek no other refuge; let the *dharma* be your lamp and your refuge, and seek no other refuge."[3] Here "*dharma*" refers to the teachings and, most concretely, the texts containing the Buddha's teaching, thus establishing sacred scripture in a special position of authority in the tradition. But, at the same time, the authority specifically of the sacred text and more generally of the Buddhist

148

teachings is here understood as appositive to, and thus inseparable from, being a lamp unto oneself and a refuge unto oneself, relying on nothing else. Here we have our paradox again, in a different form, in this asseveration of a literal authority that is ultimately not different from the solitary individual entirely "on his own."

Here then are two sides of the paradoxical attitude of Buddhism toward its sacred texts: on the one hand the authoritative text whose authority derives precisely from the way in which it ultimately undercuts its own authority; on the other, the tradition of letters offered as a "refuge" in such a way that it is understood to be ultimately inseparable from an individual in his nakedness and aloneness relying on nothing but himself. It is this paradox that stands at the heart of the Buddhist approach to sacred text, and in order to understand something of this paradoxical approach we shall consider three central, interrelated issues: (1) the origin of the peculiarly Buddhist notion of sacred text in the life of the Buddha and in early Buddhism's understanding of what a Buddha is; (2) the issue of how Buddhism determines the authenticity of sacred text; and (3) the question of how authentic texts are to be properly interpreted and used.

ORIGINS

The origin of the peculiarly Buddhist notion of "sacred text" must be sought in the life and teachings of Buddha Śākyamuni, the founder of Buddhism, who lived from about 560–480 B.C.E. in Northeast India, and in how he was understood by early Buddhism. According to Buddhist tradition, the Buddha was a human being who, through his own efforts, achieved realization of the ultimate and timeless truths about human life, and thereby attained Buddahood, the transcendent goal of Buddhism.[4]

Buddha Śākyamuni was the first to discover and teach the way to enlightenment in this world age, and for that reason he is greatly to be revered among men. But, precisely because of the ultimacy, timelessness, and universality of his realization, in a larger perspective he is far from unique. Tradition holds that across the vast expanse of time and throughout the innumerable universes that host sentient life, the achievement of the Buddha has been repeated countless times by other Buddhas and will be likewise repeated until time's end. The identity of that achievement amounts to the sameness of those who have gained and identified with that achievement, and thus we find Buddhist tradition insisting on the sameness of all the Buddhas throughout time and space.[5]

The realization of the Buddha Śākyamuni and of all other Buddhas is not unique to them alone. In fact, for all human beings and indeed for all other sentient beings as well, the ideal enlightenment is not only *a possible*, but *the only proper* goal of existence. Whether that goal is to be attained in this lifetime, or in a future existence, makes no great difference. The "realm of truth" (*dharma-dhātu*) is an ever-abiding reality and enlightenment an ever-present potential, and beings are enjoined to strive to achieve the realization, freedom, and liberation first showed in this world age in the Buddha's enlightenment.

Thus Buddha Śākyamuni is not seen as a savior figure who brings to suffering humanity something that is fundamentally other or foreign to it. Rather, quite to the contrary, he is one who teaches men to look at what is already their own lives, to realize their own fundamental nature, and to accept the inheritance that is already present. Anyone who does so is held to re-experience the same illumination and the same freedom experienced by the Buddha Śākyamuni under the Bodhi tree at Bodhgayā in the sixth century B.C.E.

This basic view of Buddha Śākyamuni and of his relationship to human beings has important implications for what he has to communicate to others through his teaching.

1.　What Buddha Śākyamuni teaches will be fundamentally the same as what is taught by other Buddhas.[6]

2.　What this teaching points to is an ever-present possibility for humanity, because it abides as the fundamental reality of human life as it already is.[7]

3.　Furthermore, Buddhist tradition holds that this enlightenment is not only an ever-present possibility, but an actuality: many people throughout Buddhist history are held to have achieved a realization not fundamentally different from that of the Buddha.[8]

4.　Just as the teaching of other Buddhas is understood to be the same as that of Buddha Śākyamuni, likewise the actuality of that enlightment among Buddha Śākyamuni's followers means that what such enlightened people themselves teach will not depart from the Buddha's teaching.

The preceding allows us some important insights into the Buddhist understanding of sacred text. The "sacred text" *par excellence* in Buddhism is what is called *buddha-vacana*, the "word of the Buddha." But what does it mean to call something *buddha-vacana*? First of all, of course, the term refers to that which is understood to have been preached by Buddha Śākyamuni in his ordinary human form. As we shall see below, it refers to those texts that have been reliably received directly from the Buddha himself, or from an authority that may be reasonably judged to have received the text from him during his lifetime and accurately passed it down. But in Buddhism the term *buddha-vacana* has a wider application.

Buddha Śākyamuni manifested his mind of enlightenment, his identity with the ever-abiding and timeless reality of "things as they are," in his human preaching. But, from the earliest times, he was also understood to appear and teach in a nonphysical body, called a "mentally created body."[9] This type of body, well-known in Indian yogic traditions, refers to the ability of a person to appear in a nonphysical, spiritualized form, in a dream or vision. Significant in this context, the Buddha may also "speak" in just such a "mentally created body" and Singhalese tradition holds him to have preached the seven books of the Pāli Abhidharma in such a body to his deceased mother in a heavenly realm.[10]

Beyond this, the term *buddha-vacana* can legitimately be applied to what has been spoken not by the Buddha himself in any of his forms, but by the enlightened ones among his disciples. Thus, for example, within the Hīnayāna Sarvāstivādin tradition, one of the early Buddhist Schools, the Abhidharma section of the Tripitaka (the early canon), considered *buddha-vacana*, is composed of seven texts not attributed to Buddha Śākyamuni, but instead to disciples who are well-known historical figures including Maudgalyāyana, Vasumitra, and Kātyāyana.[11] The term *buddha-vacana* can be applied to these texts because their authors are understood to have spoken in them with an enlightenment and with words inseperable from those of the Buddha himself.

Finally, authentic enlightened teaching can also be preached by sages, gods, and apparitional beings. Included as examples of these by Buddhist tradition are the sage Araka, the disciple of a previous Buddha Vidhura and Abhibhū, and the deity Śakra.[12]

Thus Buddha word means both that which was spoken in a very literal way by the "historical," meaning physically human, Buddha, and equally, that which is spoken with the mind of enlightenment, whether by Buddha Śākyamuni in a nonphysical form, by another buddha, or by someone else. As the noted Buddhologist Etienne Lamotte aptly observes, all of this meant that the "*dharma* thus had sources that were diverse and tended, with time, to multiply."[13] The strength of this approach to sacred text is that it affirms the ever-present possibility of enlightenment within the Buddhist community, and also of the fresh revelation of "enlightened teachings" (perhaps the best translation of "*buddha-vacana*") throughout Buddhist history. At the same time, this approach raises an important question: how does one tell which texts put forward as authentic enlightened teachings are to be accepted as such? This raises the issue of textual authenticity.

THE QUESTION OF TEXTUAL AUTHENTICITY

The determination of scriptural authenticity in Buddhism rests firmly on Buddhism's general approach to the issue of religious authority. As noted above, the Buddha declined to establish any single individual or institution as supreme authority to act in his stead after his death. Rather, the Buddha counseled his disciples to rely only upon themselves and the *dharma* as their refuge.

These final injunctions on the part of the Buddha amount neither to an abjuration of the need for definite structures of authority among his followers, nor to a refusal to establish such authority. Quite to the contrary, in his final words the Buddha defines and in effect establishes the peculiarly Buddhist form of religious authority that has characterized the tradition throughout its history. This form of authority is based on two complementary dimensions: individual responsibility and the necessary guidance of legitimate tradition.

Individual Responsibility

Each individual holds final responsibility for his own development and, ultimately, for what in Buddhist tradition is to be accepted as authentic and what is not. The affirmation of such responsibility obviously implies a positive evaluation of each individual's ability to make decisions which are the right ones at his particular stage of development. And this, in turn, is based on the notion that each individual has the potentiality of enlightenment within his experience, a potentiality that is understood to become more and more actual and accessible through the Buddhist way of life.

An account from the early scriptures illustrates the Buddhist view of the relativity of external tradition and of the individual as the final resting place of authority. We are told that a certain man, Purāṇa by name, did not participate in the first council at Rājagṛha where the Buddhist canon is held to have been initially established. Arriving afterwards, he commented to the monks who had participated in the council, "Venerable ones, the *dharma* [general teachings] and the *vinaya* [teaching on monastic discipline] have been well chanted by the elders." In saying that the teachings have been "well chanted," Purāṇa is affirming that the texts so chanted have been done so from accurate memory and come unaltered from the mouth of the Buddha Śākyamuni, and thus are *buddha-vacana*. But Purāṇa continues: "Nevertheless, I maintain that I have retained the *dharma* in my memory as I have heard it, as I have received it from the mouth of the blessed one." [14]

In another account, we find the point made that even when a monk has heard the very words of the Buddha, he is not to repeat them merely out of reverence for him, but may do so only on the condition that he has heard and understood their content for himself. After a particularly important sermon the Buddha addressed the monks in these terms: "and now monks . . . that you may also understand and think, will you say, 'honoring the Master and, through respect for the Master, we will say this or that?'" "We will not do so, Master." "What you affirm, is it not what you yourselves have recognized, seen and grasped?" "It is even that, Master." [15] Here the monks' own understanding and appropriation must take precedence, even in the matter of the words of the Buddha himself.

The Role of Authentic Tradition

The Buddha points to the final responsibility of the individual, and he equally affirms the importance of the *dharma*, which is codified in the teachings that he has given and, finally, in the tradition that he has established. This *dharma* or tradition is divided in the early traditions into two main topics: (1) the *vinaya*, that establishes both the quasi-legal unit of the individual monastic establishment, as well as the life rule for individual monks and nuns, and laymen and laywomen. Individuals have the potential for enlightenment within them and bear ultimate responsibility for their development, but it is only in the strict context of a particular Buddhist community and through following the discipline of a particular life rule that the individual potential can be fully discovered and matured into enlightenment. (2) The second aspect is referred to simply as *dharma*, which includes both the literal teachings of the Buddha in oral tradition and texts and the practical and personal realization of those teachings through the practice of meditation. Whereas the *vinaya* suggests the proper context of spiritual practice, the *dharma* indicates the practices and doctrines that directly open the mind.

In the ultimate sense, then, individual intelligence and judgment must be the guide on the path. But it is just that intelligence that enables one to recognize and appreciate the legitimacy of the authentic tradition Buddhism represents and the necessity of its guidance for one's maturation.

This basic notion of authority in Buddhism as involving the interaction of personal/internal and traditional/external factors, is further fleshed out in the notion of the "three jewels," *buddha, dharma,* and *samgha* (community), to which each aspiring Buddhist "goes for refuge" (*bud-*

dham śaraṇam gacchāmi, etc.) when he becomes a Buddhist. On the one hand, each of the three jewels has an external, traditional, institutionalized form. Here the "*buddha*" refers to Buddha Śākyamuni, establisher of Buddhist tradition, whose historical and traditionally interpreted example one commits oneself to follow; "*dharma*" refers to the literal *dharma* composed of the specific texts recognized as canonical by the particular tradition one joins; and the "*samgha*" refers to the Buddhist community with its specific life rule that one is entering.

At the same time, each of these three refuges has an internal dimension that is more or less explicit, depending on Buddhist tradition and teacher. Here the *buddha* is the enlightened potential of one's own mind, the *dharma* is "things as they are," to be progressively realized through one's meditation, and the *samgha* is the vital community of fellow Buddhists who, through encouragement and critique, support and contribute to one's own development, just as one contributes to theirs.

Thus, we see that final religious authority in Buddhism does not lie in any one place, be it a person, a text, or an institution, nor is it to be located solely either in internal or external factors. Rather, final authority reposes in a "situation" affirmed by tradition, in which "person" (the *buddha*, one's own mind), a "text" (the literal text and what is understood), and the *samgha* (in its legal and intimate dimensions) each have a part to play. Granted, in the ultimate perspective, there is the final authority of enlightenment itself, but the relativity of "the world" and its inhabitants—including the Buddhist tradition and its adherents—must be frankly acknowledged and properly used to make ultimate enlightenment possible for anyone.

This general Buddhist approach to the question of religious authority had important implications for the textual dimension of Buddhism. It meant great reverence for the traditions received by the early *samgha* from the Buddha.[16] But it remained to be seen how that reverence was to be implemented. The Buddha had taught for about forty-five years and probably counted among his disciples thousands of people. One can only imagine the number of potential "texts" that must have existed at the time of his passing (*parinirvāṇa*). Which of his words should be considered most important? Which should be accepted as valid but given lesser importance? Which texts should be rejected as improperly remembered or as inauthentic? As Lamotte notes, "the disciples themselves had to determine the sources of the *dharma*, in establishing their authenticity and in furnishing their correct interpretation."[17]

This was a particularly thorny problem. Given the Buddha's particular approach to the question of religious authority, the extensiveness of his own teaching, the considerable geographical extent of Buddhism at the time of his death, and the multiple sources of *buddha-vacana*, uniformity in determination of *buddha-vacana* and of the canon was virtually ruled out. As Lamotte notes, even in the sylized accounts of the "first council" at Rājagṛha shortly after the Buddha's *parinirvāṇa*, one sees the Buddhist community not arriving at a universal canon of scriptures agreed upon by the *saṃgha* and closed to the introduction of new texts.[18] Even after the death of the Buddha, new *sūtras* were composed that held an authority equal to that of the texts originating from his lifetime, and were accepted as equal in canonicity by the Hīnayāna traditions.[19] Finally, "these canons were never closed; in fact, in the course of time, they grew without ceasing, with new compositions. . . . "[20]

Given this overall pattern of development and the attitudes it reflects, how might Buddhist tradition articulate the criteria necessary for determining the authenticity of a text? As might be expected, early and later Buddhist tradition holds that the determination of textual authenticity was to be made through the application of several interrelated criteria, containing both internal and external dimensions. In the *Mahāpadesa-sutta*, an early work, well known and considered authoritative for later tradition, the Buddha enunciates the four "great authorities" (Sanskrit, *mahāpadeśa*) from which one may reliably receive a text as Buddha word:

> In a certain case, a monk may say, "Venerable Ones, I have heard and learned this myself from the mouth of the Blessed One himself, and this is thus the Master's Dharma, Vinaya and teaching."

> Again, a monk may say, "In a certain locale, there resides a community (*saṃgha*) where there are elders and leaders; from the mouth of this community I have heard and learned this myself, and this is thus the Master's Dharma, Vinaya and teaching."

> Again, a monk may say, "In a certain locale, there reside a number of learned elder monks, in possession of the scriptures, knowing by heart the Dharma, the Vinaya and the summaries; from the mouths of these elders I have heard and learned this, and this is thus the Master's Dharma, Vinaya and teaching."

> Again, a monk may say, "In a certain locale, there lives a single elder monk, who is learned and who is in possession of the scriptures, knowing by heart the Dharma, the Vinaya and the summaries; from the mouth of this elder, I have heard and learned this, and this is thus the Master's Dharma, Vinaya and teaching."[21]

In this passage the Buddha is indicating the external criteria one may apply to determine Buddha word. This hierarchical arrangement again fully allows for the relativity of the situation: It is best to hear from the Buddha's own mouth, but failing this, one may rely upon elders of a duly constituted saṃgha (here, monastic community), elders living merely as a group, or an individual elder. However, the Buddha continues, this external set of criteria is not enough to determine the authenticity of buddha-vacana. In fact, he says, what is proposed in any of the four cases should be neither accepted nor rejected. "Without accepting or rejecting (the text in question), its words and its syllables, having been carefully understood, must be compared with the sūtra and the vinaya. If compared with the sūtra and vinaya, they are not found in the sūtra and do not appear in the vinaya, then one must arrive at the conclusion, 'Certainly, this is not the word of the Blessed One, and has been badly learned by this monk, this community, these elders or this elder,' and you should reject the text. If the words and the syllables proposed . . . are found in the sutra and appear in the vinaya, one must arrive at the conclusion, 'Certainly, this is the word of the Blessed One and has been well learned by this monk, this community, these elders or this elder.'"[22]

Should this second step necessary to authenticate a text be understood to involve a comparison of the words and phrases of the proposed document with the literal words of already established buddha-vacana? As Lamotte notes, tradition says, "not necessarily." The Sanskrit recension of the Mahāpadeśa Sūtra adds to the above passage that the proposed text "not contradict the nature of things." Furthermore, commentarial tradition, both Hīnayānist and Mahāyānist, likewise insists on this same criterion.[23]

What does it mean to say that the proposed text "not contradict the nature of things"? The goal of Buddhism, enlightenment, involves a perception of life, of reality, that is devoid of egotistical distortions. This is the seeing of "things as they are," and it is just this that Buddhism understands as the "nature of things" at once and inseparably in their most mundane and ultimate dimensions. To say that a text does "not contradict the nature of things" means that it accords with the enlightened perception of reality. This enlightened perception is what is meant by the "internal" dimension of dharma as one of the three jewels. Thus here we are being told that, other criteria being fulfilled, a text may be judged as authentic if its words (external dharma) are in harmony with the nature of things (internal dharma). As we shall see below, it is just when the inseparability of these two dimensions of dharma is fully appreciated, that for Buddhism the text is properly understood.

The Chinese translation of the *Mahāpadeśa Sūtra* confirms this interpretation:

> If a Monk says this, "Venerable Ones, in a certain village, in a certain kingdom, I heard and received this teaching," you must neither accept nor reject what he tells you. It is necessary, relying on the *sūtra*, to examine what is true and what is false; relying on the *vinaya*, relying on the *dharma*, to examine what is essential and what is adventitious. If the text proposed is not *sūtra*, is not *vinaya*, is not *dharma*, then you must say to him, "The Buddha has not said that, you have incorrectly learned it. Why? Because I have relied upon the *sūtra*, relied upon the *vinaya*, relied upon the *dharma*, and what you have just said is in contradiction with the *dharma* (teaching)."

Lamotte sums up the message of the *Mahāpadeśa Sūtra*: "Thus, in order for the text proposed from one of the four great authorities to be accepted in the scriptures; it suffices that its general tenor be in harmony with the spirit of the *sūtras*, the *vinaya* and Buddhist doctrine in general. . . ."[25]

And what is this spirit? Lamotte: "The spirit of the *sūtras* is found condensed in the sermon on the four noble truths; the prescriptions of the *vinaya* are those which tend to the abatement of the passions; and the center piece of Buddhist philosophy is the theory of conditioned co-production (*pratītyasamutpāda*). . . . The *Nettipakaraṇa* grasps perfectly the spirit of the *Mahapadesasutta*, when it remarks 'With what *sūtra* is it necessary to compare the texts? With the four noble truths. With what *vinaya* should one compare them? With the *vinaya* (which combats) passion, aggression and delusion. Against which doctrine [in the *abhidharma*] should one measure them? Against the doctrine of conditioned co-production.'"[26]

How are we to understand this quote from the *Nettipakarana*? The *vinaya*, *sūtra*, and *abhidarma* are the three components of the early Buddhist canon, the "three baskets" (*tripiṭaka*), with the *vinaya* containing texts on monastic discipline, the *sūtra* texts on general Buddhist teaching and practice, and the *abhidharma* texts on advanced Buddhist doctrine. *Vinaya*, *sutra*, and *abhidharma* have this literal meaning, but they also have a more general and nonliteral meaning, where *vinaya* articulates an effective life rule, *sūtra* the basic Buddhist perspective on the suffering human condition and its transformation, and *abhidharma* the Buddhist teaching of the conditionality of all phenomenal existence. In the above quotation from the *Nettipakaraṇa*, we find both the literal and the nonliteral meaning of these terms active. In determining the authenticity of a text, we are told in effect "don't rely on the literal words of already authenticated Buddhist texts, but use instead the 'texts' (i.e., *vinaya*, *sūtra*, and *abhidharma*) in their broad and nonliteral senses." In this context, *vinaya* refers to that life rule that leads to the abatement of the defiling passions, *sūtra* to the basic and all encompassing teaching of the four noble truths (the truth of suffering, its cause in egocentricity, its possible cessation and the path to that end), and *abhidharma* to the conditioned co-production of all of existence, insight into which is liberation. In pointing to proper life rule, the four noble truths and conditioned co-production as the "texts" against which a proposed text must be compared to determine authenticity, it is thus the *spirit* of the Buddhist textual tradition that is being held up as standard rather than its *letter*. What is important for Buddhist tradition in determining textual authenticity is thus not purely or exclusively the validity of one term, idea or monastic rule against another, but rather such elements in the context of the overall impact of the textual tradition used properly, leading to the abatement of egocentricity, the following of the Buddhist path, and the attainment of liberation.

We see, then, the development of criteria of textual authenticity that are both literal and definite and also in keeping with the nonliteral Buddhist approach to authority. On the one hand, the text must be proposed from reliable external authority; on the other, such authority must be further and finally tested against the canons of Buddhist doctrine, not as literal words and phrases, but as living understanding.

It was in the context of such perspectives that the Buddhist canons of sacred scripture, identifying what each tradition considered to be legitimate *buddha-vacana*, came into being. In general, the viewpoints discussed above ruled out the possibility of their being any one single "Buddhist canon" accepted by all traditions. The emphasis on living experience and on the integrity of each tradition generally ensured the existence of more or less different canons for each of the major Buddhist traditions.

At the same time, certain common structures did inform the various early collections of *buddha-vacana*. One of the earliest of these structures is that of the *tripiṭaka* or "three baskets," that is the most common grouping of the Buddhist canons: the *vinaya-piṭaka* contains texts on individual and community discipline; the *sūtra-piṭaka* contains expositions of the basic Buddhist teachings; and the *abhidharma-piṭaka* contains more technical formulations of Buddhist doctrine. Most of the early Buddhist schools agreed both with the centrality of the concerns expressed in this grouping, and also with the grouping itself. However, characteristically, not all of the eighteen schools concurred, for the Sautrantikas remained with two pitakas, while the Mahāsāmghikas increased the number to five.

The disposition of the early *piṭakas* shows us some important things about the early canons. First, every sect had a *vinaya piṭaka* and its internal divisions and contents were either the same, or varied only slightly. Every tradition also had a *sūtra piṭaka* and here also one finds an often remarkable similarity of both internal divisions and contents. This commonality of the traditions' *vinaya* and *sūtra piṭakas* most likely reflects a common origin of texts, dating to a time before about 340 B.C.E. when schools began to split off from one another.

At the same time, one notices in the early *piṭaka* arrangements some important and revealing differences. The Theravādins and Sarvāstivādins both have *abhidharma piṭakas*, showing a common concern for *abhidharma*, but the structure and contents of the two *abhidharma piṭakas* are very different, indicating a time of composition posterior to the sectarian divisions. The Sautrāntikas possessed only the first two *piṭakas* because they rejected the status of the *abhidharma piṭaka* as *buddha vacana*, and disputed the validity of the *abhidharma* enterprise as a preeminent Buddhist concern. The Mahāsāmghikas accepted the three *piṭakas*, but added two more, the *kṣudraka piṭaka*, which appears to have been largely a rearrangement of material already existing within the *tripiṭaka* of the other schools, and a *dhāraṇī piṭaka*, which apparently contained material not found elsewhere. The Mahāsāmghikas also possessed a *vinaya piṭaka* containing a section on rules regulating behavior toward the Buddhist reliquary mounds (*stūpa*), a special concern of theirs. Many other similar characteristic divergencies could be cited within the early schools. Thus, in the canons of the early, pre-Mahāyānist, eighteen schools, one sees the above mentioned principles of textual authentication giving rise to collections of *buddha-vacana* that have certain basic elements in common, but also considerable divergencies. These reflect both areas of common development and interest among the schools, and also areas where the historical development and interests of the schools diverge.

When the Mahāyāna tradition arose about 200 B.C.E. and after, the question of the Buddhist canons became much more complex. The Mahāyānists, while accepting the validity of *buddha-vacana* of the *tripiṭaka* (in its Sarvāstivādin form), also accepted a great many additional *sūtras*, the new Mahāyāna texts, as no less (and in fact more) profoundly and legitimately *buddha-vacana* than those of the earlier *tripiṭaka*. These new texts included the many *sūtras* on the "perfection of transcendent knowledge" (prajñāpāramitā) and the many other types of Mahāyāna *sūtras* that appeared from 200 B.C.E. onwards. With the rise of the Vajrayāna some centuries later, an additional class of texts came to be accepted within some of the Mahāyāna schools as *buddha-vacana*, namely the *tantras*. When Buddhism moved north into central and east Asia, new canons were again in formation, including as *buddha-vacana*, much or all of the expanded Mahāyāna canon, and also additional texts regarded by their traditions with special veneration, that had not even been composed in India or in an Indian language at all.

Nevertheless, in this growing and developing tradition of sacred Buddhist scripture, one would be wrong to see an unprincipled or unchecked generation of texts. The principles outlined above define an essentially conservative position, where what has gone before is determinative, and the door is left no more than ajar for the inclusion of the fruits of fresh experience. As each Buddhist tradition matured in India and later in other lands, it faced squarely, and not always without difficulty, the need to balance two complementary tendencies: on the one hand the exigencies of a living tradition and the influx of inspiration from the highest sources; on the other, the necessity of maintaining the tradition's integrity and of subjecting unprecedented religious expression to the tests of logic and experience to determine its validity. What looks to us like a continual outpouring of new documents must be set in the context of the many centuries during which these developments occurred. No doubt *in situ*, the process was very slow.

THE PROPER USE AND INTERPRETATION OF AUTHORITATIVE TEXTS

Once the authenticity of a text has been established and the document has been set within its canon, a further question arises, of great importance to Buddhism: How should the text be approached and understood? In what way is its essential content or message to be disclosed? This is a particularly important issue for a tradition such as Buddhism where "the letter" of a text is explicitly only one factor in the larger hermeneutical situation. The basic Buddhist approach to this issue is outlined in the famous "four reliances" (*catuhpratisaranāni*), those objects of reliance upon which one is enjoined to depend as one follows the path to liberation. These "four reliances" stand at the center of the Buddhist hermeneutical enterprise in providing guidelines for the proper use of Buddhist texts. The "four reliances" form the main subject matter of the *Sūtra on the Four*

Reliances (*Catuhpratisarana Sūtra*). Although this text did not receive its definitive form until a time postdating the formation of the Buddhist canons, the ideas it contains were already in preparation in the most ancient Buddhist texts.[27]

The essential matter of this text as quoted in the *Abhidharmakośa-vyākhya*, where it appears in its Sanskrit form, runs as follows:

> *dharmaḥ pratisaraṇaṃ na pudgalaḥ*
> The *dharma* is the refuge, not the man (*pudgalaḥ*).
>
> *arthaḥ pratisaraṇaṃ na vyañjanam*
> The meaning (*artha*) is the refuge, not the letter (*vyanjanam*).
>
> *nītārthaṃ sūtram pratisaraṇaṃ na neyārtham*
> Those *sūtras* which are direct in meaning (*nītārthaṃ*), are the refuge, not those which are indirect in meaning (*neyārtham*).
>
> *jñānaṃ pratisaraṇaṃ na vijñānam*
> Direct intuition (*jñāna*) is the refuge, not discursive thought (*vijñānam*).[28]

In this foundational statement of Buddhist hermeneutics, a hierarchy of values is established in the use and interpretation of texts. It is not that the second members in each phrase (the person, the letter, indirect *sūtras*, discursive thought) are here held to be without value, but rather that their place is clearly secondary to the first (the *dharma*, the meaning, direct *sūtras*, direct intuition). Once the primacy of the first members of each pair is established, then the value of the second may be properly appreciated.

1. *The* dharma *is the refuge, not the man.*

Wherein lies the power of a text for Buddhism? It does not lie in the authority of the person who originated it, however high human estimation of him may be. Nor does it lie in the authority of the group that may accept it as canonical. The power resides in the *dharma* or teaching of the text itself.

Does this mean to deny any positive value of refuge in "the person?" Not at all. In fact, reliance upon the Buddha as example and upon the rest of the external Buddhist tradition that he founded is held up as the necessary relative means which makes possible ultimate refuge in the "*dharma*." Thus, "the *dharma* is the refuge, not the man" means to set things in their proper order and establish priorities.

This "refuge" does not quite amount to a denial of the sanctity of the "person"—the Buddha or any teacher for that matter—as over against the "teaching." To hold this would be to make an assumption of the separateness of Buddha and *dharma* which would be incorrect. In fact, Buddhist tradition considers a Buddha precisely one who fully embodies enlightenment concerning what things are. In that sense, most profoundly, the Buddha and the *dharma* are not two. Thus the Buddha speaking in the *Samyutta-nikāya*: "What is there, Vakkali, in seeing this vile body? Who so sees Dhamma sees me; who so sees me, sees Dhamma. Seeing Dhamma, Vakkali, he sees me; seeing me, he sees Dhamma."[29] And this is the meaning of the oft quoted "He who sees *pratītyasamutpāda*, sees the *dharma*, and he who sees the *dharma*, sees he Buddha."[30]

In other words, he who sees the conditionedness and interconnectedness of life (and in seeing oneself as part of that conditionedness realizes that there is no autonomous entity corresponding to the term "ego"), in effect sees the *dharma*, or the fundamental message that the Buddha has to teach. And he who sees the *dharma* in that way, sees the Buddha, in other words, sees who the Buddha really and fundamentally is. Thus, this refuge is not opposing two separate realities, but insisting on a hierarchy of insight: on the relative level, the Buddha is seen as a "person" in whom one may take refuge; on the level of matured insight, one discovers the *dharma*, inseparable from the Buddha, as the ultimate refuge.

2. *The meaning (*artha*) is the refuge, not the letter (*vyañjana*).*

The second refuge addresses a question raised by the first: if one says that the *dharma* is the refuge and not the man, then what precisely is meant by the term "*dharma*"? Our discussion of the three jewels stated that *dharma*, the second jewel, is understood to have both an internal and an external dimension. It is with these two dimensions of dharma that this second refuge deals. In the present context, the external dimension of *dharma*, *dharma* as literal texts, is indicated by the term *vyañjana*, the letter. The internal dimension of *dharma*, the living understanding or realization to which the words point, is indicated by the term *artha*, or meaning. The *Laṅkāvatāra Sūtra*, an important Mahāyāna text of the Yogācāra school, further clarifies these two dimensions in the following quotation. Here the external dimension of *dharma* is referred to by the term *deśanā* or "external teaching," while the internal dimension is referred to as *siddhānta* or "personal realization."

> Twofold are the aspects of personal realization (*siddhānta*) . . . the personal realization itself (*siddhānta*) and the external teaching (*deśanā*) about it. . . . The "personal realization" itself indicates the incomparability of personal experience, and is characterized by having nothing to do with words, discriminations, and letters. . . . What is meant by the external teaching (*deśanā*)? It is variously given in the nine divisions of the doctrinal works; it keeps one away from the dualistic notions of being and non-being, of oneness and otherness; first making use of skillful means and expedients, it induces

all beings to have a perception (of this teaching) so that whoever is inclined towards it, may be instructed in it.[31]

The fact that *siddhānta* is used both as the collective term for both members ("twofold are the aspects of personal realization . . .") and as the highest member of the pair, "external teaching" and "personal realization," is important. This indicates that *siddhānta* applies to both "external teaching" and "personal realization" and that the literal, external *dharma* is seen in light of, and as a stepping stone to, the *dharma* as realized. This indicates again, that the two members of the refuge are not opposing categories, but rather the relative, pedagogical and the ultimate, realized dimensions of the same thing (*siddhānta*).

This raises a further question. What is the precise relationship between the external dimension of *dharma*, or the "letter" and the internal dimension or meaning? In this context, several issues need to be discussed, including the question of the positive and/or negative relationship between "letter" and "meaning"; the issue of whether the literal text has any value on its own; the related issue of whether adhering to texts alone has any merit; and the question as to whether the literal dimension of texts can ever be dispensed with.

a. *The resonance between letter* (vyañjana) *and the meaning or realization* (artha). Enlightenment in all Buddhist traditions is understood to be the clear, unfettered, selfless experience of "things as they are," or phenomena in their natural state. According to Buddhist tradition, the precise nature of phenomena is described by the term "conditioned co-production" (*pratītyasamutpāda*), and refers to the fact that everything that exists is conditioned: it arose from a congeries of causes, exists in interdependence, and—in conjunction with the potentially infinite number of events in the universe at this present moment—will give rise to consequences or results. As a corollary to this, life is seen as impermanent and constantly changing. The notion of "conditioned co-production" applies not only to the natural world, but to the social world of human beings and even to the most intimate workings of each human personality. Every phenomenon is conditioned, interdependent, and conditioning. The suffering that characterizes life proceeds from ignorance about this universally conditioned situation and from the attempt of each person to assert his or her own existence, autonomy, and permanence in the face of contrary fact. On the other hand, to see the universal conditionedness is to be free from that conditioning and to touch the unconditioned. This knowledge is *nirvāṇa* and frees one, so it is said, from suffering.

The particular relationship of the conditioned world to the unconditioned is seen in Buddhism as critical for the spiritual path. Language itself, as part of the conditioned world, may have either a concordant or a discordant relationship to reality. When discordant, it expresses views that are inimical to human awakening, such as "reality contains permanence; if I have not found it, it is because I have not tried hard enough." When concordant with reality, language expresses views which are conducive to awakening, such as "reality is impermanent."

This is why the notion of "right view" plays such an important role in the various expressions of the Buddhist path. In the noble eightfold path, the early and fundamental statement of the Buddhist path, "right view" is the first step on the path. One must have a conceptual understanding of reality that is harmonious, at least on the conceptual level, with reality itself, as the necessary ground upon which the practice of meditation can be carried out successfully and wisdom developed. The classical later division of the path into "view" (darśana), "practice" (caryā), and "action" (karma) establishes the same necessity for a correct view at the beginning. This need for "right view" indicates the vital importance of the philosophical enterprise in Buddhism, and why so many major Buddhist philosophical schools have developed in Indian and non-Indian Buddhism. It also indicates the secondary and pedagogical role of Buddhist philosophy as no more than a stepping-stone, in conjunction with meditation, to wisdom.

b. *The value of the literal text.* The texts of Buddhism, and above all those held to be *buddha-vacana*, are considered the prime embodiments of "right view" in literal verbal form. The commentarial tradition in Buddhism, the tradition of works by human authors, is understood to clarify *buddha-vacana*. The *buddha-vacana* and its commentaries are then typically used by Buddhist teachers who will comment on the *buddha-vacana*, using the categories and interpretations of the written commentary, adding further spontaneous commentary to elucidate the *buddha-vacana*.

The foundation of these written and oral commentarial efforts is thus the text itself, and in past and contemporary Buddhist traditions, there is great respect for the literal words of the texts, and an adherence to them that in the West might be considered almost slavish. Buddhist tradition generally holds that the closer one adheres to the literal texts, making only those commentarial bridges absolutely necessary for understanding, the more nonconceptual wisdom can be provoked in the hearers. The roots of this respect for the "letter" of the texts are found in the earliest Buddhist traditions. Lamotte quotes the *Dīgha nikāya* (one of the five sections of the

Sūtra piṭaka) to the effect that is was necessary for the competent Buddhist teacher to be equally proficient in both the letter and the meaning of the texts.[32] If, on the contrary, a religious person were proficient in the letter, but not in the meaning, "his colleagues must patiently reprimand him and say to him, 'This verbal formulation (which we accept as you do), doesn't it have this meaning here rather than that meaning there?' If a religious person grasps the sense well, but adopts a defective expression, one says to him, 'In order to articulate this sense (upon which we are in agreement), wouldn't this verbal formulation be more expedient than that one?' The good speaker is the one who is inaccurate neither with the spirit nor with the letter."[33]

Certainly the monk who limits himself to memorizing texts alone, without grasping their meaning, has not quite fulfilled the intent of the dharma. Thus, the Majjhima nikāya (another section of the Sūtra Piṭaka) states: "There are some foolish ones who learn the dharma by heart, sūtras, geya, etc., but who have learned it by heart without having examined the sense in order to (actually) understand the texts. These texts, of which they have not examined the sense in order to understand them, do not delight them at all; and the only advantage they gain from their memorization is in the area of contradicting (their adversaries) and making citations. However, they do not attain the end for which one memorizes the dharma. These texts badly understood will leave them miserable and unhappy for a long time. And why? Because these texts have been badly understood."[34]

However, there is one thing worse than not understanding what one has memorized, namely, memorizing the texts badly. As Lamotte comments, "He who memorizes the dharma like a parrot at least has the merit of transmitting it in a literal form without error. But there are some monks who 'memorize texts which are poorly understood and whose phrases are erroneously put together';[35] these monks contribute to the confusion and destruction of the dharma. In effect, when the form is defective, all hope of arriving at the correct meaning is lost: 'If the phrases and phonemes are erroneously put together, the meaning is impossible to recover.'"[36]

The literal text may not be an end in itself, but it is the necessary and revered means without which the end cannot be attained.

c. *The relative merit of adhering to texts alone.* It might be concluded from the foregoing that, in spite of the importance in Buddhism of the literal text, the tradition would not look with favor on one who adhered to the literal text alone, without understanding. Such is not quite the case. In fact, just as one whose wisdom is imperfect is counseled to rely on the authentic teacher, so one whose understanding of the meaning of the text is undeveloped does well to rely on the text alone, to prepare the way for greater insight. Thus, in the *Saṃdhinirmocana Sūtra*, (a proto-Yogācārin work), the Buddha says, "There are beings who do not understand the true meaning (of this text), nevertheless, they adhere to (the text) and have faith in it. They adhere to it saying, 'This *sūtra* preached by the Blessed One is profound, and (its meaning) is difficult to see, difficult to know, beyond (verbal) discussion, alien to (verbal) discussion, subtle and known by the wise ones. . . . The knowledge and the view of the *Tathāgata* are infinite; our own knowledge and our view are like the plodding of a cow.' In this spirit, they revere this *sūtra*, they copy it out, they transmit it, spread it abroad, venerate it, teach it and read and study it. All the while, they do not understand my true intention, they are incapable of carrying out the meditation. In this way, their accumulation of merit and wisdom grows and, finally, those who had not ripened their beings, do ripen their beings." [37]

How can reliance on the text without understanding lead one toward enlightenment? Reverence of a *sūtra* such as the *Saṃdhinirmocana* makes possible the development of positive merit, a traditional way of talking about the development of basic psychological health and positive predisposition toward the future through positive moral actions such as kindness to others, revering great texts and teachers and so on. Out of these acts, "merit" can be accumulated, and wisdom can be developed. Thus, although refuge in the meaning of a text is the best refuge, reliance on the word alone is laudable if it is appropriate to one's level of development.

d. *The question of dispensing with the letter.* In Buddhist tradition there is not only an emphasis on the need for priority of meaning over the letter. As well, one sometimes finds a rejection of the letter and of the text altogether. Thus, the great Tibetan yogi Milarepa (11th–12th centuries C.E.), who spent most of his life in retreat in the Himalayas near Mt. Everest, declares in one of his songs: "Texts? I don't need texts. Phenomena are all the texts I need." [38] And the great Indian Vajrayānist-to-be, Nāropa (11th century C.E.), while a famous scholar at the renowned Nālandā University in North India, one day realized that he knew the words of the great texts by heart, but he had not understood their meaning. In disgust, he threw the books away and headed out into the jungle in search of a teacher who could help him find the meaning. [39]

Again, this attitude has its roots in the earliest Indian Buddhist tradition. Lamotte indicates these roots when he quotes the celebrated encounter between Śāriputra, one of Buddha's chief disciples, and Aśvajit, one of the five first disciples of the Buddha. "This latter had just barely embraced the new faith when he was questioned by Śāriputra on the doctrine of Śākyamuni. He tried at first to demur: 'Friend,' he said to Śāriputra, 'I am only a novice and it is not long since I renounced the world; it is altogether recently that I have embraced this doctrine and this discipline. I cannot expound this doctrine to you in all its extension, but I can indicate briefly to you its spirit.' Then Śāriputra, the wandering monk, said to venerable Aśvajit: 'Let it be thus, my friend. Tell me little or much, but speak to me of the spirit; it is the spirit only of which I have need; why be so preoccupied with the letter?'" [40]

This example and the previous ones indicate, in Lamotte's words, that "there are cases where the letter must be sacrificed to the spirit." [41] In fact, ultimately in every Buddhist's training, there comes a time when the supports and means of the tradition must be left behind. But according to Buddhist tradition, this best happens through the agency of the (relative) methodologies of the tradition, at the heart of which is the sacred text. Only when the letter is revered, well-learned and integrated, can one take the final step, knowing what one is abandoning and how it can (and must) be abandoned. Thus, Milarepa had trained, albeit unconventionally, under his teacher Marpa in the Buddhist doctrines for many arduous years before making the above statement, and Nāropa was considered one of the most learned Buddhist scholars in north India when he left Nālandā.

3. *Those sūtras which are direct in meaning (nītārtha) are the refuge, not those that are indirect in meaning (neyārtha).*

The second refuge, "the meaning is the refuge and not the letter," raises a further important question. What is the nature of *buddha-vacana* of which one is directed to use the letter as a stepping-stone to the profound meaning? Specifically, is it held by Buddhist tradition that there is one consistent *buddha-vacana*? If so, how does the tradition account for historical diversity? If not, how is the issue of inconsistencey and contradiction understood?

The third refuge, relying on *sūtras* of direct meaning, not those which are indirect, means to acknowledge diversity within *buddha-vacana* and also to provide a hermeneutic to make sense of that diversity. In effect, the third refuge is saying that within *buddha-vacana*, as expressed in the *sūtra* literature, (a) there are significant differences, (b) these refer to differences in the ultimacy of the "view," and (c) one should rely on those *sūtras* and words which express the true and ultimate meaning (*nītārtha*) of the Buddha, not upon those *sūtras* and words wherein the Buddha speaks with a meaning that is partial, incomplete and in need of interpretation (*neyārtha*).

The recognition of inconsistency and even apparent contradiction in *buddha-vacana* is present from the very beginning of Buddhist history. Buddha's ministry spanned about forty-five years, and one can only imagine the vast extent of his teaching during this period. Moreover, Buddhism judges the validity of a teaching primarily by its situational, pedagogical efficacy, rather than by abstract criteria detached from the pedagogical context. Clearly the Buddha taught many different kinds of people, from differing backgrounds, with dissimilar psychological make-ups and with varying levels of understanding. To each he taught in a characteristic way according to the needs and capacities of the hearer.

The result is amply reflected in the earliest Buddhist texts where one finds a rich variety of metaphors, of practices, and of doctrine itself. And, as Buddhist tradition developed historically, the ongoing pedagogical emphasis of the Buddha's teaching was maintained and the original diverse trends led themselves to further diversity.

In a real sense, this original and later diversity does not pose a fundamental threat to Buddhism's own self-understanding, given its particular appreciation of conditionality in general, its affirmation of language as relative, and its pedagogical nature as a tradition. But, if texts and doctrines are to be viewed as pedagogies, then one feels perhaps particularly obliged to make sense of those texts and doctrines in a clear and methodologically consistent manner. Such in fact has been the case in Buddhism, and this is the issue with which the third refuge deals.

The earliest Buddhist schools could point to their own *sūtras* to demonstrate that the Buddha had taught differently to individuals of differing needs: "to Phālguna who believed in the existence of the soul and of the personality, and who asked what is the being that touches, feels, desires, and grasps, the Buddha replied: 'A stupid question! I deny that there is a being who touches, feels, desires or seizes.'"[42] However, "to Vatsagotra who had believed in the existence of an 'I' but believed no longer, and who asked if it was absolutely true that the 'I' did not exist, the Buddha refused to respond in the negative, 'in order not to confirm the doctrines of monks and of *brāhmins* who believe in annihilation.'"[43]

Again, sometimes the Buddha spoke in the conventional language of ordinary people, such as when he used the pronouns "you" and "he" and even when he spoke of himself as "an individual (who) is born into the world, born for the welfare of the many."[44] On other occasions, the Buddha declined to speak of individuals, but spoke of the phenomena corresponding to "individual" in terms of causes and conditions, as in the doctrine of "conditioned co-production."

These examples involve contradictions, at least when taken literally. In order to establish clarity and methodological consistency in the interpretation of their texts, Buddhists from the earliest times made the two-fold distinction originally articulated by the Buddha himself, corresponding to *nītārtha* (direct meaning) and *neyārtha* (indirect meaning). On the one hand were those words and texts where the Buddha spoke in an unsurpassed literal form with the highest degree of concordance with realtiy (*nītārtha*), as in the teachings about "conditioned co-production." On the other hand were words and *sūtras* where he spoke in a more conventional way of "I" and "he" and of "individuals," which words and *sūtras* represent a lower, more conventional form of expression, having less concordance with reality and in need of interpretation (*neyārtha*).

The logic of such a hermeneutic is ably articulated by the great second century Mahāyānist doctor, Nāgārjuna: "The *dharma* of the Buddha is immense, like the ocean. According to the dispositions of beings, it is preached in diverse manners: sometimes it speaks of existence and sometimes of non-existence, of eternity or impermanence, of suffering or happiness, of the I or of the non-I; sometimes it teaches the diligent exercise of the threefold activity (body, speech and mind) which includes all the good *dharmas*, other times it teaches that all *dharmas* are essentially inactive. Such are the many and diverse teachings: the ignorant who hear them take them for a wicked error; but the wise who penetrate the threefold teaching of the *dharma* know that all the words of the Buddha are true *dharma*, and do not contradict one another." [45]

Nāgārjuna is here acknowledging the tremendous variety of teachings understood in his own times as *buddha-vacana*, and is affirming the legitimacy of that appellation. Behind this affirmation is a recognition of the necessity of a variety of teachings to communicate with the diversity of sentient beings' dispositions and capacities.

In the course of Indian Buddhist history, major trends of early Buddhism became established in a few prominent and influential branches of Buddhism, each with its own schools and subschools. Thus, beginning already in the fourth century B.C.E., the beginnings of the eighteen Hīnayāna schools appear on the scene, schools which would exhibit most of the trends which appear later as the Mahāyāna and Vajrayāna ("Diamond Vehicle," 5th C.E., ff.) Sometime before the beginning of the common era the Mahāyāna appeared in the form of the prajñāpāramitā sūtras ("sūtras on transcendent knowledge") which were followed by other early seminal Mahāyāna *sūtras* such as the *Lotus Sūtra* and the *Samdhinirmocana Sūtra*. Alongside the *sūtras* of the Mahāyāna one finds developing in the early centuries C.E. the two major Mahāyānist commentarial traditions, both understood to be based on the prajñāpāramitā, namely that of the Mādhyamika ("tradition of the middle way"), whose chief early articulator was Nāgārjuna (2nd century C.E.) and that of the Yogācāra ("tradition of meditative practice"), whose chief early articulator was Asaṅga, (4th century C.E.) the latter drawing much of his inspiration from the *Saṃdhinirmocana Sūtra*.

Finally, in the middle centuries of the first millenium of the common era, a further Buddhist trend surfaced in North India, that of the Vajrayāna, with a strong emphasis on meditation and doctrinally aligned with, but different from, the Yogācāra. Each of these major branches of Buddhism had its own sub-schools and movements, and traditions grew up as well on the boundaries between the major branches.

Each Buddhist tradition, Hīnāyanist, Mahāyānist, or Vajrayānist, understood itself to be founded on *buddha-vacana*, and specifically on one or more of the major *sūtras* and *tantras* (literature of the Vajrayāna, understood also as Buddha word) that came to be extant in India. As one may well expect, these various *sūtras* and *tantras* and their consequent traditions speak with one voice far less even than the earliest traditions. Significantly enough, it was always the third refuge with its distinction between *nītārtha* and *neyārtha* that enabled Buddhism to clarify and to make sense of the manifold, inconsistent, and sometimes contradictory variety of Buddha word. Put briefly, the notion of *nītartha* and *neyārtha* has enabled each Buddhist tradition to affirm the unsurpassability of the *sūtras* and/or doctrines it considers ultimate (*nītārtha*), while being enabled to affirm the relative validity and usefulness of other Buddhist teachings (*neyārtha*).

As an illustration of the application of the notions of *nītartha* and *neyārtha*, we may consider the Mahāyāna tradition, which articulates nītārtha and neyārtha through the concept of the "turnings of the wheel of *dharma*," (*dharma-cakrapravartana*), understood as those pivotal occasions upon which the Buddha Śākyamuni first "turned the wheel of dharma," i.e., presented the seminal Buddhist teachings, at the Deer Park in Benares, when he taught the four noble truths (as in the *Dhammacakka-pavatana sutta*)[46] to his five former companions. Under this "turning" fall all of the Hīnayāna texts of the Tripiṭaka and their related doctrines. This is the only "turning of the wheel" accepted by all Buddhist traditions.

The Mahāyāna, however, understands itself to derive from a "second turning of the wheel of *dharma*."[47] Developing further the early Buddhist notion that the Buddha could teach in a "body" other than his human, physical one, the Mahāyāna speaks of his preaching on Vulture Peak Mountain, outside of Rājagṛha, during his lifetime, but in a celestial form. There he preached the *Prajñāpāramitā Sūtras*, articulating the Central Mahāyāna notion of Śūnyatā, emptiness. These *sūtras* are held to have been kept secret until humans had developed the maturity and insight to understand them, at which time they were spread abroad by Nāgārjuna. Grouped under this turning are the Mahāyāna *sūtras* and teachings which set forth mainly emptiness.

The Mahāyāna also knows of a "third turning of the wheel of dharma," which is presented in the *Saṃdhinirmocana Sūtra*. Like the second turning, the third turning is likewise said to have occurred during the lifetime of the Buddha, having been preached in a limitless palace in a form even more celestial than that of the second turning. In this third turning, the second turning doctrine of emptiness is accepted, and a further distinction is made between three levels of truth (*trisvabhāva*): the level of ordinary samsaric truth (such as "ego exists"), the level of relative truth devoid of conceptual distortion, as expressed in the doctrine of *pratītyasamutpāda*, and the level of emptiness itself. Grouped under this turning are all the sutras and teachings on Buddha nature (*tathāgatagarbha*).

The *Saṃdhinirmocana Sūtra* on the three turnings:

> First of all, in the Deer Park at Ṛsipatana in Varansi, for the sake of those involved in the disciple vehicle, the Lord turned a wonderful, amazing wheel of Dharma, such as had never before been turned in the world by men or gods, and he showed the (sixteen) aspects of the Four Holy Truths. Yet even that wheel of Dharma turned by the Lord was surpassable, provisory, interpretable in meaning, and subject to dispute. Then the Lord, for the sake of those involved in the Mahāyāna, turned a second wheel of Dharma even more wonderful and amazing, by proclaiming voidness, starting from the fact of the unreality, uncreatedness, ceaselessness, primordial peace, and natural liberation of all things. Nevertheless, even this wheel of Dharma was surpassable, provisory, interpretable, and subject to dispute. Finally, the Lord, for the sake of those involved in all vehicles, turned the third wheel of Dharma by showing the fine discrimination (of things), addressing the fact of the unreality, uncreatedness, ceaselessness, primordial peace, and natural liberation of all things. And this turning of the wheel of Dharma by the Lord was unsurpassed, not provisory, definitive in meaning, and left no room for dispute.[48]

The various Mahāyāna Buddhist traditions differently apply the notions of *nītārtha* and *neyārtha* to these three turnings. All agree that the first turning is *neyārtha*, and needs to be understood in light of later turnings. Traditions strictly following the Mādhyamika will accept the second turning as nītārtha, and the first and third as neyārtha. This amounts to an insistence on the ultimacy of the presentation of emptiness in the second turning. Traditions aligned with the Yogācāra and the Samdhinirmocana Sūtra will accept the third turning only as nītārtha, and will see both the first and second turnings as neyārtha, or in need of further interpretation to be properly understood. Traditions drawing equally on the Madhyamika and Yogācāra will accept both second and third turnings as nītārtha, and hold that only the first turning is neyārtha.

This heremeneutical approach of periodizing the Buddhist teachings and classifying them according to the "level" they represent was not only a central Buddhist hermeneutical strategy in India, but was used to great advantage in the new cultures to which Buddhism traveled. Thus, to give just one of many possible examples, the great Chinese Buddhist scholar Chih-i classified the Buddhist teachings according to "five periods" extending from three to five the major promulgations of the Buddha.[49] According to Chih-i, after his enlightenment, the Buddha first preached the highest teaching embodied in the Avatamsaka Sūtra during a period of some three weeks. However, most present were unable to understand it, so the Buddha then preached the four noble truths in the Hīnayāna Āgamas, for twelve years, corresponding to the first turning of the wheel above. Thirdly, for eight years, the Buddha preached a teaching of transition between Hīnayāna and Mahāyāna embodied in what are called the Vāipulya sūtras. Fourthly, he preached the Prajñāpāramitā Sūtras, with their notion of emptiness (śūnyatā) for twenty-two years, corresponding to the second turning of the wheel above. Finally, he preached the supremacy of the Lotus Sutra (Saddharmapuṇḍarīka Sūtra) for eight years, to which Chih-i as a T'ien-t'ai (Lotus School) master was particularly devoted, corresponding structurally (but not in content) to the third turning of the wheel above. The important point is that while there is a unique arrangement of contents in Chih-i's systemization, the hermeneutical device remains the same: each doctrine the Buddha taught is held to be true, but its truth held to differ according to the level of ultimacy that it represents, as intially articulated in the nītārtha/neyārtha distinction.

Obviously, the notions of nītārtha and neyārtha as applied to the turnings of the wheel of dharma and to their correlate sūtras and as elaborated in later hermeneutical systems become the way in which each Buddhist tradition can understand its own sūtras in relation to those of other Buddhist traditions. But this raises the further question: how is that relationship understood? The answer may be found by citing an example from the eighth century Mahāyānist work, the *Bodhicaryāvatāra of Śāntideva*.[50]

The *Bodhicaryāvatāra*, one of the most important and influential of Indian Mahayanist works, belongs to the central (*prasanghika*) Mādhyamika tradition, thus accepting the second turning as *nītārtha*, and the first and third as *neyārtha*. The culmination of the text occurs in the ninth chapter on *prajñāpāramitā*, where the teaching of *śūnyatā* is expounded.[51] Two parallel lines of reasoning are followed in this chapter: either the author refutes various criticisms of *śūnyatā* put forth by opponents, or he himself criticizes other prominent viewpoints current at the time, both Buddhist and non-Buddhist. In particular, the text critiques proponents of both the first turning (the Hīnayānist "Vaibhāṣikas") and the third turning (the Mahāyānist "Cittamātrins" = Yogācārins) each of whom wants to advance his own view as *nītārtha*.

What is important is that neither of these other Buddhist traditions is rejected outright as entirely wrong. In the text and its commentaries, it is merely asserted that the viewpoint put forward by the rival traditions is not ultimately true. Nevertheless, these teachings are relatively true, and have their value within the overall spiritual path of Buddhism. Thus, the Vaibhāṣika puts forward the notion of momentariness (*kṣaṇikatva*) by which he means to indicate the doctrine that reality is atomistic, composed of tiny units of experience with no duration, which beings in their ignorance take to be a world of more or less permanence and substantiality. This doctrine the Vaibhāṣika wants to put forward as *nītārtha* or ultimate.

Śāntideva, through his commentator, does not say that this doctrine is completely wrong. He replies rather, "such statements have to be interpreted (i.e., are *neyārtha*). Having in mind their mere apparent nature, the Protector Buddha taught things to be impermanent for the sake of progressively guiding ordinary people who conveive of true existence (towards a correct understanding). But, in actuality, such things are not truly momentary. . . . but rather empty."[52] In other words, this teaching was taught by the Buddha as a provisional teaching (*neyārtha*) to help beings, but is not ultimate (*nītārtha*). The same view is taken of the Cittamātra (Yogācāra) teachings of the third turning: they correspond to a more advanced stage of development than those of the first turning, but they are still *neyārtha*.[53]

In other words, the various major types of *buddha-vacana*, as defined by the turnings of the wheel of *dharma*, are all authentic Buddhism, but they are not equal. They correspond to and are efficacious at different stages on the spiritual path. The Venerable Gyalsap, Rinpoche, a contemporary Tibetan Buddhist, commenting on the *Bodhicaryāvatāra*, pertinently observes:

> In the text, one finds the various Buddhist schools refuting one another, as one moves to finer and finer understanding. As one moves from higher to higher, or from truer to truer view, these various schools point out the errors of the limited views of lesser systems. This is the ongoing spiritual process of realizing how slightly faulted a lower or previous view is. Through this process, one sees the slight error of the limited nature of one's previous understanding, and one's view becomes higher, then eventually one realizes the slight error of limitation in this view and so on. This process goes on until final realization. In Sāntideva's text, the belief in ego is refuted by the Hīnayānists, their belief in momentariness is refuted by the Cittamātrins, and their doctrine of mind is refuted by the Mādhyamika.[54]

Thus, the third refuge, through the notion of the three turnings and its later developments accomplishes several things:

a. It acknowledges the authenticity of the various major Buddhist *sūtras* and their derivative schools. Such acknowledgment permits the mutual acceptance of one another as authentically Buddhist by the various Buddhist traditions.

b. It also establishes a hierarchy among the various traditions, a hierarchy organized differently by different traditions. Thus the "truth claims" of the various Buddhist traditions that are not one's own are accepted but are qualified in the degree of ultimacy accorded them.

c. This hierarchy is practical, with each stage representing a step on the spiritual path. This enables each tradition to accept and adopt the doctrines and practices of other traditions in a relatively valued position.

d. This general hermeneutic has enabled each new development in Buddhism to approach previous developments with an attitude of incorporation rather than exclusion, a factor that has no doubt contributed to the richness and strength of the later Buddhist traditions (e.g., the Vajrayaña, Tibetan Buddhism).

4. *Direct knowledge (jñāna) is the refuge, not discursive thought (vijñāna).*

The fourth and final refuge summarizes the list of refuges and completes our discussion of some attitudes to sacred text in Buddhism. Having identified the authentic sacred text, one then approaches and makes use of that text through the agency of the refuges. First, one understands that it is the *dharma*, the teaching, not the man, however revered, that is ultimately at issue. Then, one must master "the letter" as a stepping-stone to the ultimate refuge of "the meaning." Third, one must recognize the diversity of "views" in the texts, appreciate how each represents a valuable and useful step on the spiritual path, all the while recognizing which is the ultimate teaching text. All of this done, however, one must take the final step implied by and pointed to by the previous refuges: one must oneself pass beyond the relative world of the conceptual mind or discursive consciousness (*vijñāna*) to the direct intuition (*jñāna*) of reality itself. The *Laṅkāvatāra Sūtra* characterizes *vijñāna* and *jñāna*:

> Vijñāna is subject to birth and destruction and falls into (the dualities) of form and no form, being and non-being. It is characterized by multiplicity and accumulation, and attaches itself to the multitudinousness of objects. Jñāna is transcendental knowledge, free from the dualism of being and non-being. Jñāna is not subject to birth and destruction. It belongs to (those) who see into the state of no-birth and no annihilation, and realize the egolessness of the Buddhas.[55]

It is only here, at the point of enlightenment, that the ultimate purpose of the textual tradition of Buddhism is fulfilled. The relation of "sacred text" to that goal is fittingly summarized by Jamgon Kongtrul, the great nineteenth-century Tibetan Buddhist teacher:

> The great mind of the Buddhas of the three times, loftily known as the body of reality (*dharma-kāya*) and the great symbol (*mahāmudrā*) and so revered, simply refers to one's own mind.
>
> To understand the essense of one's own mind, is the ultimate instruction of the holy ones. There certainly is no other teaching beyond that. And it is this that is the quintessence of all the collections of the *sūtras* and *tantras*.[56]

This statement is challenging in the same way that the Buddhist tradition of sacred texts as a whole is challenging. The validity of this equation of one's fundamental nature with the essence of shelves upon shelves of written texts is, at least at face value, not obvious. Since one side of the equation, one's enlightened nature, is an engaging but largely theoretical postulation, Jamgon Kongtrul leaves the reader who wishes to prove the equation little choice but to learn the language, read the texts, study their interpretations, and follow their methodologies. At the same time, what one can expect from all of this remains to be seen, and little more than suggestion is said in this regard either by Jamgon Kongtrul or by other Buddhist texts. This quotation from Jamgon Kongtrul, then, epitomizes the Buddhist attitude toward the sacred text, an attitude that is studious and reverential on the one side, but also not without an awareness of relativity and a sense of humor. And these latter are, from the Buddhist viewpoint, nothing other than an expression within the grim and struggling world, of the ultimate itself.

NOTES

1. The following article owes a special debt to the work of the great Buddhologist, Etienne Lamotte. The interested reader is referred in particular to the following four essays by Lamotte, reference to which is made below: Etienne Lamotte, "La critique d'authenticité dans le bouddhisme," *India Antiqua*, published in honor of J. Ph. Vogel, Leyden, 1947, pp. 213–22; "La critique d'interprétation dans le bouddhisme," *Annuaire de l'Institut de philologie et d'histoire orientales et slaves*, Bruxelles, No. 9, 1949, pp. 341–61; "Sur la formation du Mahāyāna," *Asiatica: Festschrift Friedrich Weller*, Leipzig: O. Harrassowitz, 1954, pp. 377–96; "Légendes et traditions bouddhiques," *Histoire du bouddhisme indien*, Louvain: Institut orientaliste, 1958, pp. 136–235. All translations from Lamotte's French below are mine.
2. T. W. Rhys-Davids, *Book of the Great Decease (Mahāparinibbāna Suttanta)*, Sacred Books of the East Series, Vol. IX, Delhi: Motilal Banarsidass, reprint, 1968, pp. 35ff.
3. Lamotte, "Critique d'authenticité . . .", p. 213.
4. Both the human and the trans-human aspects of the Buddha's personality are critical to an understanding of who Buddha Śākyamuni was. Lamotte tells us that from the earliest days of Buddhism, the Buddha was seen, on the one hand, as a human being; on the other, as a person who embodied ultimate reality (*dharma-kāya*, "body of truth itself"), bounded neither by time nor space (*Histoire*, p. 689). "Nothing is gained by seeing the Buddha in his material and corruptible body. It is rather necessary to see him in his *dharma-kāya*, that is to say, in his teaching. . . . (as the texts say), to see the *dharma-kāya* is to (truly) see the Buddha." (Ibid.) Edward Conze (*Buddhist Thought in India*, London: George Allen and Unwin, Ltd., 1962, pp. 168–72) similarly insists on the essentiality of the transcendent "body" of the Buddha in the earliest tradition. On this same issue see André Bareau, "The Superhuman Personality of the Buddha and Its Symbolism in the *Mahāparinirvāṇa* Sūtra of the Dharma-guptaka," in *Myths and Symbols: Studies in Honor of Mircea Eliade*, edited by Joseph M. Kitagawa and Charles H. Long, Chicago: University of Chicago Press, 1969, pp. 9–21.
5. Thus in the Malindapañha we are told that, regarding the components of their transcendent personalities, "all Buddhas are exactly the same," (Edward Conze [trans.], *Buddhist Texts Through the Ages*, New York: Harper and Row Torchbook, 1964, pp. 109–10). The full quotation reads, "There is no distinction between any of the Buddhas in physical beauty, moral habit, concentra-

tion, wisdom, freedom, cognition and insight of freedom, the four confidences, the ten powers of a Tathāgata, the six special cognitions, the fourteen cognitions of Buddhas, the eighteen Buddha-dhammas, in the word in all the dhammas of Buddhas, for all Buddhas are exactly the same as regards Buddha-dhammas." (Ibid.) The Laṅkāvatāra Sūtra, from the Indian Yogācāra tradition, elaborates this point in the following dialogue. The interlocutor asks the Buddha, "What did you mean when you said, 'I am all the Buddhas of the past?'" to which the Buddha replies, "What has been realized by the Tathāgatas, that is my own realization . . . The ancient road of reality has been here all the time . . . whether the Tathāgata appears in the world or not . . . What has been realized by myself and other Tāthagatas is this reality, the eternally abiding reality, the suchess of things, the realness of things, the truth itself . . . Between myself and (all the other) Buddhas, in this respect, there is no distinction whatever . . ." (D. T. Suzuki [trans.], The Laṅkāvatāra Sūtra, London: Routledge and Kegan Paul, Ltd., 1932, pp. 124–25). In fact, it is not even just the transcendent personalities of the Buddhas and their realizations that are the same. In the Mahāvadānasūtra, we learn that of the seven Buddhas previous to Śākyamuni, all in their final lives are identical with Śākyamuni even down to the smallest details. (Lamotte, Histoire, p. 721–22). Lamotte explains, ". . . the actual Buddha Sākyamuni is not the Buddha Vipaśyin of the past, but he is in all points similar because the two Buddhas participate in the same body of the dharma (dharma-kāya)." (Lamotte, "Criteria d'interprétation . . ." p. 357.

6. Thus the Laṅkāvatāra Sūtra speaks of the "sameness of words with regard to the Tathāgatas, Arhats, and Fully enlightened ones," and "the sameness of the teaching." D. T. Suzuki (trans.), Laṅkāvatāra Sūtra, London: Routledge and Kegan Paul Ltd., 1932, p. 123.

7. Laṅkābatāra Sūtra: "The ancient road of reality has been here all the time . . ." (p. 124).

8. This is exemplified in the early period by the verses of realization collected as the Theragāthā (K. R. Norman [trans.], The Elders' Verses [Thergāthā], Pali Text Society Translation Series, No. 38, London: Luzac and Company, Ltd., 1969) and the Therīgāthā (K. R. Norman [trans.], Pali Text Society Translation Series, No. 40, London: Luzac and Company, Ltd., 1971). In the later period, it is exemplified in the ideal of the Vajrayānist Mahāsiddhas' lives (cf. James Robinson [trans.], Buddha's Lions, Berkeley: Dharma Press, 1979.)

9. "Mano-maya-kāya" or sometimes nirmāna-kāya. For the description of this "body," cf. Conze, Buddhist Thought in India, Op. Cit., p. 172 and Edward Conze, Buddhism: Essence and Development, New York: Harper and Row, 1959, pp. 36–38.

10. According to tradition, the Buddha mounted in his mentally created body to the Trāyastrimśa heaven where his mother, who had died shortly after his birth, had taken rebirth. There he preached the books of the abhidharma pitaka, one by one. Each evening, he would return to earth, bathe himself,

and communicate what he had taught his mother to his great disciple Śāriputra, later the renowned *abhidharma* master. Śāriputra, in turn, taught this *abhidharma* to the 500 earthly disciples. (Lamotte, *Histoire*, p. 201). The fact that the Buddha could preach in a form disjunct from his physical humanity had, as we shall see, important implications for the later history of Buddhism.

11. Lamotte, *Histoire*, p. 203.

12. Lamotte, "Critique d'authenticité," p. 215.

13. Ibid.

14. Lamotte, "Critique d'authenticité," p. 216–17.

15. Ibid., p. 221.

16. This reverence is expressed in the four characteristics of *buddha-vacana* outlined by the *Suttanipāta*: "It is well said and not badly said; it conforms to salvation and is not contrary to salvation; it is agreeable and not disagreeable; it is true and not false." (*Suttanipāta*, III, 3, 78, qu. Lamotte, "Criteria d'authenticité," p. 214). And from the *Dīgha nikāya*: "During the interval from the night when the Tathāgata achieved supreme enlightenment until the night when he entered the Nirvāṇa without remainder, all that he said, declared and taught, all that is true and not false." (*Dīgha nikāya*, III, 135, qu. Lamotte, "Criteria d'authenticité," p. 214).

17. Lamotte, "Criteria d'authenticité," p. 214. One may well ask, how did early Buddhism respond to this patent need to establish what was authentic *dharma* and what was not? As one may well imagine, there was more than one response. From a more conservative and institutional veiwpoint—and this trend existed even with more or less strength within every important Buddhist school—the diversity of potential sources of dharma presented a problem. There was within the various schools the desire to claim possesison of *the* valid canon and *the* authentic teachings. But, at the same time, owing to the initial form of authority established by the Buddha, and the stress on individual responsibiltity and on meditation practice in the tradition, the conservative trends were generally balanced by a sensible recognition of the relativity of all traditions, and one acknowledgement of the validity of other Buddhist traditions besides one's own.

18. Lamotte, "Criteria d'authenticité," p. 216.

19. Ibid., p. 217. I use the term "Hīnayāna advisedly. The term, meaning "small" or "narrow" (*hīna*), vehicle (*yāna*) was coined in the Mahāyāna to refer to all of those schools preceding the Mahāyāna relation to which the Mahāyāna wished to set itself apart, and to which it viewed itself as superior. Thus in its original usage, the term is pejorative. However, in contemporary Western academic usage, the term is by far the most frequent one used to refer to the pre-Mahāyāna traditions, and scholars characteristically use the term in a purely descriptive sense, the sense in which I also use it. Other terms occasionally used to refer to the same phenomenon are "the 18 schools" (although in fact about 25 schools are known to have existed), the "pre-Mahāyāna schools" (although "schools" has a connotation of separate and distinct units which in fact

applies to only a portion of pre-Mahāyāna tradition) and "*nikāya* ('sect') Buddhism," (perhaps the best choice if it were more widely known).

20. Ibid.
21. Lamotte's translation from the *Mahāpadesasutta*, Lamotte, "Critique d' authenticité," p. 219.
22. Ibid., p. 220.
23. Ibid. Lamotte cites the *Nettipakarana*, the *Abhidharmakośa*, the *Mahāyāna-sūtrālamkāra* and the *Bodhicaryāvatārapañjikā*, all of which require that a text accord "with the nature of things" in order finally to be judged to be Buddha word. (Ibid.)
24. Ibid., p. 221.
25. Ibid., p. 222.
26. Ibid.
27. Lamotte, "Critique d'interprétation," p. 342.
28. *Abhidharmakośavyākhyā*, p. 704, cited by Lamotte, "Critique d'interprétation," p. 342.
29. *Samyutta nikāya*, III, 120, quoted in Edward Conze, *Buddhist Texts Through the Ages*, p. 103.
30. *Majjhima nikāya* I, 190–91, quoted by Lamotte, *Histoire*, p. 689.
31. Suzuki, *Lankāvatāra Sūtra*, pp. 128–29; P. L. Vaidya (ed.), *Saddharmalankā-vatārasūtram*, Buddhist Sanskrit Texts Series, No. 3, Darbhanga (India): Mithila Institute, 1963, pp. 60–61.
32. *Dīgha nikāya*, III, 129, quoted by Lamotte, "Critique d'interprétation," p. 345.
33. Ibid.
34. *Majjhima nikāya*, I, 133, quoted by Lamotte, "Critique d'interprétation," p. 346.
35. *Añguttara Nikāya*, II, 147, quoted by Lamotte, "Critique d'interprétation," p. 346.
36. *Nettipakaranya*, 21, quoted by Lamotte, "Critique d'interprétation," p. 346.
37. Etienne Lamotte (ed. and trans.), *Samdhinirmocana Sūtra: l'Explication des Mystères*, Université de Louvain, Recueil de travaux, 2e serie, 34e fasc. Paris: Maisonneuve, 1935, p. 199–200.
39. Garma, C. C. Chang (trans.) *The Hundred Thousand Songs of Milarepa*, 2 vols. New Hyde Park, New York: University Books, 1962, pp. 380–81.
39. H. V. Guenther (trans.) *Life and Teachings of Nāropa*, London: Oxford University Press, 1963, pp. 23ff.
40. *Vinaya I.*, p. 40, quoted by Lamotte, "Critique d'interprétation," p. 347.
41. Ibid.
42. *Samyutta nikāya*, II, 13, quoted in Lamotte, *Histoire*, pp. 55–56.
43. *Samyutta nikāya*, IV, 400, quoted in Lamotte, *Histoire*, p. 56.
44. *Añguttara nikāya*, I, 22, quoted by Lamotte, "Critique d'interprétation," p. 349.
45. Etienne Lamotte (trans.) *Le Traité de la Grande Vertu de Sagesse de Nāgār-juna, Mahāprajñāpāramitāśāstra*, Bibliothèque de Muséon, No. 18, Louvain:

Bureaux du Muséon, 1944–1970, 3 vols., p. 1074, quoted by Lamotte, "Critique d'interprétation," pp. 349–50.

46. T. W. Rhys-Davids (trans.), *The Foundation of the Kingdom of Righteousness (Dhamma-cakka-ppavattana Suttants*, Sacred Books of the East Series, Vol. XI, Delhi: Motilal Banarsidass, reprint, 1965, pp. 137ff.

47. For a summary of the Mahāyāna understanding of the second turning of the wheel of dharma, see Lamotte, "Sur la formation du Mahāyāna."

48. Translated by Robert A. F. Thurman, "Buddhist Hermeneutics," *Journal of the American Academy of Religion*, No. 46, 1978, p. 26.

49. For a summary of Chih-i's systemization see Kenneth Ch'en, *Buddhism in China*, Princeton: Princeton University Press, 1972, pp. 305–8.

50. Stephen Batchelor (trans.), *A Guide to the Bodhisattva's Way of Life (Bodhicaryāvatara)*, Dharamsala (India): Library of Tibetan Works and Archives, 1979.

51. Ibid., pp. 131–66.

52. Ibid., p. 133.

53. Ibid., pp. 135–38.

54. Taped Seminar given by H. E. Gyal. tsap Rinpoche in 1982 at the Kagyu Samye-ling Tibetan Centre, Eskdalemuir, Langholm, Dumfriesshire, Scotland, DGI30QL, copyright: Kagyu Samye-Ling.

55. Suzuki, *Laṅkāvatāra Sūtra*, p. 136.

56. Jamgon Kongtrul, Lodros Thaye, *Nges.don.grn.me* (Torch of True Meaning), pp. 556a-b.

CONFUCIANISM:
Scripture and Sage

Rodney L. Taylor

It is often only with some difficulty that the Confucian tradition is spoken of as a religious tradition; words such as humanism and ethics tend to predominate. Yet fortunately there is now a good deal of work that indicates quite clearly the religious dimension of the tradition.[1] This applies to whether one is referring to Classical Confucianism, the teaching associated with the major figures of the tradition during the late Chou dynasty (1111–249 B.C.E.), Confucius (551–479 B.C.E.), Mencius (371–289 B.C.E.) and Hsün-tzu (fl. 298–238 B.C.E.), as well as several major works, or what is called Neo-Confucianism, the major Confucian teachings that emerged during the Sung dynasty (960–1279) and maintained a position of preeminence until quite recent times. The locus of the religious dimension has been seen in terms of the role of Heaven whether described as a law-giver in potentially theistic terms in the Classical Confucian worldview or viewed as an immanental principle, *li*, underlying the universe as well as man's nature in the Neo-Confucian view. In turn the religious life has been measured through man's capacity to perfect his moral nature and thus emulate or even seek union with the ways of Heaven or the underlying principle. Such elements point to the depth of the religious life within the Confucian tradition that has only very recently been fully appreciated.

One component of the Confucian religious life that has remained virtually unexplored is the role of the holy book or scripture. In fact in many ways its mere mention seems almost inimical to the tradition itself: a Confucian scripture or holy book? One is tempted to ask whether this is not simply the wrong term! And yet having demonstrated the religious dimension of the tradition and delineated salient features of the religious life of the Confucian, it is appropriate to take a new and fresh look at the role of scripture in the Confucian tradition. It is, after all, frequently observed that the Confucian tradition is one that emphasizes the role of learning, specifi-

181

cally book learning. In light of the new-found religious dimension of the Confucian tradition there is a need to adjudicate the attitude towards these works by an analysis of the nature of the authority these works possess as well as the role they play for the tradition and the individual.

THE SOURCE OF THE HOLY BOOK—THE AGE OF SAGES

The exemplar of the understanding of Heaven's ways from the Confucian point of view is the sage, sheng, a designation assigned to early rulers of Chinese antiquity and increasingly applied by later Confucians to major figures of their own tradition. The books which may be described as the scripture or holy books of Confucianism are intimately linked to this tradition of the sages. The works are a record of the deeds and in some cases the words of the sages. In turn for the later tradition there was an attempt to see Confucius himself, a sage from the point of view of later generations of his followers, as instrumental in the process of the formation and transmission of these works. First, however, I want to focus upon the figure of the sage and the reasons why it was of such importance that there be a record of his activities and why in turn these records took on the nature of a holy book from the Confucian perspective.

The word sage, sheng (archaic pronunciation *śiĕng, ancient pronunciation śi̯äng) is defined in the earliest and standard etymological dictionary, the Shuo-wen, as t'ung, a word whose meaning is either "to penetrate" or "to pass through."[2] Thus the general meaning of the term suggests that the sage is one who thoroughly penetrates things or by extension, thoroughly understands things. To thoroughly penetrate or understand things means primarily that the sage understands the ways of Heaven and it is on the basis of this knowledge of the ways of Heaven that he is an able and wise ruler, for the knowledge of the ways of Heaven is that which best serves the ways of human society. The philology of the word itself indicates something more of the complex nature of the sage and in turn the extraordinary status both historically as well as religiously associated with the designation. In the commentaries to the Shuo-wen provided in the Shuo-wen chieh-tzu ku-lin we find a fuller explanation of the term.[3] The character itself is composed of the radical or signific.er, the word for ear. This is combined with the phonetic ch'eng. The phonetic is glossed by Karlgren as "to manifest" and thus "to disclose" or "to reveal."[4] With the signific er playing a prominent role, we have the sense of the sage as the one who hears.

As Boltz has recently suggested,[5] there is an intriguing contrast to be made between China and the classical antiquity of Europe in terms of the visual and auditory metaphors of wisdom; while the Greeks saw, the Chinese heard! Thus the sage hears the ways of Heaven. There is also a very close philological relation between the word for sage, *sheng*, and the word *t'ing*, to hear, to acknowledge, to listen. In fact the word sage was often written as *t'ing*, emphasizing the capacity of the sage to hear. It is somewhat more speculative to suggest a semantical significance in the phonetic component; however, it is perhaps telling that the phonetic alone carries the meaning of "to manifest." If there is a significance to the meaning of this phonetic, then the sage is he who hears the ways of Heaven and in addition manifests or reveals them to mankind. As the *Hsi-ch'uan t'ung-lun* commentary to the *Shuo-wen* says, "There is nothing he does not penetrate. . . . The ear component does not mean simply to use the ear; it means instead that the mind penetrates the feelings of all things as the ear penetrates all sound. . . . It is said that the sage penetrates the feelings of Heaven and earth and understands the nature of man and the world."[6] As such, those works that record the deeds of the sages bear a major import for the development of man and society alike, for they represent the deeds of those who understood the ways of Heaven.

THE CLASSICS—CONTENT AND MEANING

The term most generally used to describe the literary works that record the deeds of the sages is that of *ching*, translated as classic. It suggests even in translation a work that stands the test of time, a work that has an appeal as well as an importance to each new generation. This is also the word that frequently renders scripture in both Taoist and Chinese Buddhist traditions.[7] The question that remains central for our examination is the degree to which the term classic carries for the Confucian perspective a significance that can render its import as nothing short of scripture or holy book.

The term itself is quite clear in its etymology. Its origin, as evidenced by its signific which means thread, is weaving and its meaning is warp, as opposed to weft.[8] Karlgren glosses the term as rule, law or norm, suggesting the underlying sense of warp as that which creates continuity as well as regularity in a piece of cloth.[9] The extended meanings are orthodoxy and heterodoxy for warp and weft respectively.

There have been various groupings of the Classics at different points in the history of the Confucian school. The designation can be applied as a group designation even when a work does not actually bear the term in its title, but is judged to be of the magnitude of importance to warrant the designation. In general there are groupings of Five Classics, Six Classics, Nine Classics, Twelve Classics and Thirteen Classics. The most essential collection, the Five Classics, includes: the *I-Ching*, Classic or Book of Changes, a divinatory work with philosophical commentaries which explain the patterns of change inherent in the universe; the *Shih-Ching*, Classic or Book of Poetry, a collection of some three hundred poems thought to exemplify the quintessential expression of poetic beauty and moral virtue; the *Shu-Ching*, Classic or Book of History, a record of the deeds of the early sage-kings; the *Li-Chi*, Book of Rites, detailed accounts and philosophical meanings of the rituals of the ancient sage-kings: and the *Ch'un-Ch'iu*, Spring and Autumn Annals, a record of the events in the state of Lu, the native state of Confucius.

The collection of Six Classics adds to these five a work referred to as the *Yüeh-Ching*, Classic of Music, which purportedly discussed the philosophical meaning of music but is no longer extant. By the T'ang dynasty (618–907) this collection had expanded to twelve including the basic Five Classics. Two additional ritual texts, the *Chou-Li* and the *I-Li* were added to the *Li-Chi*. The *Ch'un-Ch'iu* which had already included the *Tso-chuan* commentary had two additional commentaries added to it, the *Kung-yang chuan* and the *Ku-liang chuan*. The *Hsiao-ching*, Classic of Filial Piety, the *Erh-ya*, an early lexicon, and the *Lun-yü*, Analects of Confucius, were added to bring the number to twelve. Finally within several centuries the *Meng-tzu* or the Mencius, the works of Mencius, were added, bringing the total to thirteen. Each of these texts has its own significance as a Classic and each in turn is connected with the tradition of sages. They also each contain complex questions in terms of textual history and authorship.

Textual questions were made far more complex in the history of Chinese literature through the infamous "burning of the books" carried out by Ch'in Shih Huang-ti (reign 221–210 B.C.E.), the first emperor of the Ch'in dynasty who attempted through such a measure to guarantee uniformity of thought and agreement with his own legalist idealogy. The result in succeeding generations was the appearance of not just one version of many of the supposedly lost texts, but two versions that differed markedly from each other. These became known as the New Text versions and the Old Text versions.[10] The New Text versions tended to present a form of Confucianism in accord with much of the prevailing spirit of Han dynasty thought. It centered itself around complex schemes of *yin/yang* cosmology and tried to ascribe various hagiographic features to the life of Confucius. In general the New Text interpretation tended to see a major role for Confucius himself in the composition of the Classics. The Old Text versions tended instead to reinforce the strictly humanistic interpretations of Confucian teachings. There was little or no *yin/yang* cosmology and Confucius remained a human and historical figure. They also tended to see the composition and editing of the Classics as the product of an earlier age than Confucius, specifically in the figure of the Duke of Chou, the paradigm of Confucian virtue from the early Chou period. They then assigned to Confucius the task of transmitting the texts, not creating them, to paraphrase Confucius' own admission that he himself was a transmitter not a creator. As in any such textual issue, however, the solutions are not black and white and as a result the questions of New Text versus Old Text have been argued over a substantial amount of time. Let us begin, however, by returning to the founders of the tradition, Confucius and Mencius, to understand their attitudes towards the literature that purportedly came from the age of the sages themselves.

CONFUCIUS AND MENCIUS ON THE CLASSICS

To both Confucius and Mencius, the major issue remained a return to the virtuous ways of the sage-kings, particularly the founders of the Chou dynasty. The literature that they felt themselves responsible for transmitting was thought to be the record of the times of such paradigmatic figures of the early Chou period. It is this literature that became for later Confucians the Classics. For Confucius and Mencius its significance rests less with a sense of textual authority than a living contact with the virtuous sage-rulers of China's past.

To Confucius the study of this literature or *wen*, which meant literature in its broadest category, was critical, for it was seen as the means whereby individual and society alike might fully become humane and virtuous. The ideal of the *chün-tzu*, the virtuous man, who has developed his own inner sense of humaneness, *jen*, and displays it through the outward perfection of propriety, *li*, is central to the teachings of Confucius. The literature, *wen*, is invoked by Confucius as the means whereby such development can take place. Confucius says, for example, "It is by the Odes that the mind is aroused. It is by the rules of Propriety that the character is established. It is from Music that the finish is received." (*Analects* VIII:8)[11] The reference may well be to the *Shih-Ching*, Book of Poetry, the *Li-Chi*, Book of Rites or Propriety and the Classic of Music, though there is little indication of the form in which these would have been seen by Confucius. However, one can see the direction of Confucius' remark; man will develop and perfect his moral nature through a thorough learning and assimilation of such sources. In describing the *chün-tzu*, the virtuous or superior man, Confucius says, "The superior man, extensively studying all learning, and keeping himself under the restraint of the rules of propriety, may thus likewise not overstep what is right." (*Analects* VI:25) [12] We see again the degree to which for Confucius the study of literature which has been transmitted from the period of the sage-rulers is viewed as the method through which man and society alike will return to virtuous and moral ways, ways that will accord with the Way of Heaven.

One additional passage from the *Analects* is an indication of Confucius' expression of faith in the Book of Poetry's ability to contribute to the learning as well as moral and spiritual development of the individual. "My children, why do you not study the Book of Poetry? The Odes serve to stimulate the mind. They may be used for purposes of self-contemplation. They teach the art of sociability. They show how to regulate the feelings of resentment. From them you learn the more immediate duty of serving one's father, and the remoter one of serving one's prince. From them we become largely acquainted with the names of birds, beasts and plants." (*Analects* XVII:9) [13]

Confucius' interpretation of the Book of Poetry, the only such interpretation he offers of a Classic, suggests that the salient and overriding meaning of the Book of Poetry is that it is pure and uncorrupted. "In the Book of Poetry are three hundred pieces, but the design of them all may be embraced in one sentence—'Having no depraved thoughts.'" (*Analects* II:2) [14] This short passage goes a long ways towards explaining Confucius' attitude towards the *wen* or literature and in turn sets the ground for the approach by later Confucians to the Classics themselves. Confucius has in a sense established an article of faith in the moral and spiritual purity of a collection of poems. This is based upon the presupposition that the age out of which this collection of poetry emerged was itself an age of purity, for it was the period of the founding sage-rulers of the Chou dynasty. Thus from the Confucian point of view these poems embody the very spirit of their age. In turn if one thoroughly studies such works, they will have nothing short of a transforming effect upon the individual. Certainly this approach to the Book of Poetry which will be mirrored by later Confucians with this Classic as well as other Classics is the very seed from which the Confucian scriptural tradition developed.

Mencius refers to the Classics far more frequently than Confucius, quoting or referring to the *Book of History* and the *Book of Poetry* extensively and the *Ch'un-Ch'iu* and *Li-Chi* less frequently. In addition to sim-

ply quoting or referring to these works he also in several passages dis-
cusses the significance as well as the interpretation of the Book of History
and the Book of Poetry. It is through passages such as these that we have
perhaps the clearest view of how these works were understood. In the case
of the Book of Poetry, Mencius suggests in one passage that an interpretation of one of the poems by a contemporary who had suggested the poem's
limitations and accused it of expressing bigotry was quite inaccurate.
From Mencius' point of view the poem displays true humaneness and be-
nevolence, *jen*, the central virtue in Confucian thought.[15] Without getting
into the specific issue of the poem itself, Mencius' correction of the interpretation suggests a good deal about his own approach to the Book of Poetry. In a similar fashion to Confucius, Mencius views the work as the em-
bodiment of virtue. As such the key to interpretation is to be seen in the
uncovering of the moral content, recognizing that the work is permeated
with sagely wisdom. In another passage Mencius agrees with Confucius
that the author of one of the poems was versed in the Way itself, again suggesting the degree to which the founders of the Confucian tradition presupposed the immediate connection between such works and the age of
the sages.

This might lead one to think that in this veneration of the ancient
wen, we are dealing with a literal and unquestioning acceptance of such
sources as the recorded deeds and words of the sages themselves. To a
large degree the admiration and veneration seem unceasing, yet Mencius
expresses a qualification on the interpretation of the Book of History suggesting that a literal interpretation can under some circumstances lead to
misunderstanding. He notes a passage in which the Book of History states
that the blood of the people flowed unmercifully when fighting on behalf
of a benevolent prince[16] and suggests that this is simply an inaccurate recording. What do we make of his reaction? He is certainly not a literalist,
otherwise there would be some attempt to explain what the passage means
to avoid any inconsistency let alone a challenge to the text itself. On
the other hand, presupposed behind his caution is still the notion that the
Ways of Heaven are inviolable. It simply could not be the case that the
blood of the people would be spilled unmercifully for a benevolent prince.
Thus it is not a question of unqualified acceptance of the authenticity of
the sources, but it clearly indicates the degree of belief in the Confucian
teachings that Heaven operates in moral ways and any violation of this
principle could only indicate an inaccurate source.

Literature, specifically what became known as the Classics, is then for
Confucius and Mencius an immediate link to the age of the sages if not the

sages themselves. The continued role of the Classics is critical in the program of moral and spiritual learning Confucius and Mencius envision as vital to the reshaping of man and society. Yet for all the importance these works play, there is a strange paucity of reference to the overall significance they possess. We have cited most of the references that give some general sense of the interpretation and significance of the Classics. This is all the more marked when contrasted with Hsün-tzu, for whom the conscious articulation of the signifance of the Classics was significantly more important.

HSÜN-TZU AND THE ARTICULATION OF THE CLASSICS

Unlike Confucius and Mencius, Hsün-tzu seems to be far more conscious or at least conversant with the significance of the Classics, particularly when spoken of as a group. We find, for example, the following statement in his writings. "The *Shu* records political events. The *Shih* establishes the standard of harmony. The *Li* sets forth the rules governing great distinctions, and is the regulator of social classes. . . . The reverence and elegance of the *Li*, the harmony of the *Yüeh*, the comprehensiveness of the *Shih* and *Shu*, the subtleties of all creation." [17] There is a sense of wholeness about the Classics from Hsün-tzu's point of view; they each make their contribution, but together they provide for the whole development of individual and society. A statement from Tung Chung-shu (c. 179–c. 104 B.C.E.), one of the major Confucians of the Han dynasty (206 B.C.E.–220 C.E.), suggests a similar admiration for the Classics taken together as a group. "The *Shih* describes aims, and therefore is pre-eminent for its unspoiled naturalness. The *Li* regulates distinctions, and therefore is pre-eminent in the decorative qualities. The *Yüeh* intones virtue, and therefore is pre-eminent in its influencing power. The *Shu* records achievements, and therefore is pre-eminent concerning events. The *I* takes Heaven and Earth as its basis, and therefore is pre-eminent in calculating probabilities. The *Ch'un-Ch'iu* rectifies right and wrong, and therefore stands pre-eminent in ruling men." [18] Other examples would indicate the same shift in focus to the significance of the total grouping of texts, particularly among generations of Confucians during the Ch'in and Han periods. Considering that the position of Hsün-tzu is prominent during this period, it is not an exaggeration to pinpoint this effort to him specifically.

In suggesting of Confucius and Mencius that there is an apparent lack of articulation of the nature and significance of the Classics either individually or as a group we may simply be posing the wrong question. If instead the question is turned around, we might ask why Hsün-tzu felt the need to speak in terms of the Classics as a group. Looked at in this way it may very well be the case that we are dealing with a different political and ideological reality of the Confucian school from the time of Confucius and even Mencius. For Hsün-tzu the Confucian school was in more direct competition for dominance in the marketplace of schools of thought. As such, the claim to the Classics as the source of one's ideas necessitated major attention to the texts themselves as the source of authority. This does not minimize Confucius' and Mencius' admiration for the Classics, but it does suggest that the focus for both remained primarily the teachings of the sages rather than textual authority.

The situation for Hsün-tzu is different. He felt the necessity of defending and preserving the learning of the sages and, from his point of view, the very foundations of civilization itself, from the Taoists who he saw as antithetical and inimical to all culture. Thus there arises the gradual recognition of the need to articulate a body of teachings, teachings soon to be established as orthodox by the state itself, and support the teachings with the authority of a textual tradition.

THE ESTABLISHMENT OF CONFUCIANISM—CANON AND CULT

It is during the Han dynasty that Confucianism is officially established as state orthodoxy. There are several aspects to this official establishment including the emergence of a state orthodoxy, a Confucian canon, and an official cult of Confucius. Under the reign of Emperor Han Wu-ti (140–87 B.C.E.) we see much of the activity responsible for the emergence of the Confucian tradition to a position of major significance. Acting at the suggestion of the noted Han dynasty Confucian Tung Chung-shu, the Emperor Wu-ti sought to carry out measures that would virtually guarantee a major role for the Confucian school. He established the position of "Scholar of the Five Classics," *wu-ching po-shih*, and on the basis of the recommendation of Tung Chung-shu, sought to exclude from office those who did not share the Confucian perspective. In 136 B.C.E. he established official positions for the "Scholars of the Five Classics." [19] These scholars served in the capacity of advisor to the emperor as well as teachers. Their role as teachers was enhanced by the establishment and opening under Emperor Wu-ti of an imperial university, *T'ai-hsüeh*, in 124 B.C.E. The university was to provide a training center for learning in the Classics and those who achieved expertise were given official positions. The result was of course what became the commonly known feature of the Confucian tradition— training in the Classics at the imperial university, the passing of a series of examinations, and official appointment to governmental position. With the increased role of the Confucian scholar as well as the official recognition of their status, the Confucian school became a dominant and major element of the Han period.[20]

At the same time that these efforts were being undertaken, much of the focus of the Confucian school itself was directed towards the editing of texts and the attempt to establish definitive editions. Subsequent to the infamous "burning of the books" carried out under the first emperor of the Ch'in dynasty and the appearance of two versions of many of the texts, the New Text and the Old Text versions, there was a need to settle questions of variant texts. The emperor eventually commissioned a committee of scholars to deal with the variant versions and produce a definitive edition. The eventual result of this effort was the production of orthodox versions as well as interpretations of the Five Classics. As an indication of the official establishment of a canon, the Five Classics together with the *Analects* of Confucius were engraved in stone.

The fact that the *Analects* was included among those works engraved in stone is not surprising when one realizes the increased role and status given to Confucius. With the emergence of Confucianism to a position of prominence there is an equal elevation in the status of its founder. Some of the ways in which he was elevated were only short-lived, particularly the tendency of Tung Chung-shu and his school to suggest hagiographic features in Confucius' biography. Within a matter of years such interpretations were declared heterodox and subsequently Confucius has remained a founder remarkably human in personality and character. Of these features that did, however, play a lasting role there is the establishment of an official cult and subsequent temple to Confucius. Confucius had already been the patron of scholars prior to the official establishment of Confucianism during the Han dynasty, but with official recognition the cult of Confucius became a regularized part of the official state orthodoxy and in particular the state orthopraxy. Scholars offered sacrifice to Confucius and the ritual came to be included among those sacrifices officially performed by the emperor himself.[21] Though the attempt to deify Confucius was declared heretical, he remained at the center of a cult that was eventually institutionalized as the Confucian temple. As a cultic object Confucius appears to have remained human. Sacrifice was simply viewed as the perfection of ritual, not a sacrifice *to* Confucius. The cultic ritual provided a means for perfecting one's own ritual or propriety and thus one's moral and spiritual nature. It also provided a focusing upon the teachings of the founder. Nothing more was to be involved.

As an outgrowth of the New Text interpretation which had far reaching ramifications, Confucius himself was assigned a far larger role in the composition and editing of the Classics. Ssu-ma Ch'ien's (c. 145 – 86 B.C.E.) biography of Confucius in his monumental *Shih-Chi* shares in this influence by suggesting that Confucius was instrumental in the composition of all of the major Classics.[22] Tung Chung-shu, a direct follower of the New Text interpretation states that Confucius is the author of the *Ch'un-Ch'iu*. The *Shih-Ching* is described as being edited by Confucius. Confucius is given a major role in the composition of the commentaries or wings of the *I-Ching*. The *Chin-ssu lu*, a major source of neo-Confucian teachings, states this same view succinctly, saying of the Classics that they are the product of the writing of the Sage, i.e., Confucius.[23]

We have then the confluence of several factors at this stage of the official establishment of Confucianism. On the one hand the tradition has engaged in conscious self-reflection in which it views itself as a repository for the preservation and interpretation of the teachings of the sages. On the other hand, it sees its own founder as a critical link, what the later tradition will call *tao-t'ung* or the transmission of the Way, in the establishment of the proper sources of authority to transmit such teachings, the Classics themselves.

HAN CONFUCIANISM AND HOLY BOOKS

The fact that Confucianism is officially established during the Han dynasty is a major development in the clarification of the role of canon in the Confucian tradition. The official establishment of Confucianism goes hand in hand with the concern for clarification and adjudication of variant versions of the texts, the intention of which is the production of an authoritative version of each of the Five Classics. The question may well be asked whether the issue here is simply to have correct versions such that the student of the classics will have a consistent body of knowledge in the context of the examination system. Is the issue, however, only an issue of the pragmatic concern for textual accuracy and consistency? It seems rather more likely that the issue runs deeper than this. Not unlike the Scholastics of Europe, the Confucians of the Han dynasty could express genuine sincerity as well as personal depth in the establishment of the authority of the texts of the Confucian teachings. The issues separating the New Text and Old Text versions were not entirely pedantic philological differences. The concerns were also existential; for either side it was an attempt to understand what the teachings were such that one might live one's life accordingly. It is not in this sense an abstract issue, and thus even the debate over variant texts bears the full weight of the sincerity as well as authenticity of those who participated in such debates.

One might still say, however, that all of this only indicates a concern, though a very genuine one, with the establishment of the correct teachings such that the full extent of Confucian humanism might be felt by society. In other words, what is it that permits these Classics to be called holy books? The designation canon can perhaps be a bit misleading by implying too readily the religious orientation of a work. There is no doubt that the works Confucians study are Classics in the full sense in which we use that word, a cross-generational statement that remains basic to the entire cultural milieu. It is a very different category to imply that these same works are scripture. The difference is certainly located in the source of authority each relies upon. The Classics are not revealed scriputre, at least in the sense in which the term is usually employed, often presupposing a theistic world-view. However, at the same time the paradigm of the Confucian tradition, the sage, is directly involved in the Classics either in terms of exemplifying their own deeds or contributing to the composition itself. As such, while not "revelation," the sage is he who hears the ways of Heaven and manifests them to the world. Thus the Classics become the repository of such manifestations. They bear an authority as well as a source that is religious in nature. On the basis of the primary religious dimension, even though this dimension for the Confucian may be seen primarily in terms of non-revelatory ethical and humanistic tradition, it is proper to discuss the Classics as holy books. Their official recognition may then be interpreted as the establishment of a Confucian canon with its implication of religious authority.

THE NEW SCRIPTURAL TRADITION OF NEO-CONFUCIANISM

Neo-Confucianism, the major development of Confucian thought that began in the eleventh century in China and became one of the dominant teachings of Korea and Japan as well as China until the recent past, was in many ways a reaffirmation of the basic teachings of Confucius and Mencius though within the context of increased philosophical speculation. One of the many features of the Neo-Confucian movement, and one particularly relevant to the present discussion, was a gradually increasing doubt as to the authority of the Classics.[24] During the T'ang dynasty an orthodox interpretation of the Five Classics had been established in a work entitled *Wu-ching cheng-i*, "The Correct Meanings of the Five Classics."[25] It was this interpretation that the Neo-Confucians rejected, suggesting instead that the interpretation of the Classics was a far more individual matter. Thus new commentaries appeared, commentaries that differed substantially enough to warrant the designation "new learning," hsin-hsüeh. For Ch'eng I (1033 – 1107), one of the major Neo-Confucians of the Sung period, a commentary on the I-Ching was simply an occasion for the expounding of his own point of view. Thus the commentary becomes a philosophical essay in its own right.

W. T. Chan has suggested that in addition to a challenge to the orthodox interpretation of the Classics, there was also a growth of skepticism towards the authenticity and authority of the Classics themselves.[26] Ouyang Hsiu (1007 – 1072), for example, doubted the authenticity of the commentaries or wings to the I-Ching as well as the introduction to the Shih-Ching and the three commentaries connected with the Ch'un-Ch'iu. Chu Hsi (1130 – 1200) also shared in this same general attitude though as Chan is careful to point out, Chu Hsi still worked closely with the Classics and wrote commentaries to at least four of them.[27] However, his attitude towards them has changed. It is this change that is critical for the Neo-Confucian movement. Chu Hsi was skeptical as to questions of authenticity and he was also flexible and individualistic in the interpretation of the text. This can be seen clearly, for example, in the following statements from the Chin-ssu lu, a work compiled in part by Chu Hsi which represented a kind of practical guide to the essentials of the Neo-Confucian learning.[28] "In reading books, we should not rigidly stick to one meaning because the words are the same or similar. Otherwise every word will be a hindrance. We should see what the general tone of the passage is and what the preceding and following ideas are."[29] Or the following: "The Six Classics are vast and extensive. At first it is difficult to understand them completely. As students find their way, each establishes his own gate, and then returns home to conduct his inquiries himself."[30] As a mode of interpretation, the neo-Confucians suggest a certain flexibility and thus the possibility of a quite individual interpretation.

There are limits of course as the following passage suggests. "In interpreting the Classics, there is no harm in differing from their original meaning, except for important points, on which we must not differ."[31] Such passages represent a challenge to the authority of the Classics, a challenge which, as W. T. Chan argues, reaches its height in the viewpoint that the Classics might not be necessary at all.[32] Quoting Chu Hsi, "We make use of the Classics only to understand principle. If principles are understood we do not have to depend upon them."[33] Or even further: "If we understand principle, we do not have to have the Classics."[34] The meaning of the Classics has shifted from the concreteness of the historical deeds of sages of antiquity, to a more philosophical capacity to reveal the principle or *li*, the underlying metaphysical structure of Heaven's ways revealed in all things. Yet we have come even further than this with Chu Hsi's statement that having pursued and attained the understanding of principle or the ways of Heaven, the source itself might well be declared unnecessary. However, having removed the authority of the Classics, we find that the result is not simply perseverence in the light of skepticism, but rather the establishment of a new source of authority, specifically a new scriptural authority.

The new scriptural authority was found in a new collection of writings, the Four Books. The works that make up the Four Books were not new, but the combination as well as the authority given the collection were all very new. The Four Books are composed of the Analects, the Mencius, and two chapters from the *Li-Chi* which had for some length of time been considered as having philosophical merit as separate works, the *Ta-hsüeh* or Great Learning and the *Chung-yung* or Doctrine of the Mean. From Chu Hsi's point of view, as W. T. Chan has analyzed, there are at least three major differences between the Four Books and the Classics.[35]

First, the Classics remained secondary in comparison to the actual teachings of Confucius and Mencius. What was of major import to the Neo-Confucians was the centrality of the teachings of Confucius and Mencius and there was obviously little of relevance to be found in the Classics as far as the teachings of Confucius and Mencius were concerned. Thus the teachings focused upon are found in the Analects and the Mencius while the Classics simply add what might almost be called historical footnotes.

Second, Chu Hsi considered the Four Books as the source of knowledge of principle, *li*. They provided solid and pragmatic teachings for the ethical and religious growth of the individual as well as the implementation of man's moral nature into the daily affairs of the world. These concerns, from Chu Hsi's point of view, simply are not met in the Classics.

Finally, it was Chu Hsi's opinion that the grouping of the Four Books provided a unique combination of works that served as an entire program of learning and self-cultivation. In a sense the whole was greater than the sum of its parts, for taken together the works served the needs of the individual and society in their entirety.

The works were also arranged to reflect a cumulative learning experience. The Great Learning was placed first, that it might provide a framework in terms of its enunciation of stages of learning. The Analects was placed second to reinforce the primacy of Confucius' teachings as the foundation upon which learning is built. The Mencius was placed third to indicate its basis as the interpretative tool and elaborative text of the basic Confucian teachings. And fourth was the Doctrine of the Mean, a text that was appreciated for its subtlety and abstraction as well as the depth it displayed. In terms of the process of learning Chu Hsi states, "I want people first of all to read the Great Learning to set a pattern, next to read the Analects to establish a foundation, next to read the Book of Mencius for stimulation, and next to read the Doctrine of the Mean to find out the subtle points of the ancients." [36]

Out of the content of the Four Books Chu Hsi derives a number of his specific teachings and doctrines that occupy a major position in the Neo-Confucian tradition. Certainly one of the most prominent of these teachings is that of ko-wu, the investigation of things, and chih-chih, the extension of knowledge, fundamental processes from Chu Hsi's point of view in the gradual accumulation of the understanding of principle, li, and also the center of controversy as an interpretation of the Great Learning that will in part explain a major division in the teachings of the Neo-Confucians.

What is particularly important for our purposes, however, is the new authority Chu Hsi places in the Four Books. Comparing the Four Books and the Classics he states, "The student should first read the Analects and the Book of Mencius. If he has studied them thoroughly, he will get the fundamental points. He will save a great deal of effort if he reads other Classics on the basis of these. The two books are like the measure and the balance." [37] The Four Books are thus the proper interpretative tool with which to approach the Classics. In such a case, however, the authority rests with the Four Books rather than the Classics and one might even suggest that much of the interest stops with the Four Books as well. A number of passages indicate the authority given to the Four Books. "The student should use the Analects and the Book of Mencius as the foundation. When these have been well studied, the Six Classics can be understood without study." [38] Chu Hsi's commentary upon this passage states, "The Analects and the book of Mencius require less effort but will yield more result, whereas the Six Classics require more effort but will yield less result." [39]

The actual approach to the texts themselves is for Chu Hsi and other Neo-Confucians, as we have already indicated, an individualistic enterprise within certain limits, but it provided one of the reasons certainly that the T'ang commentaries were ignored. From Chu Hsi's point of view the T'ang approach to a text remained primarily philological. Thus the key to understanding the text in the T'ang interpreter's eye was primarily a philological one: to understand the text one understands the words that make it up. In due fairness to the T'ang approach which may also be compared to the European Scholastic model, a philological engagement with the text does not necessarily lessen the sincerity or faith of the individual. From Chu Hsi's perspective, however, such approaches missed the inner depth of the Classics. For Chu Hsi the understanding of a text was not an exercise in philology, but rather an exercies in moral and spiritual self-cultivation.

Thus the unearthing of meaning in a text was measured from the Neo-Confucian perspective in terms of the ability to penetrate to the deepest layers of one's own nature, in a sense to establish a correlation between self-understanding and the understanding of the text. In the metaphysical language used by Chu Hsi all things were said to contain principle, *li*, the underlying moral nature immanent in the phenomenal world. Man's task of learning was to discover it through a process linked in Chu Hsi's mind to the investigation of things, *ko-wu*, and the proper attitude of reverence or seriousness, *ching*. The meaning of a text becomes then a subjective experience for it is a matter of adjudicating inner dimensions of the self with the text itself. From Chu Hsi's perspective the Four Books represented the quintessential expression of *li* or principle and as such could serve as a guide for the interpretation of the Classics, but more importantly as a template to the unraveling of the depth of man's moral and spiritual core, his true nature and mind.

There are many other points of view within the framework of Neo-Confucianism that present a different metaphysical structure. Chu Hsi focused upon the underlying *li* within things and one's own nature which was to be understood gradually through the process of *ko-wu*, investigation of things. This school became known as the School of Principle, *Li-hsüeh*. A challenge was offered to this school by Lu Hsiang-shan (1139–1193) during the Sung dynasty and in particular Wang Yang-ming (1412–1529) during the Ming dynasty (1368–1644),[40] suggesting that the investigation of things for principle only served to miss the fundamental metaphysical importance of the mind, which from this point of view was a repository of principle itself. While the Chu Hsi school focused upon learning, particularly book learning, necessary to accumulate an understanding of *li*, the so-called School of Mind, *Hsin-hsüeh*, suggested that learning and self-cultivation were primarily a process of realization of what was already the ground of the mind rather than an accumulation process. While this led men such as Lu Hsiang-shan to say of the Classics that they were merely footnotes to the mind,[41] the practical ramifications in terms of learning and the reverence shown the Classics and in particular the Four Books in most cases seems to have changed little.

One of Wang Yang-ming's major debates with Chu Hsi's thought, for example, is centered around the interpretation of the Great Learning. Yang-ming is critical of Chu Hsi's standard interpretation and commentary, particularly the sections dealing with the process of investigation of things. Yang-ming writes his own commentary to the text to answer Chu Hsi's interpretation.[42] The authority of the text itself is not debated or even questioned, instead it is only a question of the limits of interpretation in terms of the moral and spiritual methods of self-cultivation discussed by the Great Learning.

For Chu Hsi the first stage of learning is ko-wu, the investigation of things, to uncover li. There are some complex textual questions in terms of this interpretation of the stages of learning of the Great Learning and Yang-ming felt that Chu Hsi had overstepped the boundaries of interpretation.[43] Thus for Yang-ming the first stage of learning was not an investigation process, but rather a turning within, a proces of rectification, cheng, such that one's mind of principle might manifest itself.[44] Much of the debate between the School of Principle and the School of Mind might be seen in this difference of opinion as to the proper ordering of the stages of learning of the Great Learning. In a sense this may appear as a pedantic textual issue, but for both men the practical ramifications in terms of the religious life were immediate. And though there are differences in interpretation, neither rejects the authority of the Great Learning, nor the other texts that make up the Four Books.

In a recent study of the nature of the Neo-Confucian orthodoxy during the Sung and Yüan (1271–1368) dynasties, W. T. de Bary has pointed to the major importance attached to the Four Books, particularly in those years of struggle to establish Neo-Confucianism in the several generations following the death of Chu Hsi.[45] Followers of Chu Hsi such as Chen Te-hsiu (1178–1234) during the Sung and Hsü Heng (1209–1281) during the Yüan clearly display the extraordinary importance attached to the Four Books, and at a time when, as de Bary suggests, Neo-Confucianism had not emerged into a position of prominence and in many ways resembled a religion of the oppressed.[46] Hsü Heng represents perhaps the clearest example of an almost fundamentalist approach[47] towards the Four Books as well as several other writings he felt to capture the essential Confucian teaching. Hsu has a virtual conversion experience in which he suddenly comes to the point of radically adopting in its totality the Neo-Confucian point of view, particularly that represented by Chu Hsi. He then recommends to his disciples that they only study the Four Books and a work called the Hsiao-hsüeh, the Elementary Learning: all other works are deemed unimportant and unnecessary. He writes to his second son, "I revere and have faith in [these books] as if they were divine."[48] The response is not atypical and suggests the degree to which these works were accepted as scripture within the living day-to-day context of the life of a Confucian.

CONFUCIAN SCRIPTURE IN DAILY LIFE

The daily life of moral and spiritual self-cultivation and learning of the Neo-Confucian is perhaps no more exquisitely expressed than in the following passage from the *Chin-ssu lu*, "The way of the Sage is to be heard through the ear, to be preserved in the heart, to be deeply embraced there to become one's moral character, and to become one's activities and undertakings when it is put into practice."[49] The focus of the religious life from this perspective is the internalization of the teachings and at the same time the realization of one's own internal moral and spiritual nature. The vehicle for such learning is in part the give and take of teacher and disciple, a model salient to the tradition from the recorded dialogues between Confucius and his disciples that make up the *Analects*.

It is also in part the individual efforts of learning and self-cultivation, efforts that for many indicated the sheer pertinaciousness of the religious life. Both of these pursuits return to the fundamental authority of the Four Books, the Classics and other selected writings dependent upon the particular interests of the individual. Thus to hear the way of the sage is to understand the teachings preserved in the scriptures of the tradition. And from what we can see in a number of different writings, the scripture was internalized by the individual through repetition and memorization as well as self-understanding.

Repetition and memorization in themselves were of course always viewed as empty and sterile. The focus of ones efforts was to be true self-understanding. Some efforts, at least for certain individuals, were directed towards the successful passing of the civil service examinations, exams that were based upon the knowledge of the Classics and the Four Books. The idea of orthodoxy, however, needs to be shown in all of its diversity[50] and while there is an official state orthodoxy and the motivation religious or otherwise is dependent upon individual cases, at the level of a Chen Te-hsiu or Hsü Heng we are seeing men who have embraced the Confucian perspective as a religious world view. Such a motivation is also illustrated by works such as the *Chin-ssu lu*, a guide to self-cultivation and spiritual perfection, as well as the often contemplative lives of individual Neo-Confucians who chose not to serve in government but to pursue their own form of learning both moral and spiritual.[51]

Thus the *Chin-ssu lu* cautions against considering learning as a mere process of memorization. "In studying books, search for moral principles. In compiling books, appreciate what ultimate purposes they have. Do not just copy them."[52] A further and similar point: "Master Ming-tao considered memorization, recitation and acquiring extensive information as 'trifling with things and losing one's purpose.'"[53] The commentary on the passage states, "Merely to memorize what one has recited and to have extensive information, but not to understand or to reach the point of thorough understanding and penetration, is to chase after what is small and to forget what is great. . . ."[54]

Part of what is being suggested in these passages is a certain tension within the character of the scholar-official. On the one hand a certain amount of basic memorization and recitation of the Classics and the Four Books is essential to pass the examination system, and this remains as an important if not critical step within the individual's maturation process.[55] However, on the other hand, to have as the object only a successful placing in the examination and thus the assurance of a prestigious appointment is not characteristic of the virtuous man, the *chün-tzu*, who had remained the paradigm of the Confucian tradition. Thus what these passages as well as many others suggest is that while rote learning is necessary, so too is the preservation of a larger motive, one that sees learning as the way to the realization of one's own moral nature and thus the way to accord with the ways of Heaven or the immanental principle. We find then the following kind of statement exhorting the student on to study. "The Six Classics must be gone through one after another, in repeated cycles. The student will find that their moral principles are unlimited."[56] Or a very personal statement about the nature of reading and the way in which it should deeply penetrate one's nature: "In reading a book, one should recite it silently. Often excellent thoughts will come to him at midnight or while he is sitting in meditation. If one does not remember what he reads, his thoughts will not arise. After one has thoroughly understood the great foundation of a book, however, it will be easy to remember."[57]

Based upon statements such as this it is easy to see why the practice of writing out passages or phrases from the Classics or the Four Books or simply from the many writings of Confucian authors became as well a central activity in study and self-cultivation. This is the art of calligraphy and one that the Confucian scholar practiced frequently in the quiet of his study. Calligraphy was not simply to perfect certain styles of writing as an end unto themselves, nor was the focus a method for the memorization of passages and phrases. It was seen as a direct means to deep and profound understanding of the wisdom of the Classics or other sources and the reflection of such wisdom in the gradually developing moral nature of the individual. To write the words was to identify with the words and to manifest in one's own nature the meaning of the words. Thus calligraphy too was seen as a part of the path of self-cultivation towards the goal of sagehood, always central, always salient.

Let me conclude this essay with one last example of an individual whose life can be seen oriented around the religious dimension of Confucianism and the sources of Confucian teaching as scripture. This is Kao P'an-lung (1562–1626), a late Ming dynasty member of the Tung-lin Academy and a proponent of the Chu Hsi School of Neo-Confucianism.[58] His learning and formal study of many years culminating in the highest degree of the civil service system indicates his commitment to the formal and orthodox, state orthodox, view of the Classics and the Four Books. His involvement with the Tung-lin Academy as well as his own pursuit of self-cultivation indicates his focus upon the Chu Hsi school as a means towards individual religious fulfillment in the goal of sagehood. Confucian scripture for someone such as Kao functions at both a state capacity and an individual capacity. Even at the ritual level these two levels can be seen in operation. State ceremony involved liturgical hymns, the source of which were passages, phrases, and allusions to the classics. The private academies also performed ceremonial functions, and there again scriptural sources played a key role.[59] For Kao it is ultimately the individual life of cultivation that is the centering force of his own life, and this serves as the primary basis for his discussion of scripture. He states in his autobiography that through the life of learing with all of its toils and setbacks he has still mangaged to reach a point where he can express true faith, *hsin*. His faith is expressed in terms of coming to truly believe in three of the *Four Books*, the *Great Learning*, the *Mencius*, and the *Doctrine of the Mean*.

Others in autobiographical genre express this same manner of resolution of a life, a life with purpose and a life with fulfillment.[60] To call the source of inspiration of this kind of activity anything less than scripture and holy book is simply to miss the full significance of the Confucian religious life and its focus in the realization of the ways of the sage.

NOTES

1. See, for example, W. T. de Bary (ed.), *The Unfolding of Neo-Confucianism* (New York: Columbia University Press, 1975); Wei-ming Tu, *Humanity and Self-Cultivation: Essays in Confucian Thought* (Berkeley: Asian Humanities

Press, 1979); R. L. Taylor, *The Cultivation of Sagehood as a Religious Goal in Neo-Confucianism: A Study of Selected Writings of Kao P'an-lung (1562– 1626)* (Missoula, Montana: Scholar's Press/American Academy of Religion, 1978).

2. *Shuo-wen chieh-tzu ku-lin* (Taipei, 1977) Vol. 9, p. 1086.

3. Ibid.

4. Bernhard Karlgren, *Grammata Serica Recensa* (Stockholm: Museum of Far Eastern Antiquities, 1964), p. 222.

5. William G. Boltz, "The Religious and Philosophical Significance of the 'Hsiang-erh' Lao Tzu in the Light of the Ma-Wang-Tui Silk Manuscripts," *Bulletin of the School of Oriental and African Studies* 45, Part 1 (1982), pp. 101–2.

6. *Shuo-wen chieh-tzu ku-lin*, Vol. 9, p. 1086.

7. One of the few studies to have been written on the nature of scripture in Chinese Buddhist sources is a short article, Roger Corless, "The Meaning of Ching (Sutra?) in Buddhist Chinese," *Journal of Chinese Philosophy* 3, No. 1 (Dec., 1975), pp. 67–72.

8. *Shuo-wen chieh-tzu ku-lin*, Vol. 10, p. 527.

9. Karlgren, pp. 219–20.

10. For a more detailed account of the issues that divided the New Text and the Old Text scholars see Fung Yu-lan, *A History of Chinese Philosophy, Vol. II, The Period of Classical Learning* (trans. Derk Bodde) (Princeton: Princeton University Press, 1953), Chaps. 2, 4.

11. For the convenience of readers who may want to consult more of the text, I am using the standard translation by James Legge. See James Legge, *The Chinese Classics, Vol. I, Confucian Analects, The Great Learning, and The Doctrine of the Mean* (Oxford: Clarendon Press, 1893), p. 211.

12. Legge, p. 193.

13. Legge, p. 323.

14. Legge, p. 146.

15. James Legge, *The Chinese Classics, Vol. II, The Works of Mencius* (Oxford: Clarendon Press, 1983), pp.426–28.

16. Legge, Vol. II, p. 479.

17. Quoted in Fung Yu-lan *A History of Chinese Philosophy, Vol. I, The Period of the Philosophers* (trans. Derk Bodde) (Princeton: Princeton University Press, 1952), p. 400.

18. Quoted in Fung, Vol. I, pp. 401–2.

19. John K. Shryock,*The Origin and Development of the State Cult of Confucius* (n.1.: American Historical Association, 1932; reprint ed., New York: Paragon Reprint Corp., 1966), p. 41.

20. Shryock, p. 70.

21. See Shryock, Chap. 3 for an excellent summary of this development.

22. See the translation of this material in Fung, Vol. I, pp. 44–45.

23. Wing-tsit Chan (trans.), *Reflections on Things at Hand, The Neo-Confucian*

Anthology Compiled by Chu Hsi and Lü Tsu-ch'ien (New York: Columbia University Press, 1967), p. 104.

24. See Wing-tsit Chan, "Chu Hsi's Completion of Neo-Confucianism," *Etudes Song—Sung Studies, In Memoriam Etienne Balazs*, ed. Françoise Aubin, Ser. II, no. 1 (1973), p. 82.

25. Ibid.

26. Chan, "Completion," p. 83.

27. Ibid.

28. While the *Chin-ssu lu* contains one chapter considered essential to the Neo-Confucian metaphysical system, the majority of the text deals with practical details in learning and self-cultivation. As a guide to the life of cultivation it is one of the most important works available in translation that exemplifies the Confucian religious life. For a complete translation see Chan, *Reflections*.

29. Chan, *Reflections*, p. 98.

30. Chan, *Reflections*, p. 97.

31. Chan, *Reflections*, p. 101.

32. Chan, "Completion," p. 85.

33. Ibid.

34. Ibid.

35. Chan, "Completion," pp. 85–86.

36. Chan, *Reflections*, p. 102.

37. Ibid.

38. Chan, *Reflections*, p. 103.

39. Ibid.

40. For general reading on the differences between the major schools see Wing-tsit Chan, *A Source Book in Chinese Philosophy* (Princeton: Princeton University Press, 1963) Chaps. 33–35. For an excellent study of the School of Mind see Wei-ming Tu, *Neo-Confucian Thought in Action: Wang Yang-ming's Youth (1472–1509)* (Berkeley: University of California, 1976).

41. Chan, *Source Book*, p. 580.

42. This is included in the translation of Wang Yang-ming's writings by W. T. Chan. See Wing-tsit Chan (trans.), *Instructions for Practical Living and Other Neo-Confucian Writings by Wang Yang-ming* (New York: Columbia University Press, 1963), pp. 271–80.

43. The criticism is focused on Chu Hsi's revision of the text of the Great Learning in which he placed *ko-wu*, the investigation of things, and *chih-chih*, the extension of knowledge, prior to *ch'eng-i*, the sincerity of will, in the chapters of commentary dealing with the eight stages of learning. To Chu Hsi this was a logical arrangement which placed the beginning stages of learning in an investigative and accumulative process. For Yang-ming there was no justification for such a revision. See Chan, *Source Book*, p. 89.

44. Chan, *Instructions*, p. 279.

45. See W. T. de Bary, *Neo-Confucian Orthodoxy and the Learning of the Mind-and-Heart* (New York: Columbia University Press, 1981), pp. 1–66.

46. De Bary, *Orthodoxy*, p. 17.
47. De Bary, "Some Common Tendencies in Neo-Confucianism," in D. Nivison, A. Wright (eds.) *Confucianism in Action* (Stanford: Stanford University Press, 1959), pp. 34–35.
48. De Bary, *Orthodoxy*, p. 137.
49. Chan, *Reflections*, p. 35.
50. The different dimensions of orthodoxy are summarized by W. T. de Bary in W. T. de Bary, Irene Bloom (eds.) *Principle and Practicality: Essays in Neo-Confucianism and Practical Learning* (New York: Columbia University Press, 1979), pp. 16– 17.
51. The seminal article on the life of learning and self-cultivation in W. T. de Bary, "Neo-Confucian Cultivation and the Seventeenth Century 'Enlightenment'," in de Bary, *Unfolding*, pp. 141–216. See also R. L. Taylor, "Meditation in Ming Neo-Orthodoxy: Kao P'an-lung's Writings on Quiet-Sitting," *Journal of Chinese Philosophy* 6, no. 2 (June, 1979), pp. 142– 82.
52. Chan, *Reflections*, p. 83.
53. Chan, *Reflections*, p. 52.
54. Ibid.
55. I have found this to be reflected in autobiographical expression. See R. L. Taylor, "The Centered Self: Religious Autobiography in the Neo-Confucian Tradition," *History of Religions* 17, nos. 3 & 4 (Feb.–May, 1978), pp. 266–83.; R. L. Taylor, "Journey Into Self: The Autobiographical Reflections of Hu Chih," *History of Religions* 21, no. 4 (May, 1982), pp. 321–38. An excellent study of the Confucian view of learning and maturation is found in Wei-ming Tu, "The Confucian Perception of Adulthood," *Daedalus* 105, No. 2 (Spring, 1976), pp. 113–27; reprinted in Tu, *Humanity*, pp. 35– 56.
56. Chan, *Reflections*, p. 122.
57. Chan, *Reflections*, p. 121.
58. See Taylor, *Cultivation of Sagehood*.
59. For a discussion of Confucian ceremony see Spencer Palmer, *Confucian Rituals in Korea* (Berkeley: Asian Humanities Press, 1984) and R. L. Taylor, *The Way of Heaven: An Introduction to the Confucian Religious Life* (Leiden: E. J. Brill, 1985).
60. See Taylor, "Journey" and a comparative study of the autobiographies of Kao and Hu Chih entitled, "Acquiring A Point of View: Confucian Dimensions of Self-Reflection," *Monumenta Serica* 34 (1979–1980), pp. 145– 170.

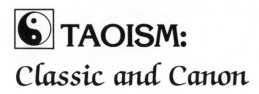

TAOISM:
Classic and Canon

Laurence G. Thompson

The Western religious tradition predisposes one to a certain assumption about "scripture," namely, that it is sacred or, more specifically, holy. To speak of a text as scripture implies that it has religious authority, which is to say, that it is subject to exegesis but not criticism. In Chinese the word *ching* (originally the warp of a textile) is applied to translations of the holy books of Christianity or Islam and to the *sūtras* (words spoken by the Buddha) of Buddhism. The word *ching*, is, however, also appellative of texts that, while authoritative in some sense, are not necessarily so in a *religious* sense, as for example the *Ch'a Ching*, or *"Scripture" of Tea*. For this reason many translators have preferred to render *ching* as a Classic. The trouble is, of course, that the word Classic in English has no religious connotation, and therefore fails to convey the religious authority that *is* attributed to many *ching* in Chinese.

In the case of the Tao Tsang, the corpus of Taoist texts, many of the works included are entitled *ching*, and have religious or scriptural character because they are revelations from divine authority. Many others of the text are not, however of this nature, but may more accurately be described as Classics. And a great many more would fall outside of either of these rubics. The name Tao Tsang indicates nothing more specific than a "collection" (bibliotheca) of works on Taoist subjects, and was coined in imitation of the name of the Buddhist Tripiṭaka in Chinese. In the Taoist case the original meaning of *tsang*, "secreted or hidden," is—perhaps not altogether fortuitously—quite apt, as many Taoist texts are esoteric. In fact some scholars use the expression "esoteric Taoism" to indicate what others call simply "religious Taoism."

This "Bibliotheca Taoica" is a huge assemblage of texts that range in date from as early as three or four centuries B.C.E. to as recently as the beginning of the twentieth century. Its contents were not early on circumscribed and defined, as were those of the Western Bible or the Qur'an. Historically, various efforts were made to bring them all together in a rational system, but these efforts were not "finally" successful until the mid-fifteenth century woodblock printed edition. Even so, the finality was elastic, a Continuation appearing in 1607; while new items were added even after that in abridged collections. It should be understood that through the ages texts were lost, collections were disbursed or their printing blocks burnt, and that at best the Tao Tsang in whole or in part was available only in severely limited numbers of copies stored in a few institutions generally inaccessible to the public. When earlier in the twentieth century, Chinese and foreign scholars became seriously interested in Taoist studies, one of their most exigent problems was the extreme rarity of complete or even partial collections of the Tao Tsang.[1]

It will be obvious, then, that the Taoist Collectanea should in no way be imagined as widely in use amongst Chinese as the Bible is among Protestants. The situation is more comparable to the limitations of usage in the ages when the Bible existed only in the original tongues and was thus understood only by scholars. The language of the Taoist texts is not only literary rather than colloquial, but highly technical and sometimes deliberately esoteric. Here we have the case, common in other historical cultures as well, where study and application of the texts is the province of adept and priest. Still, even adept or priest could hardly "know" the Tao Tsang in the sense that his counterpart in the West would know the Holy Book in its entirety. The immensity of the Tao Tsang, supposing it to be available, made such complete mastery out of the question for all but those, perhaps, with photographic memories. The practitioner or priest would usually be an adherent to one of the several major "schools" or traditions of Taoism, and would specialize in those texts relevant to his school's interests. Individuals might utilize a few of the technical manuals for guidance in practices leading to longevity or even immortality, without any particular concern for other aspects of Taoist philosophy or religion. Those inheriting the functions of community priests would need to study required texts such as the "registers" and liturgical manuals, but a lay scholar would probably find such texts of little or no interest.

Again, it should be realized that in any case almost nobody at any time had access to the Tao Tsang as a whole. Even after the use of woodblock printing could have insured the wide spread and reproduction of texts,[2] they probably continued to be disseminated mostly in handwritten manuscripts. Possession of certain specific texts was, in the tradition of Chinese craft-skills, the means by which the profession of community priest was passed down through the generations within a family. These texts were treated as family treasures and protected from the eyes of outsiders. To become acquainted with even a small number of texts required that one be accepted as a disciple by some Taoist who possessed these texts.[3]

HISTORY OF SCRIPTURE

The Tao Tsang had a somewhat complicated history.[4] Collections of handwritten texts were made in the eighth century (T'ang dynasty) and the beginning of the eleventh century (Northern Sung dynasty). The first collection to be block printed was completed a century later (beginning of the twelfth century, likewise Northern Sung dynasty). Unfortunately, none of these earlier versions survived. It is particularly regrettable that the blocks for the second Sung edition were destroyed when the monastery where they were housed burnt to the ground. Under the Mongols (Yüan dynasty) another version, based on a surviving text of the second Sung edition, was block printed (1244); but within a few decades fickle imperial favor turned to displeasure, and these blocks were in their turn mostly destroyed (1281). The Tao Tsang that we possess today dates from 1445 (Ming dynasty), although its blocks do not survive. In 1607 a Continuation of the Ming Tao Tsang was published. Some idea of the size of the Tao Tsang with its Continuation may be gained from the fact that 121,589 blocks (from each of which would be printed both recto and verso sides of a page) were required to print it.

Recognizing the exorbitant cost in labor and money of reproducing many copies of such a monumental work, and the difficulties facing anyone trying to find materials within its endless pages, various abridged versions have been made from time to time. There is, for example, the *Anthology of the Most Important Texts of the Tao Tsang* (*Tao Tsang Chi Yao*) that was compiled in the Ch'ing dynasty (1644–1911), and is still to be found in many libraries. The most important abridgment by far is that done by Chang Chün-fang, the scholar who served as editor-in-chief of the early eleventh-century Tao Tsang. His work was called *Flowers of the Seven Sections of the Cloud Bookbox* (*Yün Chi Ch'i Pu Chih Ying*), but it is now universally known as the *Seven [Sections of] Bamboo Slips of the Cloud Bookbox* (*Yün Chi Ch'i Ch'ien*).[5] This great work, which happily has survived and is today readily available in photographic reprint and modern format, is of such fundamental importance because in it are preserved a considerable amount of the contents of earlier Tao Tsang that have not descended to us. It is itself a collection on a grand scale, consisting of 122 "chapters" (the word *chüan* refers to the scrolls of earlier book formats). The edition preserved in the Abbey of the White Clouds (Pai Yün Kuan) at Peking, from which the current Taiwan edition derives, was in 2,460 pages bound as 26 volumes (*ts'e*). There is a very recent abridgment selected from the Ming Tao Tsang that likewise attempts to prune the Canon to manageable size.

Of course such abridgments necessarily involve selective judgments that may distort the total picture of the Taoist scriptures, but they are the only means of bringing a "Taoist Bible" within the possession of individual devotees or scholars. As for the Tao Tsang of the mid-fifteenth century that represents that complete surviving collection, it was reproduced photolithographically in Shanghai during the years from 1924 to 1927 and published by the Commercial Press under auspices of the Han Fen lou. It has been republished in Taiwan in 1962. Bound in 60 Western-style volumes, it contains a total of 49,087 pages, each page containing two pages of the original block printed work. The Continuation of 1607 is included in this edition. The Taiwan reprint also has an index volume which is in fact the reference work compiled in Paris under the editorship of K. Schipper (1975).

SCRIPTURAL CONTENT—RELIGIOUS AND PHILOSOPHICAL

It would not be possible to give a résumé of the contents of the Tao Tsang within the limits of this brief survey, especially as this would assume an understanding of Taoist religious concepts and language that few—even among Sinologists—possess. Instead, we shall have to be content to take note of a few historical records that indicate in a general way what sorts of texts were included at various times.

In the first place we should dispose of a notion that continues to be asserted in works on Chinese studies, namely, that a clear-cut distinction is to be made between the philosophical and the religious texts of Taoism. This notion is usually expressed in the statement that the pre-Ch'in dynasty (221–207 B.C.E.) texts of *Lao Tzu* and *Chuang Tzu* (and sometimes including *Lieh Tzu*) are works of "pure philosophy," while the religious writings are products of a late- and post-Han (*ca.* 200 C.E. *et seq.*) mentality that would have shocked those "classical" philosophers. While of course we have no way of knowing how the earlier thinkers would have regarded later Taoist developments, the Tao Tsang demonstrates very clearly that the later Taoists considered the ancient texts of the classical period as scripture. A leading Western scholar has estimated that

> . . . more than a third of the Canon is constituted solely of a score of different texts, for the most part compilations of the Sung and Yüan epochs. Two of these twenty texts are commentaries on the *Chuang-tzu*. If one adds to them the sixty-nine other commentaries on the *Lao-tzu*, the *Chuang-tzu*, the *Lieh-tzu* and the *Wen-tzu*, one will see that *more than half the Canon is occupied by commentaries on these fundamental texts*.[Translated from Strickmann 1981, p. 4; *emphasis added*]

It is without doubt the *Lao Tzu* (*Tao Te Ching*) that has remained the basic source of Taoist inspiration throughout history, and to continue to think of this text as merely one of the "pre-Ch'in philosophers" is completely to miss its significance.[6] It is not only Taoist texts of the classical period that are found in the far reaches of the Tao Tsang. One finds in this great depository also such writings as the *Scripture of Change* (*I Ching*) with many commentaries, *The Art of War* (*Ping Fa*) by Master Sun of the late pre-Ch'in period, the *Kung-sun Lung Tzu*, the *Mo Tzu*, the *Han Fei Tzu* (all philosophical works not ordinarily considered to be of Taoist provenance), the *"Scripture" of Mountains and Seas* (*Shan Hai Ching*), a sort of "Book of Marvels," the eclectic *Philosophers of Huai-nan* (*Huai-nan Tzu*) compiled late in the second century B.C.E. . . . . There are also many texts deriving from the Han period "technicians of the occult" (*fang-shih*) on such subjects as astrology, numerology, and cabalistic diagrams.

The earliest record we have of works that eventually formed the basis of the Tao Tsang is in the "Bibliography of Texts of the [Six] Arts" (*Yi Wen Chih*, a memoir in the *History of the Former Han Dynasty* (*Han Shu*) by Pan Ku (32–92 C.E.). This bibliography lists the titles and numbers of bundles of bamboo or wooden slips or rolls of silk comprising each text. The whole represents the holdings of the Imperial library of the time. Books that are Taoist in tenor are of three types: (1) 37 Taoist philosophers in 913 bundles; (2) 8 writers on *yin-tao*, or sexual techniques, in 186 bundles; (3) 10 writers on immortal transcendency (*shen-hsien*) in 205 bundles. Unfortunately many of the texts listed by Pan Ku were lost, mutilated, or replaced in later ages by forgeries. Still, quite a few were preserved to appear in what came to be the Canon.

Another early list, precious for its information, is found in the great work of Ko Hung (283–343), appearing under his pen name *Pao P'u Tzu, The Master Who Embraces [Uncarved] Simplicity* (a reference to a famous metaphor in *Lao Tzu*). Chapter 19 of the Inner Chapters (*nei p'ien*) contains an interesting account of the author's studies under a famous Taoist Master called Cheng Yin, and during the course of this reminiscence Ko Hung recites the names of some 205 titles of texts current in those times.[7] Many of these texts are still to be found in the Tao Tsang.

A third early list is contained in the "Bibliography of Scriptural Works" (*Ching Chi Chih*) of the *History of the Sui Dynasty* (*Sui Shu*) compiled by Wei Cheng (580–643). Under the heading of Taoist writings we find (1) 301 works on Scriptures and Precepts (*ching chieh*) in 908 scrolls; (2) 46 works on Ingestion (*er-fu*), presumably referring to breath-yoga, diet, and taking of the elixir (?) in 167 scrolls; (3) 13 works on Sexual Techniques (*fang-chung*) in 38 scrolls; and (4) 17 works on Talismans (*fu*) and Registers (*lu*) in 103 scrolls. Altogether this bibliography lists 377 works in 1,216 scrolls pertaining to Taoism.[8]

By the time the Tao Tsang was first block-printed at the beginning of the twelfth century, it had grown tremendously. In his *Comprehensive History [of China]* (*T'ung Chih*), the historian Cheng Ch'iao (1104–1162) gives a breakdown of the contents: (1) *Lao Tzu*, 90 works in 290 chapters; (2) *Chuang Tzu*, 49 works in 516 chapters; (3) Various Other Philosophers, 46 works in 294 chapters; (4) *Yin Fu Scripture*, 39 works in 54 chapters; (5) *Huang T'ing Scripture*, 39 works in 57 chapters; (6) *Ts'an T'ung Ch'i*—purportedly the earliest work on alchemy (the title means something like *Alchemical Correspondences [to the I Ching]*)—19 works in 31 chapters; (7) Bibliography, 11 works in 144 chapters; (8) Biographies, 103 works in 404 chapters; (9) Historical Records, 32 works in 93 chapters; (10) Treatises, 58 works in 151 chapters; (11) "Writings" (*shu*), 44 works in 452 chapters; (2) Scriptures, 85 works in 186 chapters; (13) Rituals, 54 works in 78 chapters; (14) Talismans and Registers, 103 works in 159 chapters; (15) Breath-Yoga, 74 works in 94 chapters; (16) Embryonic Respiration, 30 works in 39 chapters; (17) Interior Vision, 23 works in 25 chapters; (18) Gymnastics, 20 works in 22 chapters; (19) Abstinence from Cereals, 8 works in 8 chapters; (20) Inner Alchemy (i.e., through yogic concentration), 40 works in 44 chapters; (21) Outer Alchemy (i.e., concocting and ingesting substances), 203 works in 310 chapters; (22) Drugs of Gold and Stone (i.e., Cinnabar), 31 works in 35 chapters; (23) Ingestion, 48 works in 86 chapters; (24) Sexual Techniques, 9 works in 18 chapters; (25) Self-Cultivation, 74 works in 118 chapters. The total comprises 25 categories with 1,323 works in 3,706 chapters. A truly diversified and gigantic collection![9]

THE ORIGINS AND FORMS OF SCRIPTURE

It is unfortunate for the student that the rational categories of historian Cheng Ch'iao do not in fact reflect the organizational schema of the Tao Tsang, which is considerably more confusing. As to this actual schema, it was not the result of editorial logic, but rather of sectarian interests in the real world of Taoist activity. Scholars agree that it results from the rise of various sects, each provided with its own scriptures—revealed texts that established its claim to divine authority. These movements were very early, coming in the period between the breakdown of the Han Empire (before the end of the third century C.E.) and the eventual reunification of China by the Sui dynasty (589–618). During this age China was divided politically in complex ways, the most distinct of which was the division between the "barbarian"-occupied North and the Chinese-ruled South.[10] Taoist cults arose primarily in the latter area, whereas Buddhism was more congenial to the foreign Courts of the North. It was the rise of such cults—which may likely be an assertion of Chineseness vis-à-vis the foreign Buddhism that was becoming so popular—that brought about the creation of a recognizable "Taoist religion," in the sense that there was a sort of "united front" based on mutual acceptance of Taoist texts and Taoist beliefs.

The major divisions of the Tao Tsang that evolved from this situation reflect the rise to prominence of several of the sects, their particular texts having been grouped within what are called the Three Caverns (*San Tung*). In the Cavern of the Perfected (*Tung Chen*) there are placed the scriptures that were revealed from the Heaven of Highest Purity (*Shang Ch'ing*). These were texts recorded in automatic writing by the medium Yang Hsi during the mid-360s while he was staying in the Hills of the [Three] Mao [Brothers], i.e., Mao Shan (modern Kiangsu province). The sect for which these texts are primary is therefore usually called the Mao Shan Sect.[11]

In the Cavern of the Mysterious (*Tung Hsüan*) there are placed the scriptures revealed from the Heaven ruled by the Lord of the Spiritually Efficacious Treasure (*Ling Pao Chün*). Scriptures of this origin are already mentioned by Ko Hung in his *Master Who Embraces [Uncarved] Simplicity* of the early fourth century. According to him, they included recipes for attainment of immortal transcendence as well as information about "protective days." He repeats a fascinating story that tells of the revelation of the *Scripture of Spiritually Efficacious Treasure* to Yü the Great (legendary times), who had it buried in a cave on a mountain. The text was written in "purple ideographs on slips of gold." Many centuries later it was discovered and brought to Master K'ung (Confucius), who recognized it for what it was. The sectarian movement based upon the Ling Pao scriptures arose after Ko Ch'ao-fu (putative descendant of Ko Hung) claimed to have found them in the writings of his ancestor, at the very end of the fourth century, and these writings were expanded and edited by the master Lu Hsiu-ching (406–477). They were strongly oriented to liturgical rites of abstinence and penitence, which gave them a central position in Taoist priestly profession.

In the Cavern of the Numinous (*Tung Shen*) there are placed the *Texts of the Three August Ones* (*San Huang Wen*).[12] It is again Ko Hung who tells us a little about these scriptures, most interestingly that they are to be found hidden in caves in famous mountains including the Five Sacred Peaks. But they are of course revealed only to certain immortal transcendents. These texts are especially powerful magic against malevolent spiritual powers. Unfortunately, we still know little about the sectarian history connected with them.[13]

While we may thus matter-of-factly describe the historical circumstances connected with the scriptures of the Three Caverns, it will be well to keep in mind the religious origins that would have been far more important to the Taoists:

> The teachings of the Cavern of the Perfected (*Tung Chen*) are considered to be Evidences of Doctrinal Master the Lord of the Heavenly Treasure (*T'ien Pao Chün*); they are considered to originate in the Vital Breath (*ch'i*) of the Supreme Originless Highest Jadelike Augustus of the Cave of Chaos. The teachings of the Cavern of the Mysterious (*Tung Hsüan*) are considered to be Evidences of Doctrinal Master the Lord of the Spiritually Efficacious Treasure (*Ling Pao Chün*); they are considered to originate in the Vital Breath of the Supreme Originless Jadelike Vacuity of Ruddy Chaos. The teachings of the Cavern of the Numinous (*Tung Shen*) are considered to be Evidences of Doctrinal Master the Lord of the Numinous Treasure (*Shen Pao Chün*); they are considered to originate in the Vital Breath of the Supreme Jadelike Vacuity of the Profoundly Still and Mysteriously Penetrating Origins. . . . [from Chang Chün-fang's *Seven Slips*]

At a secondary level in the formal organization of the Tao Tsang are the so-called Four Supplements (*Ssu Fu*), one to each of the Three Caverns, and a fourth to the whole ensemble. In fact, these are the texts that antedate the revealed scriptures of the sects, on which the latter were based. The Four Supplements may be briefly described as follows:

1.   The Supreme Mystery (*T'ai Hsüan*). Includes the *Lao Tzu* and its commentaries as well as works of various Taoist philosophers. It supplements the Cavern of the Mysterious (*Tung Hsüan*).

2. The Supreme Peace-and-Equality (*T'ai P'ing*). Consists of two very long works, the *Scripture of Supreme Peace-and-Equality* (*T'ai P'ing Ching*) in 170 scrolls, attributed to one Yü Chi of the second century;[14] and the *Scripture of Supreme Peace-and-Equality of the Cavern of the Infinite* (*T'ai P'ing Tung Chi Ching*) in 144 scrolls, received from Lao Tzu by Chang Ling (or, Chang Tao-ling), also in the second century.[15] It supplements the Cavern of the Perfected (*Tung Chen*).

3. The Supreme Purity (*T'ai Ch'ing*). Includes many texts devoted to the techniques basic in the Taoist quest for immortal transcendency, especially those of "gold and cinnabar" (i.e., "outer" alchemy, *wai-tan*, the alchemy of concocting the elixir) and dietary regimens. All of these texts are supposed to be of very early date—Han dynasty or Three Kingdoms, 221–265—although of course they were of supernatural origin. It supplements the Cavern of the Numinous (Tung Shen).

4. Scriptures and Registers of the School of Orthodox Unity personally received by Chang Ling from the Supreme Lord Lao, to be taught as the New, but Orthodox, Dispensation. Most important among these texts are the registers of supernaturals by means of which the Taoist can impeach or summon the spirits.[16]

At the tertiary level of organization, each of the Three Caverns is divided according to subject-matter into twelve sections, whose nature will be indicated in the quotation that follows. This quotation tells us in the words of the editors of the Ming Canon how they conceived of the origin and organization of the Tao Tsang:

The Origin of the Taoist Doctrines
The origin of the Taoist Family from its very beginning: It arose from that before which there was nothing (i.e., the Tao), whose Evidences were let down in response to influences, giving birth to the Mysterious One. From the Mysterious One there came about the division into the Three Primordials. Further, from the Three Primordials there came about the division into the Three Vital Breaths. Again, from the Three Vital Breaths it changed and gave birth to the Three Powers (i.e., Heaven, Earth, and Man). The Three Powers being nourished, the ten tousand (i.e., all) things-and-beings came to completion.

Of the Three Primordials, the first was the Supreme Non-Existent Primordial of the Cavern of Chaos; the second was the Supreme Non-Existent Primordial of the Ruddy Chaos; the third was the Mysteriously Permeating primordial of the Dark Stillness. From the Supreme Non-Existent Primordial of the Cavern of Chaos was born by transformation the Lord of the Celestial Treasure (*T'ien Pao Chün*); from the Supreme Non-Existent Primordial of the Ruddy Chaos was born by transformation the Lord of the Spiritually Efficacious Treasure

(*Ling Pao Chün*); from the Mysteriously Permeating Primordial of the Dark Stillness was born by transformation the Lord of the Numinous Treasure (*Shen Pao Chün*). Their Evidences in the Great Caverns came forth separately as transformation-lords, governing in the Three Pure Realms.

These Three Pure [Realms] are Jadelike Purity, Superior Purity, and Supreme Purity. They are also named the Three Heavens. The Three Heavens are the Pure and Subtle Heaven, the Abundantly Flowing Heaven, and the Great Ruddy Heaven. The Lord of the Celestial Treasure (*T'ien Pao Chün*) governs in the Realm of Jadelike Purity, the Pure and Subtle Heaven, and his Vital Breath is Pristine Blue. The Lord of the Spiritually Efficacious Treasure (*Ling Pao Chün*) governs in the Realm of Superior Purity, the Abundantly Flowing Heaven, and his Vital Breath is Primal Yellow. The Lord of the Numinous Treasure governs in the Realm of Supreme Purity, the Great Ruddy Heaven, and his Vital Breath is Profound White. Therefore the *Scripture of Sections on the Nine Heavens Giving Birth to the Numinous Beings* says, "These three appellations, though different, are originally one and the same thing. These three Lords are each Heads of the Doctrines, that is, they are the Venerable Numina of the Three Caverns."

The Three Caverns are the Cavern of the Perfected (*Tung Chen*), the Cavern of the Mysterious (*Tung Hsüan*), and the Cavern of the Numinous (*Tung Shen*). The Lord of the Celestial Treasure spoke scriptures in twelve sections, and is the Head of the Doctrines of the Cavern of the Perfected. The Lord of the Spiritually Efficacious Treasure spoke scriptures in twelve sections, and is the Head of the Doctrines of the Cavern of the Mysterious. The Lord of the Numinous Treasure spoke scriptures in twelve sections, and is the Head of the Doctrines of the Cavern of the Numinous. Therefore the Three Caverns altogether contain 36 sections of venerable scriptures. Those of the First Cavern are the Great Vehicle, those of the Second Cavern are the Middling Vehicle, and those of the Third Cavern are the Small Vehicle.[17]

In addition to the Three Caverns there are the further divisions of the Four Supplements, called respectively Supreme Mystery, Supreme Peace-and-Equality, Supreme Purity, and Orthodox One. The Supreme Mystery supplements the Cavern of the Perfected, the Supreme Peace-and-Equality supplements the Cavern of the Mysterious, and the Supreme Purity supplements the Cavern of the Numinous; while the Orthodox One supplements all of the Caverns. [Within Caverns and Supplements], there are altogether seven parts.

Furthermore, the scriptures overflowing and revealed from the Three Caverns are [in each case] divided into 12 categories: The first is Basic Texts, the second is Spirit-Talismans, the third is Jadelike Esoterica (i.e., explications of texts), the fourth is Spiritually Efficacious Diagrams, the fifth is Genealogical Registers, the sixth is Precepts, the seventh is Correct Deportment, the eighth is Methods of Self-Discipline, the ninth is [Occult] Arts, the tenth is Biographies, the eleventh is Hymns of Praise, and the twelfth is Memorials (i.e., petitions to the Divine Powers).

Pen Wen (the first category, that we have rendered as Basic Texts) is another name for Ching (Scriptures), the basis for the techniques of preserving life. Having been born, it is then necessary to nurture [one's life], and therefore next we have the Spiritual Talismans. If one is not versed in the "Cloud Writing of the Eight Assemblies," the Jadelike Ideographs of the Three Primordials, how can one get benefit from them?—hence we have the Jadelike Esoterica to explain their Principles. All beings are dull and obtuse, and when they directly hear the sounds of the doctrines they are unable to comprehend; hence Diagramatic Symbols were drawn as aids to clarification. The accomplishments of the Saints having been manifested, should the true condition of things concerning these "ancestors" not [be made known], this will permit falsehoods [to be substituted]; hence the need for Genealogical Registers. In these five items the living being is defined; if we want to supplement and complete them, it is necessary to examine and be on our guard against evil practices and fraudulent texts; hence we have the Precepts. Having abandoned worldly ways and entered the Way, left one's home and become an assistant to one's treasured Master, one must have good appearance and deportment; hence next there is clarified that Correct Deportment. Having previously taken steps to prevent evil, the sins of one's past existence are still not swept away, and one must Discipline Oneself by Abstinence and Ritual, repenting of the evil to which one has oneself given rise. One's ritual deportment being good, and one's root from the previous existence being purified, one must advance to the study of the principles of the Occult Arts. In due course one will rise to the study of the essentials of the Perfected, availing oneself of the mysteries of the Arts of the Tao revealed on bamboo and silk.[18] Discussion of becoming a Saint, and the practice and study conducing thereto, follow next. Accomplishments due to such studies being manifested, therefore we have the recording of Biographies. When, beginning from the birth of a living being and ending with the perfection of his deeds, all is praiseworthy, then next we have Hymns of Praise. Furthermore, the foregoing words of all the doctrines are mostly in long lines and discursive talk. Now, speaking of Hymns of Praise, these are gāthās in phrases;[19] their cohesive words being apt, their effect is full and their virtue perfect. Hence, one must show what is in one's heart, as in the recitation of merits [of the deceased] at the close of the ritual of abstinence and penitence (chai); therefore we have the Memorials.[20]

Although the grand design of the Tao Tsang, with its Caverns, Supplements, and Sections can thus be explained both in historical and religious terms, its lengthy development through time, its many partial destructions, and its openness to the inclusion of new materials because of the lack of any ecclesiastical authority to pronounce decisions upon the contents, have effectively ruined any neat arrangement. The collection as it exists in its Ming version is not only dauntingly huge, but bafflingly disorganized. It will take the work of experts a long time yet before research aids have been developed adequate to serve as guides to the perplexed.

CONTENT OF THE "LITTLE TAO TSANG"

In any case, as has been explained, because the complete Tao Tsang is seldom available to devotees or scholars even today, most of these will consult either individual texts published by Taoist organizations or commercial presses, or collections of texts selected from the Canon. If we may try the patience of our readers with one more schematic presentation, we shall give here an outline of the contents of the "Little Tao Tsang" of Chang Chün-fang (i.e., the *Seven [Sections of] Bamboo Slips of the Cloud Bookbox. Yün Chi Ch'i Ch'ien*) dating from the beginning of the eleventh century. The 30 major subject-divisions of Chang's anthology, taken together, give a reasonably concrete idea of the concerns represented in the Tao Tsang:

I–V.[21] Section on The Tao and Its Power; Section on Cosmology and Creation; Section on the Founding of the Taoist Religion; Section on the Transmission of the Teachings of the Taoist Scriptures and Methods; Section on Lines of Inheritance of the Scriptural Teachings (i.e., the Sectarian Movements). Each of these, while reproducing several texts, occupies a single chapter.

VI. Section on the Scriptural Teachings of the Three Caverns. This section, reproducing texts of the major sectarian movements of early times, is very long, occupying 15 chapters.

VII–XI. Section on Heaven and Earth (2 chapters); Section on the Heavenly Bodies (3 chapters); Section on the Ten Islands (*chou*) and Three Islands (*tao*)—i.e., paradisiacal lands (1 chapter); Section on the Cave-Heavens and Happy Lands (1 chapter); Section on the 28 Parishes—i.e., the jurisdictions established by the theocracy of the Masters Designated by Heaven, *T'ien Shih* (1 chapter).

XII. Section on Holding to Life and Receiving One's Destiny (3 chapters).

XIII–XVI. Section on Miscellaneous Methods of Cultivating and Aiding Life (5 chapters); Section on Fasting and Purification (4 chapters); Section on Miscellaneous Methods According to the Seven Bamboo Slips (1 chapter); Section on Concentrating the Thought (3 chapters).

XVII–XIX. Section on Secret and Important Esoteric Methods (7 chapters); Section on Miscellaneous Important Methods of [Mental] Visualization (1 chapter); Miscellaneous and Important Esoteric Methods (1 chapter).

XX–XXIII. Section on Soul and Spirits (2 chapters); Section on the Methods of Breath-Yoga of the Various Masters (7 chapters); Section on the Secret Methods of Gold and Cinnabar—i.e., *wan-tan* or concoction of the elixir (a very long section in 11 chapters); Section on Prescriptions for Drugs—referring of course to substances that promote longevity (5 chapters).

XXIV. Section on Occult Diagrams [Used as Talismans] and Maps (2 chapters).

XXV. Section on the Day Designated by Cyclical Terms *Keng-Shen*—these texts have to do with the way to deal with the so-called Three Corpses within the body that work for its early dissolution (3 chapters).

XXVI. Section on the technique of attaining immortal transcendency by Liberation from the Corpse (3 chapters).

XXVII. Section on the Study of Important [Matters According to] Various True [Men]—i.e., perfected adepts (a long section in 9 chapters).

XXVIII. Section on Hymns of Praise (4 chapters).

XXIX. Section on Biographies (the longest section, with 28 chapters).

XXX. Section on Records of the Spiritual Efficacy of the Taoist Religion (6 chapters).

According to Hsiao T'ien-shih, who wrote the prefaces to the modern republications of Chang Chün-fang's anthology, its contents might be classified in modern terms under these nine heads.

1. Sections concerned with the theory of the "self-so" (*tzu-ran*) essence of all things-and-beings in the universe.

2. Sections concerned with astronomy and geography.

3. Sections concerned with physiology and pathology.

4. Sections concerned with hygiene (literally, in Chinese, the nourishing of life) and the prolongation of life including the study of becoming an immortal transcendent (*hsien*).

5. Sections concerned with hygiene (or, the nourishing of life) and breath-yoga.

6. Sections concerned with pharmacology and chemistry.

7. Sections concerned with occult techniques and incantations.
8. Sections concerned with ethics and self-cultivation.
9. Sections concerned with history and biography.

By considering the amount of space devoted to various subjects in the Chang Chün-fang collection we may gain some idea of which of them were most important, at least to Taoists of a thousand years ago. In the *Seven Slips* clearly Biographies (Section XXIX) are of capital importance, with the Scriptural Teachings of the Three Caverns (i.e., the early sectarian texts of Section VI) a close second, and the alchemical procedures of *wai-tan*, the Secret Methods of Gold and Cinnabar in Section XXII, a somewhat distant third.[22] Other sections that are allotted considerable space are those concerned with techniques (Sections XVII and XXVII), drugs (Section XXIII), and Taoist history (Section XXX).

These observations may be summarized:

Longest Sections—XXIX: Biographies—18 chapters, 270 pages; VI: Scriptural Teachings of the Three Caverns—15 chapters, 258 pages; XXII: Secret Methods of Gold and Cinnabar—11 chapters, 157 pages.

Other Major Sections—XXVII: Sections dealing with Techniques—9 chapters, 93 pages; XVIII—7 chapters, 86 pages; XXX: Taoist Historical Records—6 chapters, 85 pages; XXIII: Pharmacopoeia—5 chapters, 80 pages.

Total pages of the longest and other major sections: 1,029. By comparison, all the rest of the texts in this anthology combined take only 685 pages.

CENTRAL TAOIST THEMES

It will by now surely be apparent that, while the Taoist Scriptures are a heterogeneous and unsystematic lot, there are certain themes that provide some sort of unity amid all the diversity—that identify them, in fact, as Taoist. The central preoccupation of these texts is immortal transcendency, the Taoist form of the universal human hope for eternal life. While the strong emphasis upon biography is characteristic of Chinese historical writing in general, the figures in Taoist biography are of course those who have attained the goal.

Attainment, according to Taoism, is first and foremost a matter of practicing techniques, and the great number of texts in the Canon that deal with techniques of various kinds attests to this assumption. The ethical cultivation of the aspirant is by no means neglected, and it should be emphasized that a sort of general "Confucian morality" is required of anyone seeking success through techniques, but it is the latter that dominate in the Tao Tsang.

Scripture, properly speaking, is the basis of Taoist religion as of all religions in Great Traditions. Two kinds of scripture are clearly identified in the Tao Tsang. The first is the classical legacy, by far the most important text of which is the *Lao Tzu*. The second is the "sectarian scriptures" that were either deposited by Divine Beings in mountain caves, where they were discovered and their supernatural writing deciphered by advanced adepts; revealed through spirit-writing by a medium; or directly pronounced by Supreme Lord Lao (*T'ai-shang Lao Chün*, Lao Tzu defied). These texts all have the aura of sacredness or religious authority. The great Chinese tradition of textual annotation is at work on the Taoist scriptures as elsewhere, and much of the "theological" thought in Taoism is by way of commentaries on these scriptures.

What has not shown up distinctly in our exposition is the priestly side of Taoism, the exorcistic and ritual operations of ordained Taoists as community priests. The texts dealing with these matters—and there are very many of them in the Tao Tsang—do not clearly stand out in the sorts of classifications we have cited. However, their mastery (in some degree) is a prerequisite to ordination, and they must be considered as among the practically most used and thus most important sorts of Taoist scriptures.

THE STUDY OF THE TAOIST CANON

Serious scholarly interest in Taoism (aside from the so-called philosophical texts of classical times) is a recent phenomenon. The Tao Tsang, especially, has been almost literally a "seven-sealed book," with few, either among Chinese or foreign scholars, caring (or daring) to break some of those seals. It will thus be obvious why there are few samples of the contents of the Canon available in Western languages. But because our presentation has been of necessity so abstract and schematic, we wish in this concluding section to mention some of the samples that have been published, so that the interested reader may find a few concrete examples to make this rather dry outline come alive.

First, then, is the basic text, the *Lao Tzu*. As it happens, this is not only the Taoist text best represented in Western translations, but the most frequently translated book in all non-Western literature. We need not, therefore, spend any words on it, except to point out that it would be best for the reader to compare several renditions, as every translator has his own notions as to the "real" meaning of many passages. Unfortunately, these translators have seldom consulted the numerous commentaries in the Tao Tsang,[23] and most versions fail to convey the religious understanding of this text by later Taoists.

The other Taoist works of the trio, *Chuang Tzu* and *Lieh Tzu*, have also been available for a long time in English translations. As to the first, the version of James Legge, great British Sinologist of the late nineteenth and early twentieth centuries, may be found in Volumes XXXIX and XL of the Sacred Books of the East (London, 1891); while the recent translation by A. C. Graham, *Chuang Tzu; the Seven Inner Chapters and Other Writings . . .* (London, 1981) represents the most sophisticated level of current Western scholarship. Burton Watson's popular version (no scholarly apparatus), *The Complete Works of Chuang Tzu* (Columbia University Press, 1968) is both sound and readable. A. C. Graham translated the *Lieh Tzu* for the Wisdom of the East Series (London, 1960). The impressionistic renderings of Thomas Merton are valuable as the empathetic understanding brought to the text by a practicing mystic: *The Way of Chuang Tzu* (New York, 1965).

The subject of the Taoist biography, which looms so large in the Canon, has received some attention by Western scholars. One should consult Max Kaltenmark's *Le Lie Sien Tchouan; Biographies Légendaires des Immortels Taoïstes de l'Antiquité* (Peking, 1953); Lionel Giles, *A Gallery of Chinese Immortals* (London, 1948); Ngo Van Xuyet, *Divination, Magie et Politique dans la Chine Ancienne* (Paris, 1976)—see "Biographies des Magiciens"; and Kenneth J. DeWoskin, *Doctors, Diviners, and Magicians of Ancient China: Biographies of Fang-shih* (Columbia University Press, 1983).

The work of the great scholar and Taoist adept Ko Hung, who has been mentioned in our discussion several times, is available in translation by James Ware: *Alchemy, Medicine, and Religion in the China of A.D. 320; the Nei P'ien of Ko Hung* (Massachusetts Institute of Technology Press, 1966). Unfortunately the translation is not accompanied by the scholarly apparatus needed to make such a work really intelligible and useful.

Wai-tan, the attempt to make the "philosopher's stone," which was very important in the first millenium of Taoist practice, may be sampled in a translation of a well-known text of much later times, the *Essential Se-*

crets of the Scripture on the Elixir (Tan Ching Yao Chüeh) by the T'ang dynasty adept Sun Ssu-mo; see the scholarly work of Nathan Sivin, *Chinese Alchemy: Preliminary Studies* (Harvard University Press, 1968).

Nei-tan, the form of alchemy that replaced *wai-tan* in favor during the recent millenium—i.e., the alchemy of yogic concentration—is the subject of several translations. Best known is Richard Wilhelm's *The Secret of the Golden Flower* (translated from German by Cary F. Baynes), which contains two texts, and was of such great interest to C. G. Jung that he supplied it with Foreword and Commentary (2nd English edition, London & New York, 1962). A work of modern times, the *Taoist Yoga: Alchemy and Immortality*, as its translator renders it, of Ch'en Chao Pi (late nineteenth century) is the fullest available treatment in this field (London, 1970). Paul Anderson has translated a small text of very early date: *The Method of Holding the Three Ones. A Taoist Manual of Meditation of the Fourth Century A.D.* (London & Malmö, 1980). The fullest representation of texts in this field is the collection of studies by Henri Maspero translated into English by Frank Kierman: *Taoism and Chinese Religion* (Massachusetts Institute of Technology, 1981).

One of the basic doctrines of Taoism, that the human body is a microcosm inhabited by the same spiritual beings who inhabit the macrocosm, is presented in the translation by Rolf Homann: *The Hundred Questions; a Dialogue between Two Taoists on the Macrocosmic and Microcosmic Systems of Correspondence* (Leiden, 1976).

Several small texts are included in the second volume of James Legge's translations alluded to above: the *T'ai Shang Kan-yin P'ien* ("Tractate of Actions and Their Retributions")—a text that has had wide circulation among lay people; it has also been translated in Western languages several times before and since the work of Legge; the *Ching Cheng Ching* ("Classic of Purity"); the *Yin Fu Ching* ("Classic of the Harmony of the Seen and Unseen")—a text that figures prominently in the Canon; the *Yü Shu Ching* ("Classic of the Pivot of Jade")—recited in Taoist liturgies; and the *Chih Yung Ching* ("Classic of the Directory for a Day").

Kristofer Schipper's scholarly study entitled *L'Empereur Wou des Han dans la Légende Taoïste* (Paris, 1965) includes his translation of the *Han Wu-ti Nei Chuan*, the *Inner History of the Martial Emperor of Han*, which might be called an "historical romance" of the Chinese Middle Ages.

Interest in liturgical Taoism is quite recent as a field of Taoist studies, but already in 1919 the great French Sinologue Édouard Chavannes had translated and published an important study that includes an extensive translation of texts used in the *Chai*, or major Rites of Abstinence and Penitence, with copious notes: *Le Jet des Dragons* (Paris, 1919); see Deuxième Partie: Textes Littéraires (pp. 129–95) and notes (pp. 196–213).

It is perhaps needless to point out that longer or shorter quotations from and discussions on the Tao Tsang are an integral part of many studies of Taoism. However, it would exceed our commission here to go into the detailed bibliographical information concerning such materials.[24]

NOTES

1. Today this problem has been alleviated through photographic reproductions.
2. Block-printing was probably already in use in Chinese Buddhist monasteries as early as the eighth century, although the oldest extant example of a printed text is the *Diamond Sutra* of 868 (a printed charm written in Sanskrit and produced in Japan *ca.* 770 is the oldest extant example of printing from blocks). The Confucian Canon was block-printed in mid-tenth century, and the Buddhist Tripitaka shortly thereafter. See, Thomas F. Carter, *The Invention of Printing in China and Its Spread Westward* (New York: Columbia University Press, 1925).
3. For a vivid image of such a Taoist (ordained priest) of contemporary Taiwan see Michael Saso, *The Teachings of Taoist Master Chuang* (New Haven: Yale University Press, 1978), chapter 3.
4. For which see the thorough study by Liu Ts'un-yan, "The Compilation and Historical Value of the Tao-tsang," in D. Leslie, C. Mackerras & Wang Gungwu, eds., *Essays on the Sources for Chinese History* (Australian National University, 1973 & University of South Carolina Press, 1975), pp. 104–19, and the technical article by Ninji Ofuchi, "The Formation of the Taoist Canon," in Holmes Welch & Anna Seidel, eds. *Facets of Taoism* (New Haven: Yale University Press, 1979), pp. 253–67.
5. The "seven sections" refers to the major divisions of the Tao Tsang, the Three Tung and Four Fu.
6. For a major study of this subject see Isabelle Robinet, *Les Commentaires du Tao Tö King jusqu'au VIIe Siècle* (Collège de France, Institut des Hautes Études Chinoises, 1977)
7. The bare list, romanized and in Chinese ideographs, is given under the title, "A Taoist Library" and is followed by a list of fifty-eight Amulets mentioned by Ko Hung in James Ware, *Alchemy, Medicine, Religion in the China of A.D. 320* (Cambridge: The M.I.T. Press, 1966), pp. 379ff.
8. Fu Ch'in-chia, *Chung-kuo Tao-chiao Shih* (History of Chinese Taoism), (Shanghai, 1937), pp. 201ff.
9. Ibid.

10. These terms should not be equated with what one thinks of as North and South China today; the latter, in those times, was centered upon the Yangtzu River.

11. For authoritative studies, see Edward Schafer, *Mao Shan in T'ang Times* (Boulder, Colorado: Society for the Study of Chinese Religions, Monograph Number 1, 1980) and Michel Strickmann, *Le Taoïsme du Mao Chan* (Collège de France, Institut des Hautes Études Chinoises, 1981).

12. Always mentioned in conjunction with these texts are those called the *Maps of the True Forms of the Five Sacred Peaks* (Wu Yueh Chen Hsing T'u).

13. Relevant sources for the above are cited in Ch'en Kuo-fu, *Tao Tsang Yüan Liu Kao* (Studies in the Origin and Development of the Tao Tsang) (Taiwan reprint of 2nd edition, 1975).

14. For a brief but authoritative discussion of this text see Max Kaltenmark, "The ideology of the *T'ai-ping ching*," in Holmes Welch & Anna Seidel, eds., *Facets of Taoism* (New Haven: Yale University Press, 1979) pp. 19–52.

15. Chang Ling is accepted as the actual founder of organized Taoism, although he is only semihistorical figure. His cult developed into the Sect of the Orthodox One (*Cheng-yi p'ai*), and his descendents were given the title of Master Designated by (the Three) Heavens (*T'ien Shih*). This school is still the major form of professional Taoism.

16. The relevant sources are quoted in Ch'en, pp. 78–101.

17. These terms obviously derive from Buddhism. We are told that the Great Vehicle is the Way of the Saints (*sheng*), the Middling Vehicle is the Way of the Nine Perfected Ones (*chen*), and the Small Vehicle is the Way of the Nine Immortal Transcendents (*hsien*), i.e., for beginners. See also Ofuchi's discussion of the three vehicles (Ofuchi, pp. 260–63).

18. Ancient expression for books, which were written on those materials.

19. Using the Sanskrit term for Buddhist hymns of praise.

20. Weng Tu-chien, compiler, *Harvard Yenching Concordance No. 25: Tao Tsang Tzu-mu Yin-te* (Peking, 1925).

21. My grouping of the sections is not in the original design of the book.

22. It should be noted that this strong emphasis on *wai-tan*, an "alchemy of substances," gave way almost completely to *nei-tan*, the internal alchemy performed by meditative concentration, after the period during which Chang Chün-fang compiled his work.

23. One of the most important interpretations of the Tao Tsang has been translated (though poorly). See Eduard Erkes, *Ho-shang Kung's Commentary on Lao-tse* (Ascona, Switzerland, 1950).

24. The best introductions to Taoism and the Tao Tsang in English for the nonspecialist are three articles in *Encyclopædia Britannica 3* (Chicago, 1974). See *Macropædia* Vol. 17: Anna K. Seidel, "Taoism," pp. 1032b–1044b; Michel Strickmann, "Taoism, History of," pp. 1044b–1050b; *Idem*, "Taoist Literature," pp. 1051a–1055a. The best overall discussion of Taoist religion

is Kristofer Schipper, *Le Corps Taoïste* (Paris, 1982). The most nearly comprehensive bibliographical information on all aspects of Chinese Taoism is Laurence G. Thompson, *Chinese Religion in Western Languages* (University of Arizona Press, 1984; published for the Association for Asian Studies). On a question that it has not been feasible to discuss in the present article, but which is of obvious importance, the best information to date is the article by Erik Zürcher, "Buddhist Influence on Early Taoism; A Survey of Scriptural Evidence." *T'oung Pao* n.s.66.1/3 (1980) pp. 84–147.

NONLITERATE TRADITIONS AND HOLY BOOKS:
Toward a New Model

Sam D. Gill

There is radical incongruity in the title "Nonliterate Traditions and Holy Books." A "holy *book*" is a volume of writings, and we might assume that it is to be read. Nonliterate peoples obviously neither read nor write. It therefore seems clear that nonliterate peoples can neither create nor use "holy books."

Why then would I want to consider such a topic? Have I not in my opening sentences thoroughly exhausted the topic? The choice of title for this presentation is a self-conscious one and its incongruity is intended not to stifle thought, but to stimulate it. I avoided alternate titles like "Holy Book in Primal Societies" or "Myth as Scripture in Nonliterate Traditions." Such titles resolve too quickly the issues regarding the study of religion and the role of scripture in this study. We might consider the title "Nonliterate Traditions and Holy Books" something of a koan, but I assure you that what I have to say will proceed at only the most preliminary stages in the enlightenment process. Nonetheless I hope that by following it we will be led toward a reinvention of religion.

THE ADVERSITIES OF "THE BOOK"

Our original observation that, because of their mode of communication, nonliterate peoples cannot create or use holy books, does not preclude that such people may be aware of literacy and books, that they may comprehend such a notion as writing, that they may evaluate writing and express clearly their views on it. When placed in the context of literacy, nonliterate peoples have often consciously chosen to maintain their exclusively oral mode of communication, and they expound the benefits of the oral mode of communication over against what they see as the degradation and dangers of literacy. I am yet to be convinced that nonliteracy need be displaced with literacy, hence I caution against the use of the term "pre-literate." On this point, let me relate a story.

In 1879, Frank Hamilton Cushing was assigned the position of eth-nologist on a Smithsonian expedition to study the Zuni people of New Mexico. Cushing was a frail man, but he worked with unusual dedication. While the research party he was with made an encampment near the vil-lage of Zuni, Cushing soon found even this short distance from the Zuni a barrier to his goals. He moved uninvited into the home of the governor of Zuni where he would stay for the remainder of the study, a period ex-pected to be two months. He was so fascinated with the Zuni, that he em-barked upon the effort to become Zuni so that he might understand them fully. His stay stretched to four and a half years and then he left only be-cause his devotion to the Zuni threatened to prevent the illegal acquisition of Zuni lands by relatives of a U.S. Congressman. After a period of adjust-ment, the Zuni accepted Cushing and attempted to make him Zuni. He was initiated into a priesthood and given the high office of War Chief, a position that being held by this white man, had obvious advantages to the Zuni. In his correspondence, Cushing used the peculiar epithet, "1st War Chief of Zuni, U.S. Assistant Ethnologist."[1]

Cushing became fluent in Zuni language. He was initiated into reli-gious societies. He lived like and claimed to think like a Zuni, yet there remained differences, at least from the Zuni point of view. The Zuni call attention to one of these differences in a song they sang for him. It was remembered for many years after Cushing left. The song recalls the time when Cushing was initiated into the priesthood of the Bow Society.

> Once they made a White man into a Priest of the Bow
> he was out there with other Bow Priests
> he had black stripes on his body
> the others said their prayers from their hearts
> but he read his from a piece of paper.

The subtlety of observations made in this song is enhanced when we learn that for the Zuni, the term for written page literally translates as "that which is striped." Thus Cushing whose white body was painted with black stripes was, to the Zuni, a walking page of writing.[2]

Perhaps contrary to our expectations, the Zuni do not remember Cush-ing as some greatly superior figure because he had the power of literacy. They seem to distinguish the very character of their religion by contrast with Cushing's dependence upon literacy. They see their religion as being of the heart, not of the head. They see their religion as performed and lived, not written and read.

We may find ourselves surprised that these people are making comparisons of themselves with us, that they are using us and writing, our emblem of civilization, to state their own superiority . . . and in a poetic form at that! The Zuni are the Native Americans of whom it was said less than a century ago that their language was so crude that they could not make themselves understood without extensive use of the hands. Thus, it was insightfully concluded that they could not communicate with one another in the dark. For me, there is a particular pleasure to find that they are looking at, evaluating, and imagining us as we are doing the same to them.

Such self-conscious distinctions are commonly made by nonliterate peoples the world over when confronted by literate peoples. This confrontation has invariably taken place in the situation of colonization and conquest. Thus, the responses of nonliterate peoples have been in the context of oppression and disruption. This situation has clearly shaped the character of the comments they have made. Nonliterate peoples in these situations have typically been confronted first by missionaries who have tried to teach them to read so that they might read scripture, then by governmental agencies who presented written documents as authority for their rights to the lands and possessions of the nonliterate peoples. They have been confronted by a whole system of economic exchange that is mediated by written orders, letters, and printed paper money. Then, when they ceased to be threatening or disruptive to colonial efforts, ethnologists, folklorists, and anthropoligists have rushed in to study them before they lost their "primitive" characteristics or became extinct. These observers have taken *notes* and written *books* about the peoples they observe.

It is this background of oppression that frames many of the comparisons nonliterate peoples have made between themselves and the intruding outsiders. Here are some examples.

A member of the Carrier tribe in British Columbia compared his people's knowledge of animals to that of European-Americans. He said, "The white man writes everything down in a book so that it might not be forgotten; but our ancestors married the animals, learned their ways, and passed on the knowledge from one generation to another."[3] This Native American suggests that writing promotes forgetfulness and that the fullness of knowledge is gained through intimate experience and through face-to-face transmission. He voices the superiority of Native Americans over European-Americans on the basis of the natives lack of writing. It is also notable that many peoples identify the unity of language, its mutual intelligibility among peoples, including animal peoples, as a designation of the primordial or paradisiacal era.

The Reverend Mr. Cram, a Boston missionary, visited the Seneca in the summer of 1805. In a formal setting he spoke to the Seneca in an attempt to persuade them to become Christians. After he spoke for some time, he invited the Seneca to discuss his remarks among themselves and give him a reply. Red Jacket was selected to respond on behalf of the Seneca. Among his remarks he made the following statements.

> *Brother*: Continue to listen.
> You say that you are sent to instruct us how to worship the Great Spirit agreeably to his mind, and, if we do not take hold of the religion which you white people teach, we shall be unhappy hereafter. You say that you are right and we are lost. How do we know that to be true? We understand that your religion is written in a book. If it was intended for us as well as you, why has not the Great Spirit given to us, and not only to us, but why did he not give to our forefathers, the knowledge of that book, with the means of understanding it rightly? We only know what you tell us about it. How shall we know when to believe, being so often deceived by the white people?
> *Brother*: You say there is but one way to worship and serve the Great Spirit. If there is but one religion; why do you white people differ so much about it? Why not all agree, as you can all read the book?[4]

Red Jacket raised herein some profound issues: the nature of scripture as authority; the access to scripture and thus the access to truth being seemingly incidentally dependent upon literacy; and the issue of multiple and conflicting interpretations of scripture, especially as manifest in the observed actions of Christians.

In the context of missionary contact, in a somewhat humorous, yet biting, comment, Vine Deloria, Jr., wrote in *Custer Died For Your Sins*:

> One of the major problems of the Indian people is the missionary. It has been said of missionaries that when they arrived they had only the Book and we had the land; now we have the Book and they have the land. An old Indian once told me that when the missionaries arrived they fell on their knees and prayed. Then they got up, fell on the Indians, and preyed.[5]

There is an element of irony in the fact that the homophonic base for Deloria's humor exists in English, not in Native American languages, and has its clearest effect only when written.

Another example. In the latter half of the nineteenth century, a Wanapum man named Smohalla lived in the Washington Territory. This was a period during which an enormous transformation of the area took place.

The first missionaries had entered the area at the end of the first quarter of the nineteenth century. The first treaties opening the way to settlement did not take place until after mid-century, but by the end of the third quarter of the century virtually all Native Americans had been confined to reservations. Smohalla was one of the few unshakable hold outs. In several of his statements that were recorded and have survived, he spoke critically of his oppressors, but he also criticized his own people who had given up their ways in an attempt to take up European-American ways. Notably, the token acquisition of Christianity and literacy is captured in the image of "the book Indian." Of such persons, Smohalla said,

> Many Indians are trying to live like white men, but it will do them no good. They cut off their hair and wear white man's clothes, and some of them learn to sing out of a book. . . . No one has any respect for those book Indians. Even the white men like me better and treat me better than they do the book Indians.[6]

There are many other examples, such as the following one from Africa. Mamoudou Kouyate, a historian, poet, and storyteller or griot, of Mali in West Africa said,

> Other peoples use writing to record the past, but this invention has killed the faculty of memory among them. They do not feel the past anymore, for writing lacks the warmth of the human voice. With them everybody thinks he knows, whereas learning should be a secret. The prophets did not write and their words have been all the more vivid as a result. What paltry learning is that which is congealed in dumb books![7]

And finally, I quote Russell Means, an Indian activist, who, in a recent statement focused on writing as the distinguishing feature between "Indian" and "White." It appeared in an article entitled "Fighting Words on the Future of the Earth." The article begins:

> The only possible opening for a statement of this kind is that I detest writing. The process itself epitomizes the European concept of "legitimate" thinking: what is written has importance that is denied the spoken. My culture, the Lakota culture, has an oral tradition, so I ordinarily reject writing. It is one of the white world's ways of destroying the cultures of non-European peoples, the imposing of an abstraction over the spoken relationship of a people.
>
> So what you read here is not what I've written. It's what I've said and someone else has written down. I will allow this because it seems the only way to communicate with the white world is through the dead, dry leaves of a book. I don't really care whether my words reach whites or not. They have already demonstrated through their history that they cannot hear, cannot see; they can only read.[8]

IN DEFENSE OF WRITING

Upon reflecting on these several statements, we can easily laud the tenacity of those noble savages who, like the Zuni, choose to reject our faculty of writing and our holy books. They are the few and besides we know that in our generation, of all of the generations of human existence, these few are the last of their kind, the last ones to forego, in their noble ignorance, the pleasures of civilization. We can overlook the threat, the challenges of Smohalla's statement about pathetic Indians who try to become like us, to dress like us, and to take up our holy books. We cannot expect them to acquire the full measure of holy book traditions by merely learning to read. They are like children playing dress up in our adult clothes. We can sympathize with Red Jacket for his observation of the divisions and degradations of some Christian communities. We can even chuckle at the humorous criticism Vine Deloria, Jr., thrusts at missionaries, and at his dependence on English and on writing for the bite of his humor. We identify the mission approach he refers to as one of the past or nearly past.

But our tolerance, our acceptance, becomes more difficult, the threat more caustic, in the words of the African bard and especially the Native American political activist. We find it difficult to quietly accept these statements without rejoinder. Let me focus particularly upon the *written* words of mean Mr. Means and imagine how our response to him might go. It might include something like this.

Now wait just a minute, Mr. Means, you are imagining us entirely too superficially. What of the great works of literature that writing has made possible? What of the great thinkers, the ancient prophets, the poets, the rulers? It is quite clear you have read many of their works. We know and we can be enriched by them only because they wrote. What of writing as the great tool of creativity and learning? What of the power of communication that brings the world closer together, the power that even you, Mr. Means, acquire by letting your speech be written. I think that you care more than you say that we read your words. This written form of your hostile remarks will survive your voice, and even your flesh and bones.

Then too, Mr. Means, as we begin to think of it, even as peoples of the book, we are not limited to the written word. If you would only read the first words in the Genesis account of creation, and I suspect that you have, you would find that we do not believe that God *wrote*, but that He *said*, "Let there be light" and because of this act of speech, light came to be. And if you had studied the first words of the Gospel according to John you would know that our conception of "the Word" in the opening verse that says "In the beginning was the Word, and the Word was with God, and the Word was God," is rooted in the Greek *logos* and refers to God's creative *action*, a concept not unlike that so commonly espoused by your peoples.

And even one of our greatest teachers, the Greek philosopher Socrates, once said, "The discovery of the alphabet will create forgetfulness in the learners' souls, because they will not use their memories; they will trust to the external written characters and not remember of themselves. . . . You give your disciples not truth but only the semblance of truth, they will be hearers of many things and will have learned nothing; they will appear omniscient and will generally know nothing; they will be tiresome company, having the show of wisdom without the reality."[9]

Then too, Mr. Means, now that you have us thinking, when you consider even holy book people, in the many generations through which their traditions have existed, the great majority of these people have been illiterate; they didn't know how to read! Most of these book people couldn't read the scripture if they wanted to and doubtless many of them never even had it read to them. While they have been affected by the impact of literacy on their world and their religious beliefs, they have maintained and practiced their religion through oral forms, through action, and through their way of life.

This personal level of the debate need be carried no further, but there are implications in it for the academic study of religion that I would like to pursue.

IMPLICATIONS FOR THE STUDY OF RELIGION

What features of exclusively oral traditions are being emphasized as positive in character? Let us listen again to the kinds of things that nonliterate peoples have said.

They emphasize the immediacy of their oral traditions—the immediacy of their religious experience. They stress the extent to which people must accept responsibility for tradition; that, in fact, their traditions, the accumulation of wisdom, the features of their cultures and ways of life are always on the critical endangered species list, for they are held exclusively in the minds of the living members. Religion, tradition, and culture must be transmitted face to face among the living members. What is forgotten is lost.

Still, to forget is not necessarily bad. I well remember trying to talk a Navajo elder into recording, with my assistance of course, his stories of creation. I believed them to be of a variety that differed from those that had been recorded. The old man even became defensive and argumentative when I compared what he told me with what I knew were the views of other Navajos. I asked him if any Navajos were learning his wisdom. When he replied that there were none, I presented the argument that upon his death his wisdom would be forever lost, unless of course, I wrote it in a book for him. His response required no time for reflection. he said, "If no one sees value in learning my stories, it is time for them to pass. If they are needed again, they will appear again."

What features of writing, of book-based traditions, are held forth as negative in character? Let us listen again to what these nonliterate peoples have suggested.

They note the tendency toward abstraction and depersonalization that may accompany writing. They point out that writing and reading may remove one from the immediacy of experience, particularly social experience. They point out that writing permits one the avoidance of responsibility, the false luxury of never having to learn, the possibility of detachment— all of which, from their point of view, amounts to a loss of meaning and a threat to existence.

While we are used to thinking of nonliteracy as a negative attribute, a sign of cultural deprivation, the very emblem of "the primitive," we may find ourselves surprised by these evaluations of nonliterate peoples and we doubtless find ourselves sympathetic to what they say. We cannot deny the importance of immediacy of experience and the acceptance of responsibility to participate in and perpetuate religious traditions. We can appreciate that a performed liturgy, a liturgy known and maintained through long and careful rehearsal and repetition, is often more emotive and engaging than a liturgy where keeping one's place in a stream of unfamiliar words on a page can become the overwhelming concern. We can appreciate the importance of accepting the responsibility for performing and transmitting religious traditions. We can appreciate the value of religion as it influences the many actions and orientations of human life, being inseparable from that very foundation that makes life meaningful. All these notions are inseparable from our ideas of what constitutes the religious dimension of human life.

What should we make of this rather frustrating experience of seeing ourselves reflected through the comments of nonliterate peoples? Can they be wholly in error? Have they no basis whatever for their comments? Perhaps it is just that their views of our world view and understanding of religion are biased because their contact has been made primarily with missionaries, governmental officials, entrepreneurs, and ethnologists whose use of writing can be linked with these potentially negative qualities. Still, we must ask if this kind of emphasis extends to our study of scripture, to our conceptions of the interrelationship of scripture to religion, and even more broadly to the modern academic study of religion. I believe we must conclude that it most certainly does. Thus, what nonliterate peoples have said may provide an insightful critical perspective on the academic study of religion, and in the light thus acquired, we may see our way toward a reinvention of religion.

There are two dimensions that I would like to discuss. The *horizontal* dimension has to do with the accepted purview of the study of religion—that is, with the data and kind of data on which we conduct our study. The *vertical* dimension has to do with the interpretive approach or style of hermeneutic we tend to use in the study of religion. Both dimensions taken together constitute our operative definition of religion.

In our discussion of literate and nonliterate perspectives, writing seems to be a crucial factor. While our work, our religious heritage, our civilization depend upon writing, the critical perspective advanced by nonliterate peoples suggests that writing is not everything; that writing does not encompass all that we would wish to consider as religious; that writing perhaps inseparable from its nature, may have certain detriments; and that the absence of writing (exclusive orality) may have assets that counter these detriments.

Even a cursory review of the understanding of religious traditions and the way they are studied confirms that we have a major imbalance toward written materials and even then toward very select writings called scripture. Canonized scripture exists in but a few religious traditions and not surprisingly they are especially important in the traditions that coexist without intellectual heritage. Our study of religion has been and presently is largely, almost exclusively, the study of sacred scriptures (texts); the history that led to their being written and established within religious institutions; and the history of their interpretation into doctrinal, theological, and cultural forms.

The academic study of religion has been extended to include the study of religions of the East and Middle East and to the missionization of Africa, the Americas, and Melanesia, but it has not considered to any significant extent the thousands of religious traditions of peoples who do not write. The study of these peoples has been relegated to social scientists.

Not only is this an issue of the extent of acceptable data, it is not just that we have limited the study of religion to certain traditions and to certain segments within these traditions, but we have also placed severe limitations on the form of the data we consider in those traditions we study. Generally our data must be in the form of text or conjoined with text. We may see how our common categories are determined by text and writing even in the terms we give to them. For example, for such categories as "verbal" and "nonverbal," "literate" and "nonliterate," and even the categories of "myth" and "ritual," the defining and conjunctive principle is that of text or literacy. We do not say "action" and "nonaction." We do not say "exclusively oral" and "partially oral" or "oral and written." When we say "verbal" and "nonverbal," we usually mean "text" and "action." When we distinguish myth and ritual we make the distinction primarily on the basis of text versus act. We commonly ignore the fact that stories are often told in ritual environments in a ritually prescribed manner. We do not account for the implications of our usage of the term "myth" by which we usually mean the written account of a story. We rarely include the oral dimensions and contexts of the story form or even acknowledge the fact that such stories are almost never written down by those for whom they are religiously meaningful. Likewise, our study of ritual is usually based upon ritual texts.

Thus even as we extend our concerns beyond text, beyond scripture, it is with text and literacy directing our thinking and the data acquired through such extensions can never be more than peripheral. As peripheral they speak only to further illuminate our understanding of text, of the written dimension of religion.

While I would advocate the expansion of religion to include more than text, more than scripture and holy book, and to include the consideration of text in broader contexts, this is not the sole issue. As I have come to see it, this is not even the main issue.

Certainly we are not about to give up writing. We are not about to turn our attention away from written documents. We cannot deny the value, the importance, the vitality of written modes of communication. The obvious foolishness of these positions should be clear to all. I believe that Mr. Means has his criticism partly misplaced. And I believe that our response to him, our defense of the creative power of writing is fully justified.

Modes of communication, the differences between oral and written materials, must be taken into consideration in the study of religion and culture. Jack Goody has shown the ramifications of modes of communication on thought and culture in *The Domestication of the Savage Mind.*[10] I have attempted to demonstrate this in *Beyond "the Primitive."*[11] But the horizontal expansion of the academic study of religion, that is, the extension of the data we study, will not lead to much revision of the study of religion or to any significant expansion of our understanding of religion. This expansion must come from another direction. Let us now consider the vertical dimension.

As I consider more carefully the comments and statements made by the nonliterate peoples we have presented, I do not believe that it is actually writing that is at the core of their criticism. The concern is with certain dimensions of behavior and modes of thought that writing tends to facilitate and encourage. And these dimensions are linked to the critical, semantical, encoding aspect of language. Certainly, the academic study of religion has, as an intellectual endeavor, and as the extension of Western intellectuality, strongly emphasized this approach. We interpret texts to discern systems of thought and belief, propositional or historical contents, messages communicated. Put more generally, we seek the information in the text. We tend to emphasize code at the expense of behavior, message at the expense of effect, and text at the expense of the performance and usage contexts. Thus the products of our studies appear artificial, abstract, and rationally and intellectually complex. And they often are. And this, in itself, is not bad. The products of our studies seem removed and isolated from the subject we study. And they often are. And this, in itself, is not bad. But the shift to expand our contextual concerns, to expand our domain of data, will not revise this at all, for we will still extract messages and decode symbols in order to describe systems of thought and belief.[12]

What is needed is a complementary expansion in a vertical dimension as well. We must recognize that to decipher information from religious data, be it text or act, is not to exhaust it. This information bearing attribute of language is but one among many meaningful attributes of religious acts. Let us call this information bearing attribute "the informative function." To designate other attributes collectively without excluding the informative, we propose the term "performative functions." This is, of course, but one kind of designation, but it serves a notion that religion, as it is actualized, as it is lived, *does* something even if that is to *say* something. To extend our attentiveness and to revise our interpretive methods in these dimensions would constitute a true revision and expansion of the academic study of religion. Coincidentally, it would distract our attention from the less productive distinctions that break on literacy and text.

This concern with the functions of religion may call up the fears of a narrow pragmatism or a logically faulted functionalism, but I'm not convinced these are valid reservations. Students of religion have expressed offense, and falsely so, at what we identify as the social scientific reduction of religion to social functions. Our concerns are with the *religious* functions of what we consider to be *religious* data. And these concerns complement and extend, rather than replace, current styles of academic study. To this point in the academic study of religion we have largely avoided any serious attempt to comprehend how religion is a creative vital force in the world even of common peoples, although we generally espouse this as an attribute of religion.

A NEW MODEL

We may clarify the discussion by a diagram (Figure 1) to illustrate the dimensions we have discussed. The horizontal dimension is the "data dimension." This is commonly divided on the distinction of text and non-text or act. The vertical dimension is the "interpretive dimension" and is commonly divided on the distinction of what is said and what is done, that is, on the "informative" versus the "performative" aspect. The combination of choices among these two dimensions defines religion as it is operative for the chooser.

While a major statement might be made reflecting the placement of various fields, schools of thought, and individual scholars in the sectors of this diagram, a brief general statement will place Religious Studies. As it tends to be centered upon the study of scripture, thought, belief, institutional and doctrinal history, the academic study of religion has remained largely confined to the text-informative sector.

Religious Studies has distinguished its domain from that of the social sciences, notably not on the basis of subject matter, for social scientists also study religion, but rather largely on the basis of the form of data considered—literate (scripture) versus nonliterate (primitive)—and more recently on the basis of interpretive method, eschewing the pragmatic, functionalist, structuralist, and systems approaches of social scienctists.

There have been some leakages from and into this sector where text and scripture reign, but, in terms of the major force of the study of religion, these have been minor. Even the field that has been called "the history of religions" has not, with some notable exceptions, expanded significantly beyond this text-informative sector.[13]

Keying on the perspective gained from statements made by nonliterate peoples, I believe we have become highly constrained in our study of religion, and even in our study of scripture. I believe that we must expand in both dimensions to maintain and regenerate vitality in our study. What might be gained?

First, on the horizontal plane we must include in the study of religion all of the nonliterate peoples—those prior to the advent of writing and those whose languages are not written. We must include all of the illiterate peoples whose spoken languages have a written counterpart, but who themselves did and do not know how to read and write. We must include all of the folk, the peasant, the worker, and the common peoples. We must include, without the degeneration usually assumed, those whose religions we call "popular." (Are the others, those on which we have focused, therefore "unpopular"?) We must include objects, acts, structures, and forms that we believe to be religious or that are engaged by peoples in religious action. In other words, we must destroy the data limitations that have made the study of religion to hinge upon literacy.

Second, the dimensions and character of our interests, our approaches, our interpretive methods must expand as we consider the broader performative functions of religion. This, as I see it, is the more important expansion. To make concrete the nature of this expansion let me begin by presenting a couple more examples from nonliterate peoples. These examples are selected to demonstrate the impact and importance of this vertical expansion on the study of scripture, the traditional center and core of our study of religion.

Along with the influx of Europeans into America, the inevitable displacement and oppression suffered by Native Americans led to waves of prophetic movements. These took a variety of forms. A Delaware man named Neolin arose as a prophet in the eighteenth century. As did others, he presented a crucial message for his followers. He held that there was a way suitable for "the white people," and a way proper for "the Indians." While the white people could drink whiskey, Indians should not. While the white people could use guns and gun powder, Indians should not. He proclaimed that Indians should abandon all "white" appurtenances. This Delaware prophet spoke this message to Indian audiences utilizing the metaphor of contrasting roads to heaven to illustrate the differences between Indians and whites. He used a map as a visual aid to his presentations. On it were drawn the respective Indian and white roads and the obstacles to be negotiated on the way to heaven. He said the map was revealed to him in a vision, and therefore it was not simply a visual aid, it was the proof and basis for his authority as a prophet. He called this map "the great Book or Writing." Notable also, the followers of the prophet were instructed to recite, morning and evening, a *written* prayer.[14]

Another relevant example occurred in a similar colonial situation experienced by the Papua in New Guinea early in this century. The example is from a cargo cult—as the millenarian movements in that area have come to be known—referred to as "the Vailala Madness." The prophet, Evara, gave his people a message just the contrary of that pronounced by the Delaware prophet. Those Papua engaged in the movement were told to be disdainful of anything reminding them of their own culture and way of life. They adopted European style clothing. They communicated with Jesus in visions. They called themselves "Jesus Christ men." They placed high value on European goods. And importantly, they began *reading* the Christian bible. Though they were not literate, those people could be seen walking about, with Bible in hand, "reading" aloud. The book, as the European style clothing they wore, was sign of the new life to come. "Reading" the Bible was instrumental to the arrival of cargo.[15]

Our first tendency, I believe, upon hearing these examples is to reflect with some humor upon the naive ways of these "primitive peoples." But, upon more thoughtful consideration, we may discern something familiar in these examples. For the Delaware and the Papua, the book and the fact of writing are signs of authority, channels of revelation, transformation, and power. And it is clear that they do not believe this source of power depends upon or arises from some semantic or informational component of the words contained in the book or writing.

When we allow ourselves to be open to the possibility that "the book," that scripture is religiously important as a religious object, not simply for what it says, we can recognize all kinds of examples where the bible, as *book*, as *object*, is religiously important. Many are the preachers who preach and have preached with bible in hand. The books they carry are tattered and worn, perhaps from being read and studied, but as likely from being carried and preached, from being presented as the basis for the authority of what the preacher says. This is precisely the use made of "the great Book or Writing" by the Delaware prophet. A considerable portion of the preachers that constitute the American Christian heritage have not been intellectually sophisticated and could likely grasp only elementary aspects of modern biblical scholarship. Nonetheless these preachers and their religious communities are in the mainstream of American religion. Another aspect of the religious importance of the scripture as object is to be seen in the common practice of owning and giving expensive and handsome editions of scripture. This often has religious merit as in the giving of Torah scrolls to *shuls* or synagogues.

Even in a highly secularized and politicized era as is the present one in America, it is upon the bible that one swears an oath of honesty in a courtroom, even by those who have never read a word of it or who expressly disavow the messages of its content and the authority it represents. The Bible is the book on which officials place their hands in taking oaths of office.

Beyond the book as object, as sign, the contents of holy books are commonly recited, chanted, and sung. In these performances, the qualities of performance—sound, repetition, movement, objects, garments, gestures, and so on—are at least as significant and as effective as the informational messages contained in the words. Beyond this there are the many contexts where scripture is applied to life, where it provides guidance, inspiration, solace, and knowledge to meet exigencies and personal needs of all kinds. This is doubtless the most extensive use of scripture and wherein it has had its most significant effects. We ignore these pragmatic and performative dimensions of scripture almost totally, apart from highly confined historical and ecclesiastical spheres, that is, apart from institutional and intellectual history.

Put one way, what I am saying is that the holy book serves religiously in innumerable ways scarcely connected to any intellectual or historical significance of the words printed therein. The holy book serves as a cultural and religious sign, a form engaged in action and human behavior. I believe that for the majority of religious people, the holy book serves more powerfully in these ways than as it informs their intellectual and historical sensitivities.

In exemplifying the proposed expansion of the study of religion in a vertical dimension to include the pragmatic and performative aspects of religion in much wider cultural contexts, I have limited our attention primarily to "the book," to the study of scriptures. Beyond "the book" there are many other forms of religious data that may be approached and interpreted when this vertical dimension is opened, such areas as liturgy, tale, prayer, song, architecture, art, tools and utensils, work activities, clothing, hair styles, kinship structures, and language. All of these and many more are engaged in and by the religious life. They are the instruments by which life acquires meaning and value and by which the world and all of its attributes are created and discovered.

NOTES

1. See Jesse Green, *Selected Writings of Frank Hamilton Cushing* (Lincoln: University of Nebraska Press, 1979) for a brief biography of Cushing.
2. Dennis Tedlock, "Verbal Art," *Handbook of North American Indians*, William C. Sturtevant, editor (Washington, D.C.: Smithsonian Institution, in press), Chapter 50, volume 1.
3. Diamond Jenness, "The Carrier Indians of the Bulkley River," Bulletin No. 133, *Bureau of American Ethnology* (Washington, D.C., 1943), p. 540.

4. First published in pamphlet "Indian Speeches Delivered by Farmer's Brother and Red Jacket, Two Seneca Chiefs," prepared by James D. Bemis (Canadiagua, New York, 1809).

5. Vine Deloria, Jr., *Custer Died for Your Sins: An Indian Manifesto* (New York: Avon Books, 1969), p. 105.

6. E. L. Huggins, "Smohalla, the Prophet of Priest Rapids," *Overland Monthly* (San Francisco), xvii, No. 98, Second Series (Jan.–June, 1891), pp. 212–13.

7. D. T. Niane, *Sundiata: An Epic of Old Mali* (London: Longmans, 1965), p. 41. My thanks to Philip M. Peek, "The Power of Words in African Verbal Arts," *Journal of American Folklore*, vol. 94, no. 371 (1981): 19–43 where I learned of this remarkable book.

8. Russell Means, "Fighting Words on the Future of the Earth," *Mother Jones* (December, 1980), p. 24.

9. As quoted in Peek, "The Power of Words," p. 43.

10. Jack Goody, *The Domestication of the Savage Mind* (London: Oxford University Press, 1965).

11. Sam D. Gill, *Beyond "the Primitive": The Religions of Nonliterate Peoples* (Englewood Cliffs, N.J.: Prentice-Hall, 1982).

12. I wish to acknowledge the lectures and writings of Michael Silverstein, Anthropology Department, University of Chicago, that have so powerfully addressed these issues in the study of the pragmatic dimensions of language.

13. I do not wish to imply that this expansion and redefinition is yet uncut or that I am in any way its designer. There are a number of scholars that are causing sector leakages. I think immediately of works in the areas of speech act theory, symbolic anthropology, semiotic studies, and ritual studies.

14. For further documentation of this prophetic era, see A. F. C.Wallace, "New Religions Among the Delaware Indians, 1600–1900," *Southwest Journal of Anthropology*, 12, no. 1 (1956): 1–21.

15. See Peter Worsley, *The Trumpet Shall Sound* (New York: Schocken Books, 1957: rev. ed., 1968), pp. 75–90.

CONTRIBUTORS

James W. Boyd, Professor of Religion and Philosophy, Colorado State University, Ft. Collins, received his Ph.D. from Northwestern University. He is a specialist in Zoroastrianism.

Harry Y. Gamble, Jr., Associate Professor of Religious Studies, University of Virginia, received his Ph.D. from Yale University. His major research and teaching interests focus upon New Testament and Early Christian Studies.

Sam D. Gill, Professor of Religious Studies, University of Colorado, Boulder, received his Ph.D. from the University of Chicago. He is one of the major figures in the field of Native American religions.

Kent P. Jackson, Associate Professor of Ancient Scripture, Brigham Young University, received his Ph.D. from the University of Michigan. His specialization is Biblical Studies and Mormon Theology.

Robert C. Lester, Professor of Religious Studies, University of Colorado, Boulder, received his Ph.D. from Yale University. His research and teaching interests include South Indian Hinduism and Theravada Buddhism.

Reginald A. Ray, Director of Buddhist Studies, Naropa Institute, Boulder, received his Ph.D. from the University of Chicago. His research and teaching interests include Indian and Tibetan Buddhism.

Jonathan Rosenbaum, Associate Professor of Religious Studies, University of Nebraska, Omaha, received his Ph.D. from Harvard University. His specializations include Hebrew Bible, Ancient Near East and Jewish History and Law.

Laurence G. Thompson, Professor of Asian Studies, University of Southern California, received his Ph.D. from Claremont Graduate School. His specialization is Chinese religions, particularly popular religion in Taiwan.

241

EDITORS

Rodney L. Taylor, Associate Professor and Chairman, Department of Religious Studies, University of Colorado, Boulder, received his Ph.D. from Columbia University. He is a specialist on Chinese religions, with a particular focus on the Confucian and Neo-Confucian traditions. His books include: *The Cultivation of Sagehood as a Religious Goal in Neo-Confucianism* (1978), *The Way of Heaven: An Introduction to the Confucian Religious Life* (1985) as well as numerous scholarly articles. He is editor of the *Journal of Chinese Religions* and is presently finishing a volume to be called *The Confucian Way of Contemplation* to be published by South Carolina, the first study of Confucian meditation in English.

Frederick M. Denny, Associate Professor of Religious Studies, University of Colorado, Boulder, received his Ph.D. from the University of Chicago. His specialization is Islam focusing upon ritual studies and Qur'an recitation from Egypt to Indonesia. His books include: *An Introduction to Islam* (1985), *Islamic Ritual Practices* (co-authored) (1983) and a number of scholarly articles. He is also the general editor of this series from South Carolina.

INDEX